THE FRICTIONLESS ORGANIZATION

THE FRICTIONLESS ORGANIZATION

DELIVER GREAT CUSTOMER EXPERIENCES WITH LESS EFFORT

BILL PRICE
DAVID JAFFE

BK®

Berrett–Koehler Publishers, Inc.

Berrett-Koehler Publishers, Inc.
1333 Broadway, Suite 1000
Oakland, CA 94612-1921
Tel: (510) 817-2277
Fax: (510) 817-2278
www.bkconnection.com

ORDERING INFORMATION

Quantity sales. Special discounts are available on quantity purchases by corporations, associations, and others. For details, contact the "Special Sales Department" at the Berrett-Koehler address above.

Individual sales. Berrett-Koehler publications are available through most bookstores. They can also be ordered directly from Berrett-Koehler: Tel: (800) 929-2929; Fax: (802) 864-7626; www.bkconnection .com.

Orders for college textbook / course adoption use. Please contact Berrett-Koehler: Tel: (800) 929-2929; Fax: (802) 864-7626.

Distributed to the U.S. trade and internationally by Penguin Random House Publisher Services.

Berrett-Koehler and the BK logo are registered trademarks of Berrett-Koehler Publishers, Inc.

Printed in the United States of America

Berrett-Koehler books are printed on long-lasting acid-free paper. When it is available, we choose paper that has been manufactured by environmentally responsible processes. These may include using trees grown in sustainable forests, incorporating recycled paper, minimizing chlorine in bleaching, or recycling the energy produced at the paper mill.

Library of Congress Cataloging-in-Publication Data
Names: Price, Bill, 1950- author. | Jaffe, David, 1963- author.
Title: The frictionless organization : deliver great customer experiences with less effort /
   Bill Price & David Jaffe.
Description: First edition. | Oakland, CA : Berrett-Koehler Publishers, [2022] |
   Includes bibliographical references and index.
Identifiers: LCCN 2021053258 (print) | LCCN 2021053259 (ebook) | ISBN 9781523000142
   (hardcover ; alk. paper) | ISBN 9781523000159 (pdf) | ISBN 9781523000166 (epub)
Subjects: LCSH: Customer relations. | Customer services—Management. | Consumer satisfaction. |
   Service industries—Customer services.
Classification: LCC HF5415.5 .P679 2022 (print) | LCC HF5415.5 (ebook) |
   DDC 658.8/12—dc23/eng/20211029
LC record available at https://lccn.loc.gov/2021053258
LC ebook record available at https://lccn.loc.gov/2021053259

First Edition

27 26 25 24 23 22   10 9 8 7 6 5 4 3 2 1

Book producer: Westchester Publishing Services
Text designer: Darryl J. Keck
Illustrations: Jon Kudelka
Cover designer: Matt Avery
Photographer for Bill Price: Leann Crosby

To Lori and Sue

CONTENTS

PREFACE

We are passionate about helping organizations deliver better experiences and less effort for their customers. In this book, we have tried to hand over our ideas and experience because we want organizations to get this right and to remove all the "friction" they have created for customers. We think this book has the potential to help every customer-facing organization deliver better customer experiences, save money, and grow revenue. That sounds too good to be true, but removing friction for customers really is a miracle cure. However, it also requires hard work and adopting a way of thinking that the whole organization must get behind. If the customer service or sales teams or the head of digital try to go it alone, you'll make some progress but get only incremental results.

This book is a methodology for the **whole of business** (terms in **bold** are defined in the glossary), and becoming frictionless, as we have defined it (see the introduction) will challenge you. We can't tell product design, finance, marketing, sales, IT, or other departments how to get it right, but we can show you where to look for the problems and solutions. As such, the book focuses on interactions with customers because of a universal truth we have learned: customers don't want to contact you; you made them do it! We focus on interactions with customers because that's where the problems and complaints wash up in every organization and where customers describe the friction they are experiencing. But first, we should go back to share why we wrote this book.

When we produced *The Best Service Is No Service* back in 2007–8, the world was a different place. It's almost hard to remember how different it was, because in 2008 . . .

- Apple's iPhone had just been launched, Samsung's first Android phone had not hit the streets, and Blackberry was still five years from its peak.
- We hardly knew what an app was, and web chat was rarely used.
- Email was often preferred to inbound calls, with email marketing supposedly the next big thing.
- Companies were starting to enable self-service via digital portals, but they were struggling to get traction.
- Walmart was 19 times bigger by revenue than Amazon. (Today, Amazon has surpassed Walmart's revenues.)
- Microsoft was two times bigger than Apple and three and a half times bigger than Google; today, the rank order is Apple, Google, and then Microsoft.
- Airbnb and Uber started operations that year, and Tesla sold its first model, the Roadster.
- The practice of offshoring service and sales was in full swing, and in many Western countries, it appeared there would be few customer care jobs left onshore.
- Speech recognition and natural language were being tested with limited success.
- Social media was still in its infancy.
- Post-contact surveys were just emerging as a tool.
- Some industry analysts started talking about **customer experience**, but the term was rarely used; the **NPS (Net Promoter Score)** was only two years old, and the **CES (Customer Effort Score)** had not yet been invented.

- London had won the rights to host the next Summer Olympics, a young Black Democrat had emerged as a surprise winner in the U.S presidential polls, and a boisterous, blond ex-journalist was standing to be mayor of London.

Even in those times we asserted that organizations needed to think more about why they were putting their customers to work. We talked about friction but hadn't yet given it a name. We'd already identified that this was a whole-of-business problem and not the responsibility of the director of customer service or the contact center director. This was based partly on Bill's experience as Amazon's first WW VP of Customer Service. We'd been refining the idea of "challenging the need for service" with our consulting colleagues in the 10-country LimeBridge Global Consulting Alliance, and the ideas seemed universal. We promoted concepts such as getting rid of **dumb contacts**, keeping customers informed, creating engaging self-service, and listening and acting on customers' inputs.

In 2015, our second book, *Your Customer Rules!* encouraged companies to focus squarely on a hierarchy of seven customer needs, including "You know me, you remember me" and "You make it easy for me," which meant reducing friction, although we didn't use that term. We coined the expression **Me2B** to place the customer front and center in the relationship with the business, in contrast to traditional business models like B2C (business to consumer) or B2B (business to business) that placed the business ahead of the customer. We saw that the customer was gaining control through information transparency, ease of switching, and the ability to rate organizations publicly.

We are proud that the frameworks we described in 2008 and 2015 are still relevant today. However, in addition to calls, mail, email, and branch or shop visits, our world now includes chat, messaging, text, and **chatbots** (also called virtual agents or avatars). Customer experience has emerged as a strategic focus. It is now seen as more important than price in influencing purchasing decisions and is one of the few areas in which companies can differentiate themselves. Surveys are everywhere, and it seems like we are asked to rate almost everything. Who would have thought in 2008 that we'd rate every taxi trip?

These new **channels** (chat, messaging, etc.) seemed to have followed "the freeway effect." Build a new freeway and more people drive on it. Build a new channel and more customer contacts flow into it.

Rather than creating "less need for contact" as we had advocated in 2008, there are now more customer contact points, more contacts, and new types of effort and friction. As one banking executive reported at an industry forum we run, "We have far more channels and mechanisms now for customers than we did ten years ago, with internet banking, mobile banking, chat, and the like, but we have the same number of people in our customer service area now as we did then."[1] Channels are proliferating, but the amount of effort required of both the customer and company seems undiminished and often even larger than before.

Organizations now have to manage more channels and contact types, so not surprisingly, they have even less time to think about "Why is this contact happening?" or "What can we do to reduce customer effort?" These new channels—and many products and services themselves—have added new friction for the customer. So while the ideas we wrote about in 2008 are still appropriate, now we have new problems to tackle, new tools to use, and the benefit of another 13 years of applied learning.

We're a little frustrated that more companies haven't taken up the ideas that we wrote about in 2008. We know that these ideas work and that they are even more needed now to reduce friction. The good news is that many of the innovative and disruptive companies seem to be getting it, leading to rising customer experience expectations. Newer businesses have made themselves easy to deal with, and customers want every organization to treat them that way; we call this **last-contact benchmarking**. As a result, the strategic landscape is changing.

We agreed that we should collect and frame the methods that are needed today to help organizations deal with this new channel complexity and the higher expectations of customers. Friends, colleagues, clients, and family encouraged us along the way, and we kept hearing stories of frustrated customers and unresponsive organizations. On the other hand, we have been excited by the many innovative "bright-lights organizations" that understand the need to make everything frictionless, and we set out to learn more about how these companies think and work. We already had lots of examples of clients that had embarked on change and reform, but they tended to be bigger, older businesses. We wanted to learn from these innovative companies, so we added their stories.

We are proud that some of the actions that we lay out in this book are similar to those we promoted in 2008 and 2015—the principles haven't changed, but the mechanisms, scope, tools, and processes have all evolved as the world has changed. After a couple of Zoom calls, we agreed that what we needed was to build on the ideas of *The Best Service Is No Service* but with a completely new methodology to remove friction for customers. As a result, *The Frictionless Organization* was born. We tried to make it as much a how-to book as possible, adding "Hints and Tips" sections throughout, which are based on the practices of organizations who seem to get it. We feature stories, quotations, and results from organizations in many different industries and geographies. We name organizations we think have it right but disguise those we think have much to learn.

HOW TO READ THIS BOOK

We hope we have allowed for all styles of readers. Those with limited time might want to read the first section of each chapter. If you want more depth, each chapter has a more detailed "How to?" section (this is free consulting for the price of a book!) and a self-check list to help you assess whether the ideas apply to your organization. The case studies span the globe, so you may not have heard of all the organizations we feature, but there are success stories and failures in all geographies. Just as we contrasted good and bad stories in our first two books, we have also done so here. We have a little fun along the way, with cartoons lampooning the ways many organizations still do not seem to get it. No matter how you choose to navigate the book, we hope that you can glean some ideas and frameworks to help your organization become frictionless! For those who want more or have ideas to share, we plan to make additional examples and methods available on the website www.frictionlessorg.com, where we aim to create a community of shared stories and methods. Please contact us there or on LinkedIn.

Thanks for joining us!

INTRODUCTION AND OVERVIEW

I've never had to contact Amazon about any matter.

—George Anders (then–West Coast bureau chief, *Fast Company* magazine)

WHAT IS A FRICTIONLESS ORGANIZATION?

A Frictionless Organization is one that has made its products and services so effective that customers never have to make contact for the wrong reasons. Everything in Frictionless Organizations works for customers and is easy for them. Using that definition, every organization should try to become frictionless! For many companies, this is almost a necessity if they are to survive, because innovative businesses are creating models with far less friction that are also low touch and low cost. Industries are being disrupted by new companies that possess frictionless characteristics: their products always work, deliveries arrive as promised, instructions are clear and understandable, and self-service is easy to use. The more everything just works to make it easy for the customer, the closer an organization gets to becoming frictionless.

Organizations that strive for perfection in product, service, and self-service design are able to deliver much better customer experiences while controlling costs. They make themselves so easy to deal with that customers feel it takes little to no effort to interact with them. It is this simplicity for the customer that we define as *frictionless*. Businesses that are frictionless have a cost advantage because the rate of assisted contacts for failure is so low. Better still, positive relationships with customers prompt them to buy more and to advocate for these organizations. Some Frictionless Organizations market solely through word of mouth, the way Amazon did for its first five years, and thrive with minimal sales and marketing spend, which makes them even harder to compete with.

Stories presented in each chapter will show how many legacy-style organizations have added or ignored friction in their product and service design and delivery. They have made it hard for customers to deal with them, and as a result, their customers are frustrated. This friction has been measured by polls, surveys, and research studies. For example, the **ACSI (American Customer Satisfaction Index)**,[1] at the time of this book's writing, was lower than its 1994 baseline level. The number of staff employed in customer care contact centers has risen year over year in the United States,[2] despite trends to offshore and digitize interactions. In Frictionless Organizations, the number of support staff drops as the companies get easier to deal with; however, organizations that are full of friction have to add staff in their contact centers to deal with problems and complaints. This pattern is mirrored across the globe.

WHY HASN'T DIGITAL MADE THINGS BETTER?

In theory, the proliferation of unassisted or digital customer contact channels, such as portals, smartphone apps, web chat, and social media messaging, should have improved life for customers. While these channels have added choice and, at times, convenience, they have also created new problems and more friction. For example, customers rightly expect that the organizations they deal with will know and understand the interactions they have had using these different channels. If a customer uses a website, then chats, and then calls, they do not expect to have to repeat themselves again in each contact. Sadly, this book will show that it is rarely the case that organizations have achieved this level of **omnichannel** integration.

Each one of these new channels has added complexity for organizations to manage and, at times, another layer of costs, since customers have come to expect this choice of channels. It was already hard for organizations to understand and track the **reasons** for customers contacting them when they only had branches and call centers. Now that there are multiple channels, it's even harder to deliver consistent and integrated experiences.

The digital age has also made it more difficult for organizations to hide friction. Customers now have many forums in which they rate the organizations they deal with and their products and services. In addition, customers have these ratings at their fingertips and can find reviews of nearly any product and service company, including reviews on how hard an organization is to deal with. Negative stories are laid bare and shared on social media. Unfortunately, research has shown that customers who have bad experiences are more likely to tell more people than those who have good experiences.[3]

Despite this increased visibility, many companies don't seem to know how much effort they are causing for customers and how likely it is that this will be their undoing. Chapter 1, "Understand," will show how few organizations measure friction well. One of the oldest sayings in business reminds us that "you get what you measure."[4] This book contends that very few organizations effectively measure the reasons customers are forced to contact them for help. Fewer of them have data on how well these contacts are resolved, and fewer still have analyzed the causes of those contacts and who in the organization is responsible for fixing the problems. The early chapters will give the evidence behind those assertions and discuss their consequences: after all, if organizations aren't measuring friction well, it's very unlikely that they are managing it.

WHY IS BECOMING FRICTIONLESS A WINNING STRATEGY?

The good news is that there are organizations that have worked hard to reduce friction across their business. It is no coincidence that they are market leaders in their categories, such as Amazon in retail and online services, Apple in consumer electronics, Dyson (UK) in household appliances production, USAA in financial services, and Xero (NZ) in **SaaS** accounting software. They also include innovative government agencies such as the Australian Tax Office (covered in chapter 4, "Digitize"), the Colorado Department of Motor Vehicles (e.g., its lost drivers' license renewal process), and the Estonian government (and its "e-Estonia" program[5]), all of which have led the way to simplifying interaction models for citizens.

Studies have shown that the quality of customer experience correlates with financial performance. Customer experience leaders have outperformed the S&P 500 Index by over 50%, according to published studies.[6] The same studies show that customer experience laggards trailed the customer experience leaders by 120%. Other studies have shown that 58% of customers with bad experiences stop buying from companies, and 79% of high-income earners avoid companies for more than two years after bad experiences.[7] Getting rid of friction would appear to be a top priority.

Friction is a whole-of-business problem because it can be created by any department. Therefore, all departments have to collaborate and integrate to become frictionless, including design and product development, marketing and promotion, and even IT and legal. As such, reducing friction is a unifying strategy. It can bring all parts of an organization together around a common purpose: a constant focus on design and delivery of low-effort products, services, and support for the customer.

In addition to achieving greater financial returns, becoming frictionless produces many other tangible benefits. It may sound contradictory, but the easier companies are to deal with, the less customers notice them—and yet the more they come back for additional products or services. The more things work well, the more likely customers are to seek future business from that organization. This produces a virtuous circle that others will struggle to match because operating costs are much lower.

Customers flock to these frictionless companies. They rave about them, are loyal to them, and are happy to do more business with them. While they may interact more frequently with them, it is in ways that they choose rather than to fix problems or query delays. Customers are happy to invest time in these companies' apps, use their websites, and give them their feedback. The important thing is that everything just works the way customers expect it to work. In other words, "If you want to be loved, just do it right."[8]

These organizations have created frictionless and low-effort experiences and have tuned in to customer needs. They make it look easy, but this book will show that it's much harder than it looks; it requires research, constant experimentation and testing, and lots of communication. It isn't by luck but by design that customers love these organizations.

Organizations that are successful in this area have worked out that becoming frictionless achieves the following:

- Reduces cost in the long run
- Drives customer and revenue growth
- Delivers true competitive advantage
- Enables business survival

The sections that follow discuss each of these in turn.

Being Frictionless Reduces Cost in the Long Run

For many years, the media has promoted the view that companies that want to cut costs will offer lower or inferior service by cutting staff or narrowing hours. It's true that having fewer checkout staff or lower headcount in a contact center saves money, but this also creates queues that quickly impact the business reputation. However, the stories in this book show that a frictionless strategy cuts costs in ways that are more sustainable by removing the need for contacts and reducing processing times. For example, if order processes are streamlined and effective, customers will receive what they want accurately and on time; they will not need to call or email the company about delays or errors, and the cost per transaction will fall. When they reduce friction, companies save a huge amount of money because they have done the following:

- Streamlined processes so that they take less time
- Reduced returns and refunds, thereby saving effort and costly make-good concessions
- Met the expectations of customers, cutting the need for queries and contacts
- Built more effective websites, apps, and other channels that reduce contacts, complaints, and queries about how these channels work
- Replaced assisted contacts with self-service channels that customers want to use

There is a cost to reducing friction that partially offsets those benefits. For example, an organization may have to build the functionality to allow customers to track their orders and be notified of major changes to a delivery schedule. However, that cost will be repaid many times over if it prevents customers from having to ask for help or express their frustration.

Being Frictionless Drives Customer and Revenue Growth

As mentioned, studies have shown that customers who have good experiences buy more. It seems intuitive that customers who have had on-time delivery from a company, when and where they expected it, are far more likely to place another order with that company, while customers who had to chase their orders or who received them late will probably shop elsewhere next time. According to one study, "77% of customers would recommend and provide a referral to a company to a friend where they've had a great experience."[4] The growth of Amazon is testament to this. It could not have been achieved if Amazon's processes didn't work so well. Amazon's ACSI scores remain some of the highest, and being frictionless has meant that customers have turned to Amazon for an increased range of products and services.

Being Frictionless Delivers True Competitive Advantage

Companies that reduce costs through less friction create a sustainable advantage via low cost and high recurring revenue. In contrast, organizations that reduce **service levels** (e.g., speed of answer, speed of delivery, or length of checkout queues) put themselves in a difficult place, since customers will leave and revenues will likely fall. The reputation and brand of organizations that offer poor experiences will be damaged, as stories in subsequent chapters will illustrate.

The lower costs delivered by becoming frictionless drive other sources of advantage. Amazon at one point compared its **CPO (contacts per order)** with that of another major online retailer and found their own to be 75% lower. This meant that the cost of each transaction enabled the company to reinvest these savings in lower prices (to drive more revenue) and greater marketing benefits like free shipping. Being the lowest-cost provider in the market is a critical advantage that can then drive further success. A strategy that delivers both revenue and cost savings is clearly a winning one.

As noted, being frictionless is not just about cost. More innovative businesses have created new ways to share value with customers. Throughout this book, we describe these types of businesses as Innovators. One example is the online car-sales business at www.carsales.com.[9] Their website is better than what it has replaced—classified newspapers and magazine advertisements—for many reasons. The company's search function, advertising, and display make it far easier for buyers and sellers to find each other, because of the following features:

- Buyers can quickly compare similar vehicles or get information on recent sales and value.
- Sellers can also research the market before listing to understand important market dynamics, such as how quickly cars of a certain type and value sell.
- The low-friction experience produces a better exchange of information between buyers and sellers that adds certainty and trust to their transactions.

In a newspaper ad, you get a bare-bones description, which is often out of date. An online ad can show more pictures, give far more detail, and even rate the seller. Carsales.com helps sellers take the right pictures of the car and explains to sellers what information and pictures work best. The online business also helps dealers run their businesses by providing information on things like the depth of market for different models and the speed with which they turn over. This is a very different business model, and by helping both buyers and sellers, the company has redefined the marketplace, having grown its market value by over 400% in 10 years.

Netflix is another Innovator and, like other digital media sites, offers a different experience to traditional TV. With Netflix, deciding what you watch and when to watch it is a low-friction and more controlled experience. The customer can select the viewing device and tailor the watching experience—no more cable and antenna constraints. Netflix's flexible experience enabled the company to invest heavily in original content, further deepening their must-watch reputation with their millions of subscribers.

Being Frictionless Enables Business Survival

One of the impacts of digital disruption and the emergence of other digital-only Innovators like N26, Uber, and Xero is that low-friction business models are now essential if others are to compete. Older-style businesses are burdened with high-cost physical networks and clumsy processes, and they face possible extinction if they don't reduce this friction. Consider these examples:

- Zoom has gobbled up market share from Cisco's Webex by being simple to use.
- Many regional high-touch banks are now challenged by "fintech" players such as N26 and TriumphPay, which even promotes its simplicity with the tagline, "We provide frictionless presentment, settlement, and payment experiences for brokers, carriers and factors so they have the freedom to grow their businesses."[9]
- Amazon has forced many conventional retailers such as BestBuy, Target, and Walmart to add an online channel with various degrees of success; others have gone under, like Borders and Toys R Us in the United States, Harris Scarfe and Dimmeys in Australia, and many others.
- European retailers Aldi and Lidl have disrupted operators all across Europe by offering a simpler product range (2,000 items in UK stores, compared to 25,000 in most supermarket chains), low-cost store formats, limited checkout, and simple self-service. Customers find them easy to use, and they have grown to be among the world's largest retail chains as a result. They have forced other supermarkets

to adapt to lower costs and hypermarket-type formats—or to collapse. In the UK (as of the writing of this book), they have over 12% market share built in the last 20 years[10] and have reduced the profit margins of the incumbents from an estimated 7% in 1990 to between 2% and 3% today.

- In insurance, disruptive businesses are emerging that can price risk more precisely to each customer's need and offer low-cost channels and self-service.
- In wealth management, digital or robotic advice models are emerging that undermine high-cost financial advice models.
- The airline industry was also disrupted by low-cost carriers with simplified business models and mostly self-service facilities, which again forced incumbents to adopt innovations like self-serve check-in and online booking.

These customer experience stories are part of the cycle of business disruption that has occurred over the last 30 years. For example, the most valuable automotive businesses are no longer the "Big 3" in the States or the Japanese manufacturers; instead, they are led by Tesla and Rivian, with some German producers closing in fast by disrupting their own 100-year practices.

Of course, there may be a case for high-touch premium providers of some goods and services. Some customers are prepared to pay a premium for bespoke tailoring or the high-service model of a Fortnum & Masons, Tiffany's, or Louis Vuitton. Note that these companies also offer seamless online solutions. However, in many markets and services, this high-end service model doesn't exist or is very limited. If incumbents are high cost and high effort, then lower-effort and lower-cost businesses will emerge to "eat their lunch." This book will explore many similar examples.

▆▆▆ HOW CAN I TELL IF BEING FRICTIONLESS IS RIGHT FOR MY ORGANIZATION?

The checklist in table I.1 will help you determine if this is the right strategy for your organization. If you answer no to any of these questions, this book will likely assist you.

TABLE I.1. Frictionless Self-Assessment

Question	Yes	No
Do you understand the cost and volume of all customer contracts across your business?	We have clear reporting of the cost of our contact channels every week and every month.	
Do you understand the top 25 to 50 reasons for contacts by total cost and how they are changing?	We can easily track improvements in contact volumes and costs across a limited number of mutually exclusive reasons, none defined as "Other."	
Do you understand which departments drive contacts and hold those executives responsible to fix them?	Customer service informs the other departments, and the entire executive team pulls together to reduce points of failure and friction. We have had many successes and tell stories about them to spur more.	
How has the rate of customer contacts trended over time?	Our contacts per X (where X = active customers, orders, claims, etc.) has fallen over a sustained period by Y% per year.	
To what extent have your customers adopted and exploited your self-service?	Our customer self-service is now our dominant mechanism for our customers and is very popular. X percent of those who use it complete their goal.	
How well do your systems and processes predict and preempt contacts?	We spot problems and tell customers before they even know about them.	
How effective have you been in improving the customer experience?	We have data that show our customer experiences are simpler, take less effort, and are applauded by customers.	

WHAT ARE FRICTIONLESS ORGANIZATIONS LIKE?

Frictionless Organizations share these traits:

- Services and deliveries occur on time and in the way their customers expect.
- Products are intuitive to use and work well.
- Websites and apps are easy to use, and customers use them frequently.
- They recover quickly if anything goes wrong.
- All parts of the organization know the role that they play in delivering for customers.

In Frictionless Organizations, every process works well. It's easy to do everything with these organizations: searching, joining, buying, moving, changing payment or contact details, canceling orders, and returning goods and services. These organizations have provided customers with a choice of interaction methods. They have put their customers in control and deliver consistent, simple, and transparent experiences wrapped around their products and services. Customers love these organizations because they make their lives easier. In contrast, consumers complain bitterly about other organizations that take too long, confuse them, or are hard to deal with.

Three different organizations illustrate how being frictionless is good for customers but requires great design and delivery: Apple, Bla Bla Car, and Uber.

Apple. Over the past 25 years, Apple has built on its product and process acumen to become the most highly capitalized company in the world at times. Much has been written about Apple's constant drive to be frictionless—on its website, in its apps and devices, and in its care centers and retail shops—and that includes its award-winning Genius Bars. Apple starts with simple and elegant designs that have been the envy of audio, video, and laptop producers. The company then follows this with intuitive out-of-the-box experiences that rarely require customers to hunt for support. Apple's retail shops are elegant and open, not closed in or cordoned, inviting customers to browse, play games, test models, and buy on the spot (or know what to order online later). Most Apple devices come without instructions. The Apple designers back the intuitiveness of the experiences they have created: they have led the world in how to interact with touch-screen devices and then made users comfortable with speech-based interaction. They epitomize the frictionless ideal by trying to design devices and related experiences that need no help and support.

Bla Bla Car. Based in Paris, Bla Bla Car exploded on the scene by matching available space in personally owned vehicles with travelers who preferred to drive with someone rather than take a bus, train, or plane. What was particularly insightful—and a great example of being frictionless—is that the company not only matched space availability but also the compatibility of the driver and passengers. They spotted the friction involved in driving with someone who was very different in personality and behavior, and then used a three-point scale to rate drivers and passengers, where "Bla" meant relatively quiet, "Bla Bla" meant somewhat talkative, and "Bla Bla Bla" meant very talkative. As a result, the company has been able to make these long-distance drives much more pleasant for everyone in the vehicle. This made repeat hosting and travel more likely. In short order, Bla Bla Car opened up identical operations across Europe and, during the pandemic, acquired the bus service of the French National Railway. It created operations that needed little or no support, and the growth of this low-friction business continues.

Uber. This company offers another great example of what frictionless experiences can be like. Uber has completely redefined the short-distance travel business, which the media refers to as "ride-sharing" or as part of "the gig economy." Uber's success can be attributed to the frictionless experiences that it has created compared to the old taxicab model. Uber passengers can see available drivers and their ratings, be informed of wait times, get an estimated travel time and cost—and all without paperwork to complete at the end of the journey: no messing around with paying fares, getting receipts, or risking a stolen card or transaction fraud. Both passengers and drivers can rate each other, creating an incentive for amicable behavior. For customers, Uber has taken so many points of friction out of the taxi experience: long and uncertain waits, the inability to communicate with drivers, and the need to place bets on the drivers they will get. Uber has also made it easier to cancel fares and get back in touch with drivers so that even when things do go wrong, the experience is better. If you ever leave a phone or wallet in the back of a taxi you hailed on the street, for example, good luck in getting it back. But with ride-sharing services like Uber, you can reconnect to the driver almost instantly—making the experience frictionless.

■ TYPES OF FRICTIONLESS ORGANIZATIONS

There are three types of Frictionless Organizations that we will feature throughout this book:

- **Innovators.** These organization have created their customer-focused business models from scratch. Many of them were far from profitable in their early years, but they invested in customer-facing processes and technologies that made life better for the customer and, many years later, reaped the benefits. None of them stated an explicit goal of being frictionless; however, all of them set out to build operating models that put customers in control and required little or no interaction through **assisted channels**. Prime examples include Airbnb, Amazon, Uber, and Xero. Other similar organizations will be featured in each chapter.

- **Renovators.** These organizations discovered over time that they needed to devote more attention to removing friction that had built up over the years. Their renovations may be in response to Innovators entering their markets, to customer frustrations, or to regulatory or shareholder pressures. Many have achieved higher levels of profitability by removing friction. Examples include the Australian utility AGL, German-based European utility giant E.ON, T-Mobile USA, United Airlines, and Vodafone.

- **Responsive Agencies.** These are public or nonprofit organizations that recognize that citizens want agencies to be low touch, low cost, and easy to deal with. The precedents set in the private sector raise the bar for the public sector and create pressure for governments to match the standards set elsewhere. Governments are also looking for sustainable mechanisms like contact reduction and digital enablement to make savings. Examples include the Australian Tax Office, the government of Estonia, and U.S. nonprofits American Prairie and Soccer Without Borders.

HOW THIS BOOK IS ORGANIZED

The strategy used to become a Frictionless Organization is presented in three stages and nine chapters, as shown in figure I.1.

Each chapter will do the following:

- Introduce the action needed and explain why it is important.
- Share stories describing which organizations have done this well (we call them "good stories") and haven't ("bad stories").
- Provide detailed how-to steps and methods.
- Present hints and tips for how to get going and how to refine the action.
- Close with a summary and a short self-assessment to determine the relevance of the actions in a given organization.

There are three stages on this path to becoming frictionless, which we will cover next.

FIGURE I.1. The Path to Being Frictionless

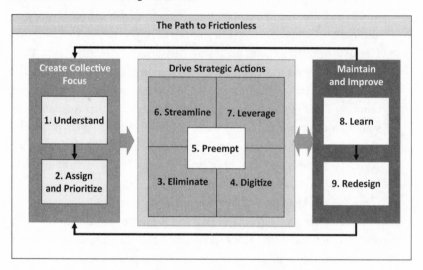

Stage 1: Create Collective Focus

The first stage sets up organizations to remove friction with two strategic actions, which we call Understand, and Assign and Prioritize. In this stage, they learn to Understand the points of friction and then to Assign and Prioritize improvements. These steps are critical, as they make sure organizations address the right problems, solve them in the order of highest priority, and then put the responsibility for solving them in the right place. The Understand strategy helps organizations to obtain data and insights that show friction by analyzing why customers need to make contact. The strategic Assign and Prioritize steps then help organizations to use mechanisms to allocate accountability for friction to the areas that cause them. In these steps, organizations determine what friction to tackle first and how to assess which strategies to apply to which friction.

Stage 2: Drive Strategic Actions

The five strategic actions in this stage enable organizations to reduce and remove friction; organizations can pursue these actions separately or simultaneously. The Eliminate strategy is described first because eradication of friction is the most complete solution. Digitize covers any self-service or automation tools that enable customers to handle their needs independently. Preempt overlaps the other strategies, as it looks to prevent the impact of various problems by reaching out to customers before they find issues. Where Eliminate removes the fundamental cause of problems, Preempt warns customers and helps them manage the impact of a problem. For example, a preemptive strategy might warn someone of a late delivery or alert them to a product fault. The flaw or problem might remain, but the impact will be reduced.

The fourth strategic action, Streamline, reduces the effort that customers have to invest in problems that can't be tackled in any other way. Streamline makes the friction slightly easier to deal with for the customer. The last strategic action, Leverage, looks at how an organization can make the most of contacts that the company and customer both want. This strategy describes how to stop turning things that customers have to do into points of friction.

Stage 3: Maintain and Improve

The last two actions, Learn and Redesign, allow an organization to "sustain the rage" and enable continuous reduction of friction. These actions include steps to measure friction constantly and to ensure that the responsibilities involved in addressing that friction remain in the right departments. The Learn action includes methods to spot new areas of friction and track improvements. Finally, the Redesign step looks at making more fundamental change to handle any work that remains and working in ways that prevent friction from developing. It also examines how to identify when products and processes need a radical overhaul.

WHY DOESN'T EVERY COMPANY BECOME FRICTIONLESS?

It makes sense to design friction-free experiences if they are also cheaper, so this should be a common strategy; however, four common obstacles prevent organizations from becoming frictionless:

- An internal culture and organizational dynamics designed to add friction

- A short-term focus
- Complacency
- Ineffective customer experience methodologies

Internal Culture and Dynamics That Add Friction

Businesses often set up organizational structures and reporting lines that have departments focused on goals that fail to surface customer issues. For example, the product and marketing heads might focus on sales and revenue and have no accountability for customer care or customer support costs that sit in other areas of the business. These consequences of issues created in one area are out of sight, out of mind. Structural silos mean that those parts of the business that cause friction for customers have limited visibility into or accountability for the resulting issues and costs. As more channels of contact like digital, chat, and social media are added and often sit in different departments, it becomes even more complex to work out what the customer issues are and who is accountable.

Short-Term Focus

Getting rid of effort and problems for customers is rarely a quick fix. It requires detailed analysis, a range of solutions (some of which are hard or expensive), and a medium- to long-term focus on the customer. It also requires close collaboration across the organization—not just change in one area.

Unfortunately, executives and shareholders looking for the next quarterly return are likely to be tempted by improvements that are quicker but less customer focused. For example, they may pursue a lower-cost offshore solution rather than do the hard yards required to fix complex friction caused by product design or hastily created websites. Many organizations have sought cost savings in customer-facing areas through mechanisms like offshoring. It has been pursued all too often as a quick way to cut costs before the organization has looked at more fundamental issues such as why contacts occur. The examples described later, however, will show that customer service areas are full of problems and complaints. The risk of moving these functions offshore is that it separates issues further from those who need to fix them. There is also a risk that the complexities and problems exposed may be a poor fit for those working offshore, because they are working in different cultures or in their second or third language.

On the other hand, successful Frictionless Organizations typically have an enlightened CEO or executive sponsor with a long-term focus. This is key to bringing all parts of the business together. Many still have the founder leading the charge or at least looming large enough to challenge everyone or to remain vigilant and embrace the long game. There are many cases that show that organizations can get results within months with the right tools and focus.

Complacency

Successful organizations develop hubris that makes it hard for them to change and identify new trends and dynamics that will undermine their business. Said another way, organizations that acquire large numbers of customers tend to become complacent and almost arrogant in their attitudes toward these customers. As organizations get larger and more complex, they stop noticing the friction that develops as internal hierarchies or increased scale and complexity prevent problems from becoming visible.

Complacency can also be supported by culture and power structures within organizations. This can take the form of managers who promote only those who support rather than challenge their views. Or it can look like people recruiting others who are like them, thereby reducing diversity of opinion. These cultures and norms tend to stamp out those who question how customers are being treated or whether customers will follow new trends being developed. Kodak saw digital cameras coming but did nothing; Nokia knew of the interfaces that Apple was developing but didn't create a smartphone. Most of the major automotive manufacturers have been holding back electric vehicle technology, watching Tesla establish the category so that now they have to play catch-up. These are all illustrations of how organizations protect the status quo and lose touch with customers and their needs.

Ineffective Customer Experience Methodologies

We've observed that customer experience improvements tend to revolve around two dominant methodologies that have become well established but don't always reduce friction: **customer journey mapping** and customer experience measurement.

Journey mapping traces the steps that customers take in complex processes (e.g., becoming a customer and operating with the product or service over time). It is a great tool to help educate different parts of an organization about what they put customers through. It also has a place to bring together product, sales, marketing, and service teams to analyze their most complex processes, like making a claim or obtaining a home loan. However, journey mapping can fail for many reasons:

- It focuses on the current state rather than on design changes or potential improvements.
- Many customer interactions are not journeys and therefore can't be illustrated this way. If paying a bill is a journey, then there is something badly amiss.
- It is hard to illustrate and capture all the variations and steps that go wrong.
- **Root causes** of and responsibility for problems often remain unclear.
- The focus tends to be on fine-tuning the journey rather than on asking fundamental questions about why major steps exist.

Customer experience measurement. Many organizations seek customer feedback on almost every interaction, from flights to website ordering. Asking customers to complete surveys is rife across all industries. The NPS is one common measure, as are CES, satisfaction ratings, and agent ratings. There are also many software options to manage all of these tools.

Promoting customer service management as the way to drive customer improvement is often referred to as listening to **VOC (Voice of Customer)**. Methods to survey the customer have become intrusive, however, so response rates are low (often only 5–10%) and falling. Customers have started hating the constant interruption of being asked for feedback, and organizations are not sure how to address their **survey fatigue**. Other failings include overly long surveys, survey bias toward well-handled processes, and lack of action or follow-up. Some businesses are so busy measuring that they don't have time to take action on the feedback.

Perhaps the biggest failing of these tools is that they encourage a focus on how to handle the contact or query better instead of seeking to answer the more fundamental question of why the contact was needed in the first place. Surveys rarely ask, "Would you have preferred not to have contacted us today?" or "What could we have done to prevent this contact?" Later chapters describe that the most recent analytical tools and other methods enable organizations to understand what customers are thinking without asking them in surveys. This book is about not needing to ask, "How did we do?" types of questions, because organizations should just know!

Now let's figure out how to become frictionless!

THE DARTBOARD METHOD OF CALL-TYPE TRACKING WAS THE MOST ACCURATE COMPANY X HAD FOUND....

UNDERSTAND

Any fool can know. The point is to understand.

—Albert Einstein

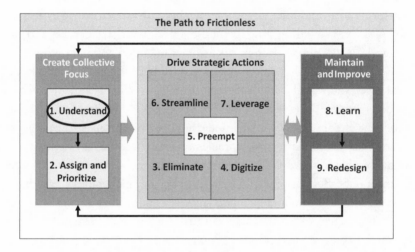

The Path to Frictionless

Create Collective Focus
1. Understand
2. Assign and Prioritize

Drive Strategic Actions
6. Streamline | 7. Leverage
5. Preempt
3. Eliminate | 4. Digitize

Maintain and Improve
8. Learn
9. Redesign

WHAT IS "UNDERSTAND" AND WHY IS IT IMPORTANT?

Most organizations have a long way to go before they are frictionless. An easy way to tell if you are close to eliminating friction is to look at how many people are in the customer service department. Let's compare the percentages of customer care staff in four different businesses:

- An online service provider has 44% of its staff in customer service.
- A telecommunications company has 37% of its staff in customer care.
- An accounting software business has 21% in customer support.
- An insurance business has 18% in customer care and 9% in claims support.

The reason you can be sure these organizations are far from frictionless is that their busy customer contact teams are dealing with frustrations and problems—not sales opportunities. Even though these businesses now offer more contact choices, including options like chat and messaging, customers are still getting stuck and needing help. Contacts typically start with expressions like, "Why can't I . . . ?" "I don't understand. . . ." or "How does this work?" It's common to have 60% to 70% of contacts represent these forms of dissatisfaction. The ISO 10002-2018 standard states that a complaint is an "expression of dissatisfaction made to an organization,"[1] so in many ways, the contact centers in most organizations are handling different forms of complaints. The more of these dissatisfaction contacts an organization is handling, the further it is from being frictionless and the larger the opportunity to improve customer retention and reduce costs.

Given the size of these customer service workforces and the associated costs, you would think that that the ability to Understand and then to reduce contact drivers would be the top priority. However, even the measurement of contacts is not well understood within businesses. Ask most boards and executive teams if problem contacts are increasing, and few would be able to answer. Very few organizations collect, and virtually none of them publish, their contact rates against an appropriate measure of business growth. Very few annual reports feature commentary about the "lower rates of contact" from customers, and it rarely gets discussed in analyst briefings. There are exceptions in companies closer to being frictionless, however. Take Amazon, for example, whose founder and CEO, Jeff Bezos, declared back in 2007,

> Execution focus is a big factor [for us], and you can see it in our financial metrics over the past ten years. It's very obvious when, for instance, we look at the number of customer contacts per unit sold. Our customers don't contact us unless something's wrong, so we want that number to move down—and it has gone down every year for 12 years.[2]

Amazon has long reported and managed contacts per unit (CPU) shipped, recognizing that the larger order (meaning the greater number of items, or units, in the order), the greater the risk of something going wrong. They still measure CPU today, but few organizations have followed suit. Tracking rates of contact has become harder to do as the number of contact channels have increased. Most organizations rarely report their call rates let alone their combined rate of chats, calls, emails, and messages.

Instead of mining these contacts to help drive improvements, organizations have focused on finding less expensive support methods. Many have moved contact operations to cheaper locations (for example, offshore to countries with lower labor costs) or have sought forms of automation regardless of the impact on the customer (as we'll explore in chapter 4, "Digitize"). Automation and **digitization**, when executed well, can be part of a frictionless strategy, but to know *what* to automate and what to digitize and *how* to do it well, you need a good understanding of *why* customers are making contact and what they are looking for. The Understand strategy is therefore an essential step in driving subsequent strategies.

Understanding the rate of and reasons for contacts is the first step to becoming frictionless. The rate of contact shows the size of the prize and the extent of the imperfections. The reasons behind customer contacts show what problems need to be analyzed and fixed. It's also great customer research, since customers are taking the time and effort to call, write, or text to show something isn't working. Every contact is telling a valuable story. Consider, for example, a contact center with 100 agents having approximately 31,200 conversations a week[3] with customers about what they do or don't like about the company's products and services. What a gold mine of potential insight! Imagine how much it would cost to engage a market research firm to interview 31,200 customers.

The recent business trend is to ask customers, "How well did we handle that?" in surveys that typically get 1% to 10% response rates. But the more fundamental question of Understand is "Why did the customer have to contact us?" There seems more to learn in understanding the reasons behind the customer contact, and looking at this data doesn't put the customer to extra effort.

There are four levels to the Understand method.

Calculate and Track How Often Customers Contact Us across All Channels

This means understanding the rate of contact—and not just the volume of contact—and how that rate is trending. While the contact volume can fall when business is trending down or during off-peak seasons or grow when business is rapidly expanding, the contact rate looks at the extent of customer contact relative to the growth or decline of an organization's customer base. Using the Understand strategy will show that most contacts are not valuable and that the goal should, therefore, be to reduce contact rates over time. Tracking the rate of contact answers two critical customer experience questions: (1) Are we getting easier to deal with or harder? and (2) Are we nearing a frictionless state?

Capture the Reasons for Customer Contacts and Associated Costs

To make sense of contact volume and trends, organizations need to understand what drove customers to make these contacts. Then they can start to analyze the root causes of the contacts and work out what related issues to tackle. This decision-making is easier when the total cost of each **contact reason** is understood, starting with the handling time and labor costs of assisted support and the cost of other actions or make-goods that happen (e.g., problem research time, refunds or replacements, sending a repair crew).

Determine Repeat Contact Rates and Causes by Channel

Repeat contacts are the greatest source of frustration for customers, since they represent multiple amounts of effort. Making a second or third contact about the same subject is more frustrating, especially if the first contact was a complaint. Repeat contacts can span channels, as well, so if a customer attempts to use a chatbot that fails; tries to check the app, which fails too; and finally ends up calling the contact center, then that's already two repeat contacts. Understanding these repeats helps an organization get a grip on the key pain points for customers and adds disproportionately more cost than an initial contact.

Assess the Customer Impact of Contacts

Contacts affect revenue and customer relationships, and they cost organizations a lot of money. This "failure demand" may well cause customers to leave or do less business with an organization. The Understand method, therefore, looks at the relationship of contacts to other key customer behaviors, like leaving, spending, and rating the organization. It shows the complete impacts of the contacts.

Understanding customer interactions is a necessary first step toward becoming frictionless because it enables a systematic and fact-based approach for improvement. Put more simply, the ability to Understand allows an organization to assess which strategic actions to take. (Chapter 8, "Learn," takes this further by describing how organizations can apply the Understand method continuously). The business world is littered with investments in self-service, digitization, and simplification that didn't deliver the business case that was hoped for. For example, recently a company accepted a business case claiming that a chatbot could automate 40% of calls, but it was based on a vague analysis of the reasons for calls. They then obtained only half of this result, or a 20% success rate, because they didn't understand the reasons for contact well enough.

As mentioned, it is getting more complex to apply Understand since customers can express dissatisfaction in multiple channels. The good news, however, is that the latest analytical and **AI (artificial intelligence)** technologies can help automate this analysis and provide rich, continuous, all-embracing insights. Executed correctly, the Understand actions help an organization to do the following:

- Expose the size of the opportunity.
- Quantify the root causes and opportunities.
- Analyze the strategies needed to exploit these opportunities.
- Identify the areas of the organization or the partners that need to be involved.
- Determine why customers are buying less or are leaving.
- Track the impact of investments and improvements.
- Cut the costs of low-sample-size surveys and research.

The following stories show how organizations have been able to achieve these results.

GOOD STORIES

The 30 Reasons That Matter

Amazon once had more than 300 customer contact reasons for emails and 60 for phone calls. The wording of the reasons given for phone calls was different from that of emails, and the reasons for each type were reported in separate tables. Worse, the company added reasons whenever a new product category was launched or whenever an executive requested that a specific issue be tracked. Amazon thought they understood what was driving their customers to contact them for help, but in reality, the combined 360 reasons didn't really add insight or drive change. Upon closer inspection, it turned out that there were really only 30 unique reasons for Amazon customers to contact the company, including "Where's my stuff?" The recognition that it was possible for **frontline staff** to classify contacts into these magic 30 reasons turned out to be a gamechanger. The company trained its customer service agents to capture these 30 reasons using a two-digit identifier, which all agents quickly memorized. As the reasons became familiar to the agents, they also became reliable in the diagnosis. The number 30 turned out to be important. It wasn't so large that each reason accounted for less than 1% of contacts and therefore appeared not worth fixing. Nor was it such an aggregated grouping that the underlying customer issues were not clear. Each of the 30 reasons also had a clear customer statement attached to it, like "I need to return X," so that frontline staff could easily select the right reason to match what customers were saying.

Each reason was assigned to a single **owner** whose team was assigned to attack the reason and deliver solutions. Jeff Bezos made it clear that he wanted reason owners to be able to explain why their contacts were rising or falling. This forced all of the owners to work more closely with customer service to understand the issues. Amazon reviewed all of the reasons every Friday, an effort led by the VP of marketing, with each owner sharing how his or her assigned reason was trending down, or not, with details on how to accelerate progress. As a result, Amazon improved and simplified the customer experience. Thereafter, Amazon reduced the rate of contacts (or CPO) year over year, leading to the steady drop in CPU that Jeff Bezos pronounced in 2007.

Standardizing Globally

Each of Vodafone's 20-plus markets (countries) across Europe, the Middle East, and Africa used to collect and report more than 500 customer intents or reason codes, each with different wording, preventing any comparison, trending, or common attack plans. An exercise in rationalization and standardization got the codes down to 102 standard intents across all three of its product groups (Prepaid Mobile, Postpaid Mobile, and Fixed Broadband). All markets then began to collect data on these codes, either from their frontline staff or by using analytics. This global standardization enabled Vodafone to share root causes and attack plans to accelerate their strategic actions and benchmark performance across the markets. Each product group's support team only had to worry about 30 to 50 reasons— far more manageable than the previous hundreds.

Vodafone then calculated costs and **KPIs (key performance indicators)** for each reason, including direct and **downstream costs, tNPS (transactional Net Promoter Scores), first-contact resolution (FCR),** and customer **churn.** In cross-functional workshops, it selected call recordings to illustrate several of the more irritating reasons, bringing those reasons and their associated costs to life so that its executives and heads of departments could also understand. This meant that each reason code could then be assigned to an owner, who could have clear insight into the costs and customer impacts, and tackle the associated issues.

Simplifying Customer Needs

OLX is one of the leading online marketplaces. It operates in more than 40 countries and enables sellers of real estate property, vehicles, and everyday objects to find the right buyers. OLX kicked off a pilot in Portugal to test how to understand customer contact reasons and tag owners with responsibility to attack the most irritating reasons. After analyzing the range of issues across its phone, email, and web contact forms, OLX Portugal completely revamped its reason codes into simple expressions such as these:

- "I need assistance to do X on your website."
- "I don't understand X about your website or services."
- "I have a problem; my account is restricted or blocked."

Then, OLX Portugal tracked its seller and buyer **customer journeys** using large A0-sized papers (33 by 47 inches), which it posted on the company's walls, enabling every company manager to understand clearly where bottlenecks drove customers to contact and express these reasons. As a result, OLX Portugal reduced its contact ratio significantly, increased its customer loyalty levels, and won numerous awards. According to the company's VP of Customer Happiness, David da Costa Mota, "In the first three months of this program our CSAT went from 65% to 80%. After one year, we are at 93% customer satisfaction."[4]

To Balance or Not to Balance

Airbnb has grown into one of the most reliable places to find a vacation rental property, valued by hosts and guests alike. Over time Airbnb discovered that trying to balance the quantitative (data and metrics to drive performance) and the qualitative (stories to create empathy and drive action) wasn't providing actionable details, so the company decided to overhaul its customer feedback system. The new system translated verbatim comments from guests and hosts into customer reasons such as "Payments—Extra Charges, Taxes, and Fees" or "Crewbie—Knowledge" (crewbies are what they call their frontline team), which were then assigned with operational impact scores that ranged from negative through positive numbers. By capturing and sharing these direct quotes widely, Airbnb further increased its ability to understand, and thereby to engage, its crewbies, hosts, and company staff in improvements.

Zip Up the Problems

Australian "buy now, pay later" short-term credit provider Zip Co experienced almost exponential growth in 2017–18. It was a classic Innovator story: a land grab for customers and retailers versus competitors such as Afterpay. Staff headcount was doubling every six months as the company's customer counts boomed; Zip Co quadrupled their support staff in just a year. The problem was their systems and processes couldn't keep up with this growth, which would leave customer care to mop up the damage. The director of customer care knew that they needed to understand and then tackle this contact demand.

Zip Co put in place a range of mechanisms to make sure they understood the problems, including the following:

- Track CPTR, or contacts per transaction rate. This showed them the macro picture of whether they were getting harder or easier to deal with.
- Define contact reasons to track, and only add more reasons if significant new issues emerged.
- Create a "wall of pain" where new problems or issues were posted on visible sticky notes. This wall occupied what became a "war room" for problem owners to meet in and understand issues and priorities. Those responsible met every month in this room to understand new issues and track how solutions were progressing.
- Separate issues into those that could be solved by an **agile** process team and those that needed deeper, more complex technology fixes.

Zip Co then used these mechanisms to understand the problems and keep a lid on problem growth. They recognized that customer contacts were key insights into potential improvements.

BAD STORIES

Call-Tag Mania

A major bank used its frontline staff to "tag" the reasons customers were calling or sending emails. The system of dropdown menus they used enabled agents to select combinations of reasons over four levels. In total, there were over 2,000 alternatives! A cursory review showed that agents were 50% more likely to select the first option in the lower menu levels. In short, no one trusted the information's accuracy, and there was too much detail. Every year the customer care team would have to justify why it needed more staff to answer queries by showing the rising level of customer calls and associated costs, but they couldn't explain why the volume and workload was increasing. While attempts were made to charge other departments for the calls they caused, the other areas had no faith that they were being charged appropriately, so they resented the charges. Rather than working collaboratively on the reasons, the other departments would try to prove they were paying too much. The lack of good information meant that no one was working on the contact causes, and the rate of contact continued to rise.

Lost in the Weeds

A major pension administration company had purchased analytics tools to help explain to their clients (the pension funds) why their customers were calling and emailing them. The analytics team let the machine loose on 80,000 calls and came back with a lengthy report that had over 1,000 different contact reasons that the analytics had found. This wasn't a great help. These 1,000 reasons were far too numerous, and the largest reason represented less than 1% of calls, meaning none of the individual reasons was worth actioning. The analysis went nowhere. The analytics didn't work because the technology was given no guidance. To the analytics tool, the customer statement "My contributions are wrong" would be seen as different from "My contributions are missing" or "I want to question my contributions." The language used was distinctive and different; therefore, the uneducated analytics tools selected them as distinct problems. In reality, they could be grouped as a single customer problem that could then highlight flaws in the organization's contribution process. The machine should have been "trained" to group these similar expressions and see them as the same reason for contact.

Same Every Week

A major utility reported the drivers of customer contacts every week in reports to senior management. The drivers were grouped into eight large buckets, such as "billing," "credit," "moving house," and "payments," based on the options the customer chose in the menus on the **IVR (interactive voice-response system)**. Each week the volume of each reason and their proportions changed very little, and there was hardly any discussion about what actions to take. The business accepted that contacts were unavoidable. A more detailed analysis that explored customer statements at the start of calls found there were about 40 common reasons. Of these, 20% of the contacts were for functions that the customer could have completed in some form of self-service. The "billing" calls included complaints about late bills, incorrect bills, and problems that customers had raised in prior calls. These real call reasons shed a much better light on the problems with the business than did the previous shallow reporting methods.

▊ HOW TO UNDERSTAND

There are four levels in the Understand process (see figure 1.1) that deliver progressively deeper insights, each with more detailed steps. The goal of each level is to help the organization understand everything about contacts they receive, from their reasons to their costs, and how all of it affects customers and the organization.

This four-level approach had its origins in Amazon in the late 1990s and has been enhanced and proven over the next 20 years. The objective of these steps is to provide the fact base to drive strategic actions, determine appropriate ownership, and set priorities. The steps are critical for understanding today's contacts, their trends, and their true costs and customer impacts. The process needs to start in one contact channel, usually in inbound phone calls, but it will be even more meaningful and actionable when all other channels are added.

Level 1: Calculate and Track How Often Customers Contact Us across All Channels and the Trends

It seems easy to say that we should "understand how often customers contact us." Shouldn't every organization be on top of this? If you pose the question to the CEO or CFO of most organizations, at most, they might know something like overall monthly or annual call volumes. But in most organizations, there is more data at the executive levels describing how quickly things get done (i.e., service levels for calls or emails) than there is trend data on contact volumes across channels. Few executives would know the volume of chat threads, the frequency with which customers used their app, or the trends in email traffic. As the number of contact channels has grown, it has become harder for leadership to stay on top of this demand picture and what it means.

In businesses where customer and transaction volumes are changing, it is also hard to assess if volume changes are proportionate or not. If the number of customers grows 20% in a year, is it to be expected that contacts also increase 20%? We'd say that it is unlikely to be a good outcome if customer

FIGURE 1.1. Understand Approach

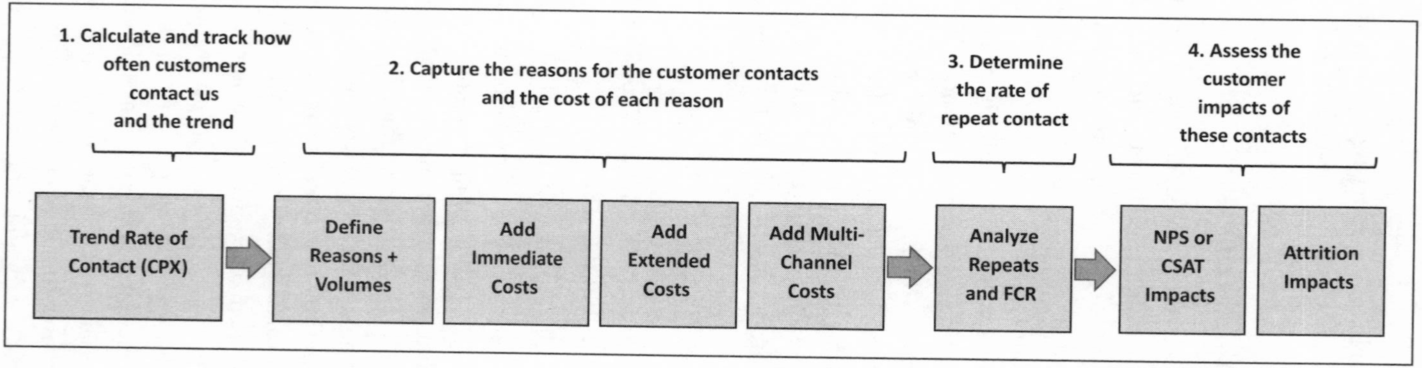

1. Calculate and track how often customers contact us and the trend

2. Capture the reasons for the customer contacts and the cost of each reason

3. Determine the rate of repeat contact

4. Assess the customer impacts of these contacts

| Trend Rate of Contact (CPX) | Define Reasons + Volumes | Add Immediate Costs | Add Extended Costs | Add Multi-Channel Costs | Analyze Repeats and FCR | NPS or CSAT Impacts | Attrition Impacts |

and contact volumes move in lockstep; this would mean that the business is adding costs and friction at the same rate that it is adding customers. In a world where customer contact channels are evolving at great speeds, it is critical to know what is happening across all channels, along with their trends, and then to understand the demand in proportion to key business drivers like customer, account, or order growth.

In table 1.1, a fictional example of a fast-growing airline illustrates the challenge.

This organization knows that calls more than doubled in two years when total customers doubled, that unique accounts grew 2.5 times, and that total flights quadrupled. Calls went up 250% in this period, and chats grew much faster. However, as noted earlier, we need to normalize the contact data to get to **CPX (contacts per X)** so that we can understand if the business got easier to deal with or added friction, as shown in table 1.2.

Examining the CPX ratios—or contacts per driver "X"—paints a very different picture. The ratio of calls per flight is falling, but adding in chat, the story is less convincing. This kind of analysis produces much greater

TABLE 1.1. Core Measures for the Airline, by Year

Measure (in Millions)	Year 1	Year 2	Year 3
Customers	1.0 m	1.5 m	2.0 m
Accounts	2.0 m	3.5 m	5.0 m
Flights	20.0 m	40.0 m	80.0 m
Calls	2.0 m	3.3 m	5.0 m
All Chats	0.5 m	2.5 m	7.5 m

TABLE 1.2. CPX Ratios for the Airline, by Year

Ratios (CPX)	Year 1	Year 2	Year 3
Calls per Customer	2.0	2.2	2.5
Calls per Account	1.0	0.9	1.0
Calls per Flight	0.10	0.08	0.06
Assisted Contacts per Customer	2.50	3.87	6.25
Assisted Contacts per Flight	0.125	0.145	0.156

insight as to whether the business is getting harder or easier to deal with (in this case, harder). Therefore, the three key actions are as follows:

1. Determine which channels and contacts to include. In this example, we added calls and chats and then removed the automated chats handled by the **bot**.
2. Decide which denominator to use as the X in CPX (contacts per X). This entails assessing which measure gives the best indicator of the growth or decline of the business. You might determine X to be the number of active customers, accounts, orders, embedded base units, or transactions. In this instance, we assumed that the number of flights is the best indicator of the volume of activity that could drive contacts.
3. Trend these key ratios over time with **visualization** tools. Figure 1.2 shows a significant increase in the number of contacts handled (both phone calls and chat messages), but since the number of customers rose less in the second chart, the company's CPX, measured as contacts per customer, increased significantly over the first three years.

FIGURE 1.2. Contact Rate Visualization for the Airline, by Year

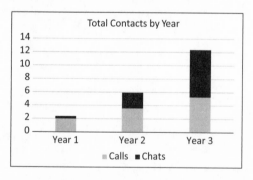

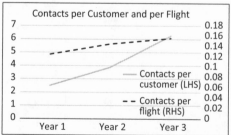

However, CPX measured as contacts per flight begins to plateau in year three, so while this is a good example of the path to becoming frictionless, this organization will need to double down going forward!

Level 2: Capture the Reasons for the Customer Contacts and the Cost of Each Reason

There are five steps that enable this level 2 action:

1. Understand the customer contacts at the right level of detail.
2. Associate all direct costs with each contact reason.
3. Attach all indirect or downstream costs.
4. Report customer contact volumes and costs by reason.
5. Add **multichannel** contacts and costs by reason.

Understand the Customer Contacts at the Right Level of Detail

Almost every organization collects contact reasons, but few of them do so at the right level of detail. Some organizations have thousands of customer reasons (the most that we've seen is 4,500, but 90% of them were never used, and 5% more were used once or twice during the year). Others have too few reasons, such as 8 to 10 major functional categories like "billing," "payments," and "maintenance," that provide no direction. Unfortunately, neither extreme works well. Once an organization gets hundreds of reasons that are manually selected, no one trusts the accuracy, and the associated costs become so fractured that there appears to be little benefit in taking action. At the other extreme, having generic categories like "billing" or "payments" provides very little insight into what needs to be fixed or how to begin to attack the problems. We could label either extreme as "Too many to trust and act" or "Too few to add insight." If there is a magic number, it is typically between 25 to 50 reasons for each product category or business function, but ideally these reasons span product categories.

Tracking the right level of detail is critical for the following reasons:

- Analysis and strategies hang off of this classification.
- Credibility with the business is dependent on getting it right.
- Other analyses, like repeat contacts and customer impacts, also depend on it.

Understanding customer contacts requires building consistent contact categories using the reasons that customers state in their language (e.g., "Where's the closest branch?"). This is different from the organizational view that sees that as an admin question. Techniques to identify these contact reasons include sampling contacts by listening to calls and reading emails or chat threads. A good way to start is to ask frontline staff via round-tables, surveys, or workshops. Germany-based fintech company N26's former global director of customer operations, Carmen Beissner, followed this path to create actionable customer contact reasons: AI-tagged reasons in their chatbot plus agent coding during the live chat sessions.[5]

Organizations should be able to consolidate down to 25 to 50 unique reasons for each product group or business function since the reasons in customer care will be different from the reasons in other areas, like claims or technical assistance. It's harder than it sounds to consolidate thousands of reason codes down to this magic 25–50 level, but one way to force the process is to sample enough volume to work out what the top reasons are. The 25–50 range is magic because it allows an organization to build the case to tackle the root causes that drive each reason. With too many reasons, the justification is harder, since each one will only account for <1% of costs. With too few reasons, either the problems aren't clear or they amalgamate so many issues that the root causes and owners aren't clear.

Associate All Direct Costs

The direct costs of each contact reason come from its handling time multiplied by the associated labor costs. But even that isn't as easy as it sounds, because in contact centers, overall average handle times are fairly easy to collect but not at the reason level. For other channels, such as retail shops, email messaging, and chat, handle times are often not tracked at all. A range of methods can be used in the channels that do not track their time against contact reasons:

- Use call listening samples to estimate handle time by reason.
- Ask frontline staff to bucket the time by reason, using levels from "very long" down to "very short."
- Task frontline staff to track time for a short period.
- Put the analytics to work to calculate durations.

- Add handle time to the tick boxes that QA teams complete when sampling customer contacts.
- Ask staff to keep logs in a tablet that can be analyzed.

Attach All Indirect or Downstream Costs

Few organizations factor in the indirect post-contact costs associated with contact reasons because those costs often lie in other areas of the business. For example, customer care may initiate a repair crew visit to a customer, but the repair costs are tracked by the dispatch or field operations team. The extent of these other costs varies by company and industry. Some industries have to roll a truck to send an engineer to the customer site or engage other suppliers in the process, such as energy network providers. The costs of these downstream activities can be far greater than the costs of handling the call or email. Additional costs can include writing off fees or issuing refunds and credits. Some contacts also kick off work in other teams, such as recalculating an invoice or revising a contract. Downstream costs therefore need to be quantified by tracking service requests, counting trouble tickets, and capturing transferred or escalated calls.

Calculating and applying direct and downstream costs will make a huge difference in understanding priorities as well as the potential benefits of tackling these issues. For example, cable TV and broadband provider Cable One knew that truck rolls to its subscribers' homes represented significant costs. But it wasn't until they associated these downstream costs with specific contact reason codes such as "My connection keeps dropping" that they were able to isolate the root causes and build the case for change.

Report Customer Contact Volumes and Costs by Reason

To ensure that all of an organization's departments understand the issues that customers face, it is important to produce robust reporting of contact reason volumes, costs, and rates. Frequent and trusted reporting helps executives understand the impact of various types of friction on the customer. Reporting, in turn, connects the owners with the problems that their teams create. Initially, the reaction may be one of hostility and denial (i.e., "What does this have to do with my department?") The steps in the next chapter, which deal with the Assign strategy, explain how to tackle that problem.

These costs and volumes become even more powerful by adding two key components:

- **Normalize each volume category against the business volume driver that was used to calculate CPX.** It may be necessary to use different denominators (*X*'s) in different areas. In an insurance business, for example, contacts per policy may make sense for the customer care area, but in the claims function, contacts/claim may provide greater insight. Possible CPX metrics include CPT (contacts per transaction), CPnC (contacts per new customers), or CPeC (contacts per experienced customers), since CPnC is often three to five times higher than CPeC, CPD (contacts per device) (e.g., different mobile phones or set-top boxes), and CPA (contacts per account), as well as the Amazon duo of CPO (contacts per order) and CPU (contacts per units ordered).
- **Include sufficient time series and points of comparison so that trends are clear.** Showing six-week trends for each reason will span monthly billing cycles, while other indicators, such as "this time last year," add even greater insight. Figure 1.3 illustrates this week-by-week trending on a CPX-indexed basis. Most of the reasons were flat or down (which is good), but the left-most reason, which has the highest CPX, is rising (which is bad).

Add Multichannel Contacts and Costs by Reason

The analytics tools available today allow organizations to report contact reasons not just in call centers but across all channels. The call center is one of the harder and more expensive channels to apply analytics because calls usually include more than one reason and are often recorded as speech, so they have to be converted from speech to text. It can also be difficult to separate what customers said from agents' responses.

Email, chat, and messages are all in text form, so basic **text analytics** engines can identify, parse, and match reasons in those channels, and they are often similar to inbound call reasons. Chat tends to be more specific to associated apps or websites, but generally for the same reasons codes can be used, with slight variations and adaptations.

Retail shop reasons (bank branches, product sales, etc.) are harder to collect because the interactions aren't generally captured in any fashion.

FIGURE 1.3. Contact Rate Pareto Chart

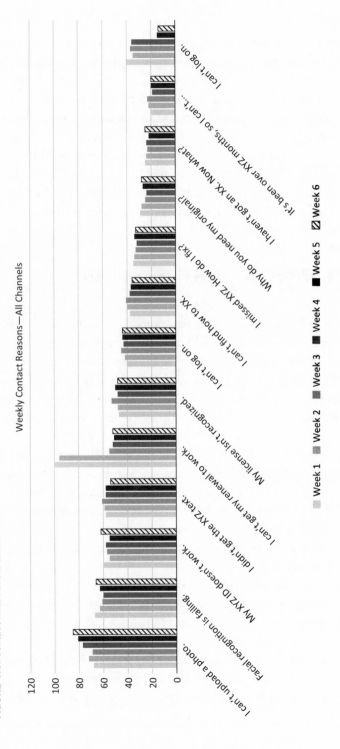

Weekly Contact Reasons—All Channels

A retail bank employee may enter a transaction or some customer notes, but conversations are not recorded or captured. For this reason, some organizations are now deploying many of their contact center tools to retail so that conversations can be captured in the same way.

Analytics tools can classify and analyze reasons in these alternate channels once they are converted to text. The harder part is allocating costs, because many interactions are often not measured and timed as they are in call centers. It is hard to measure the time agents invest in chat dialogues, for example, because they often manage multiple chat sessions at the same time. Similarly, with email, agents are often not timed per message, although it's possible to do.

Level 3: Determine the Rate of Repeat Contact

Level 3 tackles the gnarly issue of FCR. Repeat contacts, which occur when problems aren't solved the first time, and FCR are notoriously hard to measure. Customer research usually puts "Resolving my query" among the top three customer needs on any contact; if customers go to the effort to call, email, or chat, then they want an answer or a solution. The flip side of not resolving the customer query, or doing so in a way that wasn't satisfactory or that they didn't understand, is that they will make contact again. That's if the organization is lucky; some customers simply give up and never return! Repeat contacts and FCR are mirror images and inversely linked. An operation that fails to resolve problems will get more repeat contacts. When customers were limited to one channel of contact (e.g., inbound calls), the repeat tended to occur in the same channel. In a multichannel world, the secondary or repeat contacts can and do turn up in other channels. For example, if a customer doesn't get the answer to an email, they might then call or open a chat session.

Even in a single-channel world, it was hard to measure resolution and repeats, so much so that many organizations have resorted to two flawed techniques:

- **Assume that if a customer calls twice in a short period, it must be for the same reason and is therefore a repeat.** This is an approximation, at best, because many contacts are not related, and most companies use an arbitrary seven-day period, which misses many repeats where the customer may not recognize the problem that fast.

- **Ask the customer in a survey if resolution was achieved.** One problem with this is that, while an organization may commit to resolving an issue, it will still take some work, and customers usually don't know whether the organization will follow through on actions that they promised. In other instances, the customer may have been put to work to resolve the issue, and they aren't clear what will happen next.

There are four more accurate techniques to calculate FCR:

- Listen to 100 or more contacts (for each reason) to get a grip.
- Task the QA team to estimate FCR and repeats to get three for the price of one.
- Add management processes to handle **snowballs,** or repeat contacts.
- Use analytics to do repeat measurements.

Listen to Contacts to Get a Grip

To get a grip on FCR and repeats, it's useful to start by sampling contacts. It is relatively easy to ask an observer to assess whether the call or email was resolved and whether there were prior requests for help. This can be done by listening to see if customers mention prior contacts, or the analysis can assess prior history and analyze the actions that are needed at the end of a call or email. By separating solutions into buckets like "Customer to act," "Workflow to initiate actions," and "Agent to act," it is possible to unpack resolution rates. For call observations, there can be 10 to 20 possible outcomes, of which some are resolved and some are not, as shown in figure 1.4.[6]

Quality Samples—Three for the Price of One

Many organizations use a QA team, team leaders, or third parties to assess their call or contact quality, and many outsource arrangements make this a key measurement for the contract. With a typical sample rate of 5 to 10 contacts per agent, per month, a contact center with 1,000 frontline agents

FIGURE 1.4. Example Resolution and Outcome Analysis

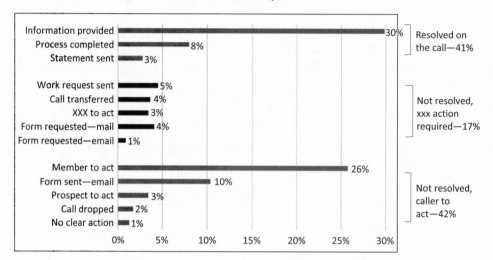

might sample 5,000 to 10,000 calls each month. These samples are used to score the agents on compliance and other parts of the process. Since the call, email, or chat is being analyzed anyway, why not add an assessment of resolution and repeats? It seems obvious, but almost no one does that.

Manage Snowballs

Bill's team at Amazon initiated a very sophisticated measurement technique, which they called Snowballs. The idea was that a repeat contact needs to be "melted" right away, or it will get bigger and become worse, creating a "snowball." Assessments usually show repeat contacts to be 50% longer than initial contacts, and each subsequent contact tends to get worse—or snowball—as irate customers insist on escalation and resolution.

The idea behind Snowballs was that agents had to log any repeat contacts they took, and then Amazon's CS team attributed the problem back to the person who didn't resolve it the first time. This achieved four results:

- Amazon could then measure each agent's "net snowball rate" (generated versus resolved).
- It focused agents on resolving both first-time and repeat contacts.

- It provided feedback for training, process improvement, and quality.
- It allowed Amazon to measure outsourced providers as well as in-house agents.

The only cost to this process was that agents had to log contacts as snowballs—a small price to pay for the benefits.

Later in the book, we'll cover how to reduce the rate of repeat contacts and improve resolution.

Analytics to the Rescue

AI-based analytics can reveal repeat contacts automatically. Once the analytics can accurately report 25 to 50 reasons, it can also be trained to look for repeats of these contacts. This can create a much more accurate measurement because the analytics can look for the same contact reason in a defined period, making it clear to the organization that it is a repeat.

There are four further refinements that can be added to FCR analyses:

- **The period for a repeat can be tailored to the process.** For example, some contacts might be related to a quarterly billing cycle. Therefore, if customers complain about a charge on the bill in month 1, they might not realize that they won't see the charge fixed until the next billing cycle. In that case, the analytics would look for repeats one to three months later.
- **The analytics can look for related reasons for the same customer that may have been "spawned" by the first contact.** For example, if a customer calls in month 1 because they believe they are on a plan different than they signed up for, then a month later, when the next bill arrives, they may call again and say, "My bill is wrong." This is the first problem repeating in a different way.
- **The analytics can look for related contacts across channels.** A chat request for an issue may lead to a call for the same thing if it isn't resolved.
- **The analytics can start to report at the agent, product, and process levels and provide an overall view of repeats and resolutions.**

FIGURE 1.5. Repeat Rates Mapped Against Contact Reasons

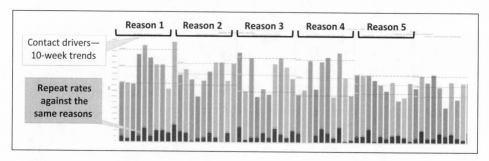

Some organizations have added repeat reporting to the same columns used to track contact reasons. The columns in figure 1.5[7] show the volume of contacts, and the sub-bars show the repeats for each reason.

We've summarized a very complex technique to identify repeat contacts and calculate FCR. This technique typically requires many workshops, analyses, and iterations to get the calculations correct; however, even using analytics to produce a simple "repeat by reason" code analysis, without sophisticated date ranges or multichannels, can produce solid insights.

Level 4: Assess the Customer Impacts of These Contacts

This final level in the Understand strategy rounds out an organization's insight into the impacts on customers and revenue.

Determine What Score Best Defines Customer Experience

Organizations use many metrics to describe **CX (customer experience)**. The most common examples are listed in table 1.3. Each one has a different purpose, benefit, and implication linked to contact reasons.

Each of these CX metrics provides different insights. Analytics techniques now enable organizations to link the data they have on reasons with these metrics; they also enable automation of some of the metrics. For example, rather than asking a customer about their effort (as many organizations do in surveys), the analysis tools should be able to calculate the effort and create a CES by combining the following:

TABLE 1.3. CX Metrics and Their Benefits, Implications

Customer Experience (CX) Metric	Benefits, Implications of Linking to Contact Reasons
Net Promotor Score (NPS) and Customer Satisfaction	Proxies of advocacy and loyalty. May help indicate future revenue and how it varies by reason.
Customer Lifetime Value (CLV)	Reveals if some contact reasons occur more with different customer segments and therefore impact higher- or lower-value customers.
Customer Attrition or Churn	Linking to rates of attrition enables analysis of which contact reasons are attrition drivers and have a more direct revenue and cost impact.
Complaint Rates	The extent to which these contact reasons lead to complaints.
Customer Effort Score (CES)	Used to measure the total impact of this reason on customers and is a much better indication of the impacts on the customer. It gets the business thinking about cost to the customer rather than the company.
Customer Process Analysis	This links reason codes to particular stages of the customer process, like joining or annual premium changes. It helps narrow the focus on which processes need to be reassessed.
Subsequent Purchase Levels	Instead of focusing on scores and numbers, analyzes customers' actual purchases after association with each contact reason and will predict how much irritation that reason causes.

- How long a customer may have taken to navigate menus or websites
- Wait times
- The contact duration
- Hold times
- The extent of repeat contacts
- The percentage of related complaints
- The extent of attempts to perform a task in multiple channels, such as in an app or chatbot

Linking these customer-pain metrics to reason codes can shape not only priorities but also the returns available after fixing the problem. This analysis can add a revenue dimension and provide a different level of analysis of which contact reasons are a priority. Associating measures like customer churn rates can turn the discussion from cost to revenue impacts. Where two contact reasons have similar costs, a customer metric will inform priorities and build a better business case. In some organizations, this can help move the focus from cost reduction to the benefits available from customer retention or greater advocacy. The other benefit of making a clearer linkage between contact reasons and these CX metrics is that contact reasons are often early warning signs of customers leaving or reducing their spend. For example, at one broadband provider, 50% of customers who called two or more times about problems with their connection later switched providers. It became very clear to this business that they had to manage those contacts better not only to prevent the problem from escalating but to prevent the loss of customers.

HINTS AND TIPS

Following are five useful lessons to learn about Understand.

Walk before You Can Run

One-off exercises to sample and unpack contact drivers get to action faster than three to six months of attempts to "boil the ocean." In an organization with no understanding or analysis of the rate of contact and reasons, a sampling exercise can be done in weeks and then get the discussion going. A proper sample can highlight call reasons, FCR, and repeat rates and then flag priority areas. These simpler sampling exercises can also show the potential for investing more in techniques that will provide understanding on an ongoing basis.

Teach the Machine

Analytics companies will tell you that AI software will figure out contact reasons. While this can be true, the AI will figure it out faster and more accurately when you show it what to look for. Building variations of the top 25 to 50 reason codes, key words, and other related expressions will help to refine the analytics tool's accuracy. Using manual sampling first can save several wasted iterations of AI analysis. In worst-case scenarios, AI may never get to the right level of detail, highlighting 1,000-plus reasons, which doesn't really help.

Produce the Right Number of Reasons

Getting to the right number of customer contact reasons is hard but essential. With more than 50, the cost of each one does not look like it is worth tackling; fewer than 25, and they start to include too many root causes and too much detail, preventing the organization from understanding what's happening. The 25-to-50 range is effective because it produces a reasonable concentration of costs and enough reasons to separate potential causes and owners.

Beware of Root Cause Seduction

Reason codes aren't the same as root causes. When a customer states, "My bill is too high," the root causes of that contact reason can be many and varied. It is tempting to try to get down to the root cause of each contact reason, but there is logic behind not doing that. First, the root cause may not be apparent; the customer may mention a cause but often does not. The cause may also not be clear to the customer-facing staff who handle the query. Asking staff to add root causes can create guesswork and waste time. For this reason, **RCA (root cause analysis)** should happen only once the reasons, volumes, and costs are clear. It may be important to distinguish among different reasons for something similar but only if the agent has to figure this out. For example, an agent who has to work out whether a customer hasn't gotten an order because it is in the warehouse, out of stock, or with the shipping company is in a position to distinguish among those three.

Apply the Ownership Test

If a contact reason has multiple departments that could own solutions (e.g., billing and marketing), then it probably isn't at the right level. It's important to have only single owners. As a business constructs reasons, it's worth considering whether there is a logical owner and, if there is more than one possible owner, deciding on how to break down and delegate that reason. There will always be situations where multiple departments have a role to play, because departments like IT and HR have functions that span many business processes. But wherever possible, it's good to aim for reasons that can be owned by a single department with IT or HR in a secondary role. Doing so will be important for the next stage of the process.

▇▇▇ SUMMARY

Understand is crucial if an organization wants to know whether it is causing or removing friction. The CPX gives an overall measure of the rate of contact and how easy an organization is to do business with. Trending this rate over time then shows whether an organization is getting better or worse. Getting insight into why contacts occur is hard to get right, but it creates the essential building blocks for deeper analysis and improvement. This insight also exposes issues in ways that help an organization focus on these problems and their solutions. It is also now possible to link all related costs to build a complete picture of the impact of problems and issues.

Organizations have talked about resolution and repeat rates for years, and many have used loose approximations that aren't accurate. Now companies can measure these important indicators much more accurately, and these measures provide even more valuable information to drive real improvement. They can also provide multiple ways to analyze the effectiveness of people and processes. Modern analytical techniques now enable organizations to link data, such as churn or customer satisfaction rates, in ways that previously weren't possible. This level of understanding equips an organization to assess how it can improve and what areas of friction to tackle.

ASSESS YOUR NEED TO UNDERSTAND

If you answer no to any of the following questions, you need to do more to understand:

Q1.   Do you have a good understanding of the volume, costs, and contact trends in all channels in the business?

Q2.   Do you understand whether the rate of contact is rising or falling relative to business growth?

Q3. Do you have clear visibility of the reasons for contacts that every executive and "head of" understands?

Q4. Are the downstream costs collected at the reason level and tracked?

Q5. Are resolution rates and repeat contact rates well understood and used to drive improvements?

Q6. Is the impact of customer contacts on satisfaction and customer loss/ growth clear?

Q7. When the volume of contacts in any channel goes up or down, do you understand why that happens?

ASSIGN AND PRIORITIZE

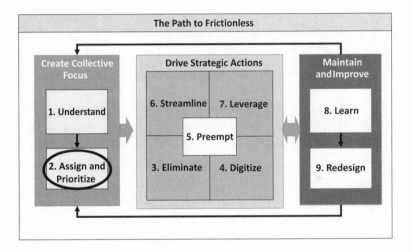

I take ownership of every mistake I've ever made.

—Jon Runyan, U.S. Representative for New
Jersey's 3rd Congressional District

The Path to Frictionless

Create Collective Focus
1. Understand
2. Assign and Prioritize

Drive Strategic Actions
6. Streamline | 7. Leverage
5. Preempt
3. Eliminate | 4. Digitize

Maintain and Improve
8. Learn
9. Redesign

WHAT ARE "ASSIGN" AND "PRIORITIZE" AND WHY ARE THEY IMPORTANT?

After an organization understands the reasons for customer contacts, it can apply the Assign and Prioritize processes to clarify who is responsible for the underlying issues, what strategies to pursue, and which actions should progress first. These process steps trigger the actions that start to remove friction for customers. Assigning contact reasons to owners involves getting consensus on who owns each problem across the business. Prioritizing includes determining what to do about each reason code and the associated causes, how important each reason is, and how feasible it is to determine solutions.

The first step—assigning tasks to owners—is critical, because most problems are caused outside of customer service and need to be owned in the right place in the organization. This step sounds straightforward enough, but getting busy departmental heads to take ownership of problems they haven't previously recognized can be quite complex. In addition, it usually means getting senior leadership to back a different way of working: since the job of owning contact reasons needs to have consequences if is to be effective, this step usually requires changing or realigning current business goals and strategies and resetting targets, all of which need to be agreed upon across the executive team.

In addition to being assigned, tasks must be prioritized, but not before there is an agreed strategy for each of the contact reasons identified in the Understand step (see the previous chapter). The strategy for each contact reason includes the outcome required for that type of contact. For example, some types of contacts might require an Eliminate strategy, while others might be digitized. Each contact reason should have an agreed target, such as "eliminate 50% of this type" or "eliminate all of this type of contact."

Finally, the organization needs to agree on the priority of actions and the feasibility of solutions that underpin those actions. Some organizations might select the highest-cost reasons to attack first, for example, while other organizations might choose a combination of high-cost and high-customer-pain options (e.g., reasons with low FCR or high customer effort) or one or two "quick hits" and one or two more gnarly contact reasons..

Two complex techniques can be used to assign and prioritize contact reasons and their actions:

- **Reverse the costs to the owners.** Cost reversal drives action quickly, since the owners feel the pain and take more interest in the data. This technique has enabled friction to be removed much more quickly.
- **Use multichannel action analysis to add more solution options.** The growth of more contact channels adds to the volume of data in this process and yields more potential solutions. It is important to include all of the customer-initiated assisted channels (e.g., inbound phone calls, emails, SMS, chat, and messaging) with clearly defined costs. The **unassisted channels**, such as chatbots, IVR, apps, and portals, contain invaluable insights about customer intentions or needs

and may represent solutions. Leaving some channels out will provide an incomplete picture of problems and solutions.

The main challenge posed in the Assign and Prioritize steps comes from the fact that every organization has more than enough to do and never enough budget to do it. To simplify the process, the organization can ask these four questions:

- Who owns which problems and what will motivate them to attack those problems?
- What is the strategy for each contact reason and the goal that everyone agrees to achieve?
- What are the current priorities?
- How feasible are the solutions?

Answering these questions as a team will enable the whole organization to move in the same direction, mustering financial resources, time, and attention across all responsible functions and departments toward a common goal. This can be a great mechanism to unite the company around customer issues. In effect, it forces responsibility on the right areas of the business and makes them listen to what customers are saying.

So why is this process hard if it is so logical?

1. First off, assignment requires a clear model of what it means to "own" a set of contacts. It also requires the involvement of stakeholders who haven't recognized the role of their departments in these problems. This can mean senior leadership, even those as high as the CEO or board members, resetting goals and rewards across the entire business.
2. Second, the process requires a change in responsibility across a business that can involve many departments, so it needs senior sponsorship at the **C-level**.
3. Last, the solutions needed to address contact reasons are often complex. They usually require investment in people, processes, products, and technology, and they compete with other investments. This requires collaboration across functions and departments to make solutions happen.

▰ GOOD STORIES

Organizations that get Assign and Prioritize right demonstrate at least one of the following key characteristics, and sometimes they display all three:

- They have always had this level of collaboration and shared ownership of customer issues (typically seen in Innovators).
- They have strong sponsorship at a very senior level of the organization, with the CEO or managing director taking a strong position on customer-facing improvements.
- They have shared goals that encourage this behavior.

Minding the Stores and Sites

When T-Mobile USA embarked on its customer contact demand-reduction program, the company wasn't capturing contact reasons. The Understand process made this clear, and the organization was then able to work out who should own what. Two examples from T-Mobile illustrate the importance of Assign and Prioritize:

Retail Stores

T-Mobile was surprised that many of the contacts they wanted to remove from the contact centers had started because of actions (or inactions) in retail shops around the country. The head of retail stores was assigned contact reasons such as the following:

- "Why is my bill so high?"
- "Where is my discount?"
- "This isn't what I signed up for; why am I being charged?"
- "I want to return this phone."
- "Why am I paying for this?"

The root causes of these five reasons were traced back to retail shops being overly hasty in onboarding new customers or making incomplete introductions of the T-Mobile billing plan or devices. The cost of these contacts showed a trade-off between the productivity of retail sales reps and the process needed to avoid subsequent calls to the care centers. To align motivations, the sales incentives provided to stores' sales staff were decreased by the costs that their actions produced. The Assign steps changed responsibility across the business and added new measures and goals. Other actions included the following:

- Additional support resources were assigned in the shops to assist with onboarding.
- The sales discussion was amended to confirm the "right fit" between the customer and the device being sold.
- A customer onboarding checklist was added to the sales process.
- Each subscriber walked out of the shop with a copy of what their first invoice might look like.

Web Self-Service

Meanwhile, T-Mobile's customer care team determined that its self-service tools were not getting sufficient attention (or "eyeballs") on the website. The focus of the site was selling new devices to subscribers. The care team argued for higher and more visible placement of FAQs and other help pages to no avail, since the website was owned by marketing. In a particularly heated exchange, the company's COO decided that the best solution would be for the care team to own the website and direct the changes they needed. The final outcome was a website with much more visible support functionality that didn't hinder the sales strategy—a true win-win. The change led to a greater uptake of self-service tools, meaning the reassignment of the website to customer care got the desired results.

These and other changes contributed to T-Mobile's 30% reduction of total customer care costs within 18 months and its regaining the no. 1 customer satisfaction rating, as awarded by JD Power.

Cable One Adds Science to Prioritization

As a Renovator, U.S. broadband and internet provider Cable One (now called Sparklight Internet) recognized that they were generating significant and unpopular customer effort and high support costs, so the company embarked upon a "challenge demand" strategy. The problems weren't limited to costs in the contact centers but also included downstream costs led by expensive truck rolls to fix equipment and by the need to refund fees.

Cable One started with the Understand process to define and quantify reasons for initial and repeat contacts. They knew that repeats were costly and frustrating. Once they were able to associate reasons with repeat contacts and determine the rate of these repeats, they could assign responsibility to different areas of the business. They then asked owners to consider the cost and time frame required to implement solutions, along with their impacts. They used a bubble chart that displayed four dimensions of potential solutions: the implementation time frame (on the X-axis), the implementation effort (on Y-axis), the size of the benefit (bubble size), and the customer/staff impact (color codes).

Cable One was able to prioritize projects that were easy to do, like narrowing appointment windows for technicians and speeding the refund process. These projects had instant impacts and reduced repeat contacts. The waves of initiatives that have followed have had a dramatic impact on the business. The company estimates that it has achieved nearly 40% in customer support cost savings and has reduced its contacts-per-customer ratio by 60%. Quite a remarkable exercise in becoming frictionless! Their quest is not yet over. According to Cable One's former SVP of Customer Operations Chip McDonald, "Our goal is to have contacts per subscriber get to zero!"[1]

Owning the Digital Transformation: Put the Innovators in Charge

In the media industry, the arrival of the internet threatened to undermine conventional media such as newspapers and television. The Fairfax business in Australia owned major mastheads, such as *The Sydney Morning Herald*. CEO Greg Hywood took control of the business when the board agreed to his strategy to create a truly digital business. He recognized the need for renovation and had persuaded the board that if they didn't embrace digital, the business would soon be unviable once advertising and circulation declined.

There were some glimmers of hope. Fairfax had established a specialist property sales business called Domain whose online revenue was rising dramatically. Hywood recognized that he had to "invert" the business. Rather than a print business with some digital assets, he saw the future as a digital business with some print. He recognized that he couldn't trust this change to the executives who owned the print mastheads because they would resist it. Instead, he assigned the strategy and more control to the owners of the digital channels. In effect, he told the Innovators in his business to go renovate the company. This was a master stroke, since it gave power and influence to the new business and undermined the change resistors.

An example of how this changed thinking was the way news stories worked. The business pivoted to one where the digital stories were created as a priority and then the physical newspaper was constructed from the digital content. This flipped the old model in which digital content was an afterthought. The Domain property business also became the prime source of property revenue and used the physical print circulation as a glossy add-on.

The net result of the changes that came from these new power structures was a business that turned the corner in terms of revenue and profitability. Readership, revenue, and subscribers grew. The Assign process, which put the ownership of problems and solutions in the right places, was critical to this turnaround.

Braving the Blizzard

Multigame-player giant Blizzard Entertainment embarked on its frictionless journey by collecting its executives together in a workshop to determine the ownership of newly defined customer contact reasons. At first, some of the executives balked and avoided assuming responsibility, but once the head of product design started raising his hand to say yes, the dam broke. Other executives from all of the company's departments chimed in and assumed ownership of their customer contact reasons. The results were nothing less than staggering: growing its revenue by over 200%, Blizzard was also able to reduce its Customer Service expenses, along with the effort extended by its gamers, by 67%, which mean a significant reduction in CPX.[2]

BAD STORIES

Still Not My Problem

An Australian bank also embarked on the process of demand reduction. The head of their contact centers knew that her team wasn't creating most of the contacts, and she needed the rest of the business to help. The contact center team did all the right things, finding ways to track and then report the contact drivers. They were able to analyze the frequency and costs of the top 40 contact drivers and then set about assigning owners. They invited these owners to monthly meetings to discuss the contacts and possible actions. The contact center's budget was allocated to related product owners each year, so in theory they already had an incentive to reduce these costs.

On the surface, they appeared to be taking a textbook approach to become frictionless: There was a clear Understanding of contact reasons, and owners were assigned. Unfortunately, even though the owners all agreed that the problems lay in their areas, almost no action occurred for several key reasons:

- The sponsorship came from customer care. Senior leadership did not overtly back this approach, and there was no support at a level above the contact owners.
- There were no shared measures and goals for the contact owners, so action was never a priority for them.
- The contact owners focused on other existing initiatives. They came to meetings about contact demand, looked interested, and then did nothing.

After a few months, many of the other departments stopped attending the meetings, and the whole process petered out. This shows the importance of sponsorship and aligned measures, without which other business areas see no reason to act.

Falling through the Cracks

A major pension fund used a third-party **business process outsourcer (BPO)** to handle calls, administration, and processing work for its members. The fund was frustrated that the contact costs and complaint rates were high and not improving. The two organizations initiated a deep-dive to understand the contact drivers. Within weeks, using a well-planned sampling exercise, the organizations started to develop a shared understanding of contact drivers. Analysis showed that both sides had areas to fix and that doing so would remove many of these contacts. The overall opportunity exceeded 70% of the contact workload, so it was a substantial prize that would dramatically improve member experience and reduce costs.

Analysis also showed that the pension fund had created process and communication problems, which they owned, including being heavily dependent on complex paper forms that customers were struggling to get right. The fund also owned the member portal, which some members couldn't log in to because the password format and requirements were too complex. The BPO also had lots of issues to fix. For example, the teams that processed customer forms seemed to take pleasure in rejecting any errors they found, emailing customers to tell them to resubmit each time.

It seemed clear that both parties should act, but neither did. The contract binding the two organizations together was part of the problem. It encouraged finger-pointing and blame rather than effective collaboration. Neither party had a clear incentive to remove the friction. With two parties involved, there was no clear sponsor and no agreed-upon measures that made the problem owners take action. Even after seeing the data, some of the owners obfuscated and wanted to do further research rather than tackle the problems. The problem stalled due to the lack of effective assignment to owners, a guiding sponsor, and a prioritization process.

No Responsible Culture

Following a Banking Royal Commission public inquiry in Australia, one of the regulators, APRA, conducted audits of the culture of some of the major institutions. These audits identified that some of the major banks established cultures in which fault was never admitted and problems were buried. Eventually these negative systems led to major fines (over A$1 billion) due to problems in regulatory reporting and regulated processes. In one famous instance, when a senior executive raised an issue with the CEO, he was told to "temper your sense of justice,"[3] and this was reported to the Royal Commission, leading to the eventual resignation of the CEO and several board members.

This culture of ignoring problems is the opposite of the Assign approach in which those who own the problems have to own them publicly and then help explore their reasons. This latter approach starts to build a culture where it is okay to make mistakes. Cultural improvement is enabled because the approach makes it a team sport: rather than blaming one executive or area, all responsible areas are involved. Problems are aired and shared, creating a culture in which it's easier for any executive to take responsibility.

◼ HOW TO ASSIGN AND PRIORITIZE

For the Assign and Prioritize process, there are four main steps to take, as shown in figure 2.1.

Step 1: Assign Contact Reason Owners and Align Motivations

The first step for Assign is to determine who owns each customer contact reason and then to find ways to motivate those owners to create solutions. It is important to design an ownership model that identifies single owners for each customer contact reason. Owners are defined as either those who manage the function that caused the issue in the first place (such as the head of billing for reasons such as "My bill is wrong") or those who are in the best position to lead the attack on the reason. Further, it's rare that only one person is involved in the solutions, so each owner must rally others to participate in understanding the causes and findings solutions.

Assigning ownership is harder that it sounds. "My bill is wrong" sounds like a clear billing problem, but it could be that the head of procurement owns the contract with the meter-reading company that is sending in poor readings. Alternatively, some customers may say their bill is wrong because they have been set up incorrectly by a new business team (think of the T-Mobile retail shop story). There could also be a combination of reasons why bills are wrong. Regardless, the first job is to establish the most logical owner, even if later analysis proves that different or multiple parties need to act.

There may be a temptation to assign ownership to IT because many of the solutions you'll need will be designed and implemented by that area. However, it is usually better to invite IT members to team with the functional heads of business functions, like product owners or marketing. Likewise, customer support often provides insight to owners but rarely owns any of the reasons itself.

It's not easy to get executives to take action, particularly when they are tasked with a new goal, such as reducing customer effort, that they don't

FIGURE 2.1. Assign and Prioritize Approach

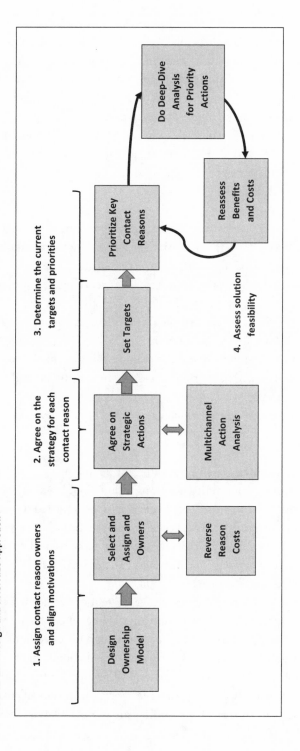

believe relates to their "day job." In many Renovators, busy execs are more concerned with other goals: marketing execs focus on marketing goals, IT execs worry about IT projects and performance, and so on. In Innovators, we observe that shared responsibility and customer focus are often part of the DNA of the business. In start-up businesses, scale and separation from other functions are less of an obstacle. The bigger an organization, the more likely that departments have become separated from the problems they created.

A range of strategies can be used to get the assigned contact reason owners to take action:

- Put into place strong sponsorship from the CEO and the senior executive team that makes it clear everyone has to take action.
- Set collective targets for all owners that are in everyone's best interest. For example, if all executives are incentivized to reduce CPX (the contacts and costs per X metric), then all have a reason to act.
- Make this a key strategic goal that is in everyone's scorecard, affecting their bonuses and promotions.
- Ensure that owners feel the pain by charging back assisted contacts' operating costs, sharing successes, and admitting failures in executive meetings.
- Create a culture in which this is seen as the way to do things. Easy to say, but hard to do!

The first challenge is to get the right people in the room to acknowledge and take responsibility for things they should own. The commitment of senior leadership is essential to get the process started. In particular, the business unit head or CEO needs to sponsor this change program. That level of sponsorship is crucial and may need to be backed up with new collective metrics or a realigned strategy. The executive sponsor may have to motivate attendance and then action.

In some businesses, "shock and awe" tactics are needed that use data from Understand to show the reality of customer effort and cost. In the early days of Amazon, for example, customer service once flooded the inbox of the head of outbound shipping with email complaints they'd received; the complaints, focused on the reason "Where's my stuff?" and were linked to one particular shipper. In another instance, the director of customer service at a water utility started forwarding all the complaints about sites that weren't "made good" to the **GM** of engineering and copied the CEO on each. In both cases, the owners got engaged, and after investigating the root causes, they took swift actions to correct them. Sometimes that kind of shock tactic is a necessary first step.

There are three possible mechanisms that can be used to assign ownership:

- **Bring all of the department heads-of together to agree who should own each reason.** This can work well because it allows for debate and consensus to emerge, but it takes time and needs really clear data from the Understand step.
- **Have the CEO or managing director assign ownership.** This is faster but doesn't build as much consensus. It may work well in a smaller organization or where the CEO is admired and trusted in that decision-making.
- **Have the customer support team recommend ownership,** based on their intimate handling of customer issues, but have the decision ultimately be made at the C-level. This is fast but creates limited buy-in and may produce resentment and rejection, as described in the bad story about the Australian bank.

In the Understand chapter, we described getting information to the right level of detail. However, shrinking the number of customer contact reasons to between 25 and 50 can still create ambiguity. A key indicator that the reasons have been broken down to the right level is the ability to identify who each owner is. Criteria that drive the ownership decisions include the following:

- Does this owner have the most at stake on this reason?
- Do they own the likely causes?
- Is their department most likely to get others to get to an outcome?

Collective decision-making and workshops explaining contact reasons and costs can help drive out who should own what, but it can be a heated debate needing both facilitation and the clout of a sponsor.

Once all major reasons have owners, these owners can then reach out to other departments to support them to create solutions, forging a team approach. There may be some reasons totally in their control, but often it can take multiple departments. Making it clear that owners can involve others is an important step in getting them to sign up. There can even be multiple levels of support. However, the critical first step is to determine who should own what and then to keep them accountable. As an example, in a telecommunications company, "Why is my bill so high?" was owned by the head of billing and collections who received support from IT, sales, and retail with a last level of support from customer care.

One technique that forces owners to take responsibility for their assigned contacts is to make them feel the pain of all the associated costs. To make this more successful (in the short term), the executive sponsor can force the owners to meet their existing budgets and plans and also carry the costs calculated for their assigned reasons from the Understand activities. In effect, these costs are reversed from support and from downstream work to the department of the owner. For example, a marketing executive who owns the reason "I don't understand this promotion" still has to deliver the target for new customers and increased revenue uplift. The existing budget now has several million dollars removed because of the costs of the contact reasons assigned to them. This is a good tactic to get action, because the owners now have other targets under threat.

For chargebacks to work, organizations will need accurate and detailed cost information, available by contact reason and owner, that is trusted; a different way to budget; and strong support from the CEO and CFO. Chargebacks can be a powerful tool to engage owners and the customer support team, but it's a significant change, since owners are being asked to go from not being involved in customer contacts to having their budgets eaten by the costs they caused.

Step 2: Agree on the Strategy for Each Set of Contact Reasons and the Associated Goals

The strategy for each customer contact reason varies depending on myriad factors for the company. In a Renovator business that sees its call centers as an asset, a reason like "Do you offer product X?" might be seen as a contact reason that should be grown and exploited; in a purely digital business of an Innovator, it might be seen as a failure in the intuitiveness of the website that needs to be digitized more fully. Departments are often at loggerheads to decide the right strategy. For example, a large bank ran a series of advertisements offering a five-dollar reward if you spent longer than five minutes in the branch, while other departments were busy closing branches and trying to virtualize the bank. Clearly these strategies were counter to one another, and communication had broken down somewhere.

One way to agree on the strategy and goals is to get C-level executives and likely contact reason owners together to thrash out strategic actions and to establish a preliminary target or goal for each reason. A proven way to do this is to workshop two related questions around the contact reasons uncovered in the Understand stage:

- Are these contacts valuable for our customers, or do they irritate them?
- Are the same contacts valuable for the organization, or do they irritate us?

While the definition of *valuable* might be clear, what we mean by *irritate* is a situation in which the customer does not want to make that contact and/or the organization doesn't want to handle the contact with assisted support in the contact center or retail shops. Using these two questions, the heads-of and other prospective owners can debate the levels of each reason's value and irritation. The combination of customer perspective and organization perspective produces the **V-I matrix (Value-Irritant matrix)** shown in figure 2.2.

Each quadrant produces a different strategic action:

- Contacts that are irritating to customers and to the organizations should, ideally, be eliminated completely. We also call these dumb contacts.
- Contacts that customers value but the organization doesn't are candidates for automation and digitization.
- Contacts that are valuable to the organization but irritating to the customer ought to be streamlined and eventually eliminated.
- The leverage strategy is for contacts that both customers and organizations value. These are the contacts the organization wants more of.

There is a fifth strategy that we call Preempt, which is an alternative or interim solution for contacts that could be eliminated, digitized, or

FIGURE 2.2. Value-Irritant Matrix Format

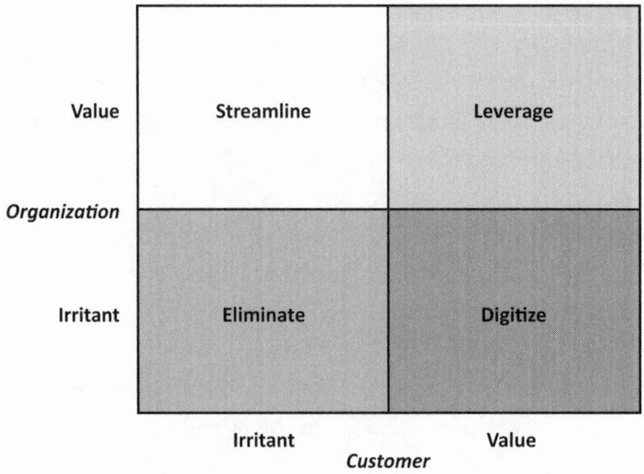

simplified. This emerges once an organization conducts an initial root cause analysis and looks at potential solutions. We will cover each of these five strategic actions in chapters 3 through 7.

The objective of debating these questions is to secure agreement on the required strategy for the most important contacts. The data gathered in the Understand process should help with this exercise by enabling the team to rank the reasons by . . .

- The volume of contacts associated with each reason
- The associated costs, both direct and downstream
- The rate of repeats
- The impacts on CX, such as customer satisfaction, FCR, and attrition or churn

In figure 2.3,[4] the organization has assigned the reasons and then associated the workload (volumes × frontline time) to rank them from most to least work:

It is harder than it sounds to gain agreement on the appropriate strategy for each contact reason. Typical problem scenarios include the following:

- Companies view all contacts as valuable because contact levels are low. For example, one pension fund saw contacts as valuable regardless of their reasons so that they could "engage with the members." This business changed its strategy when research showed that customers who never had to call were the most loyal!

- Organizations see every contact as a potential to eliminate. (Although this can be true in some functions and products.)
- Organizations become hooked on digital strategies for everything. Sometimes these companies need to be shown how eliminating is an even cleaner and cheaper strategy.
- Companies view all contacts as eligible for upsell or cross-sell, so they are loath to eliminate or digitize them. However, there is usually very little to no **sales through service (STS)** for reasons that are assigned to be eliminated or streamlined.

FIGURE 2.3. Sample Value-Irritant Matrix

	Workload

	Streamline	~15%	Leverage	~22%
	How do I do this process?	14%	I want to change my direct debit.	5%
	Please explain arrears.	1%	I want to change my address.	3%
			I need to access my super.	3%
			I want to roll funds out.	2%
			Have you got my lost super?	2%
			I want to surrender or cancel.	1%
			Send me a withdrawal form.	1%
			I want to change my premium.	1%
			I want to change payment method or frequency.	1%
			I want to roll funds in.	1%

	Eliminate	~34%	Digitize	~29%
	What is the status of my work?	8%	I need my account/policy details.	9%
	The XXX letter is wrong.	5%	I want to make a withdrawal/part withdrawal.	4%
	Did you receive my letter/form/fax?	4%	What's the status of my account?	4%
	What's the status of my application?	3%	Please explain product features.	3%
	Please explain fees or charges.	2%	What are my current values?	2%
	Where's my money?	2%	What's my account balance?	1%
	I haven't received …?	2%	I have a query about my premium amount.	1%
	Where's my statement/notice?	2%	I need your form.	1%
	Where's my form?	1%	Stop sending me …	1%
	Did you receive my money?	1%	I want to pay my premium or one-off payment.	1%

Left axis (top to bottom): Value / Company Perspective / Irritant

Bottom axis: Irritant ... Customer Perspective ... Value

The Assign and Prioritize steps can be further complicated when considering contacts across channels, as described in the Understand chapter. The multichannel view provides even greater insight because it shows the following:

- Where contacts in one channel are the tip of the iceberg
- The total cost of a particular reason
- The total effort and true pain for the customer in solving some issues
- The gaps and deficiencies in digital channels
- The poor experience triggered by underscoped chatbots

The challenge is to bring all of these contacts together into a combined set of analyses. This means an organization must be able to:

- Combine common reasons together across channels.
- Have a consistent way to name and spot the reasons.
- Recognize success and failure in different channels.
- Connect the interrelationships of contacts for a given customer across channels, where customers try and fail in different channels.
- Differentiate between the relatively high costs of assisted channels (calls and chat) and not ignore positive outcomes in self-service and digital channels.

There are two ways to do this:

- **Instead of analyzing one V-I matrix, the organization can construct multiple matrices like a layer cake, with different views into each channel.** However, this technique makes it hard to assess the combined impact of common reasons across channels and tends to perpetuate the separation of channels.
- **Create an integrated V-I matrix that adds volumes and costs across channels to a single view.** Instead of showing just call center volumes and costs, this integrated value-irritant includes the volumes and costs across all unassisted and assisted channels for the same reason.

This combined view may change priorities and move some contact types higher up the list. It may also change perspectives on who needs to be involved in subsequent solution design. For example, understanding that many calls also involve prior failed attempts for the same reason—say, in a digital app and in chat—may throw a different light on the root causes.

Step 3: Determine the Current Targets and Priorities

Once the strategies are clear, the next step is to secure agreement on preliminary targets for each contact reason (e.g., "Reduce this reason's costs—or, better yet, its CPX—by 60% by the end of the next fiscal year") and agree on which reasons to attack first.

There is no magic recipe to determine the appropriate target for each reason, and cultural norms tend to play out over detailed analysis. Some senior leaders may be gung-ho and look to set aggressive targets despite limited analysis, while other owners will be conservative and not want to set targets they may not be able to meet. The overall sponsor and the facilitator of this process need to moderate these kinds of behaviors. In most companies, it is often a useful strategy to set more aggressive goals, because it forces new owners to challenge the status quo.

Targets may need to be thought about differently in each quadrant of the V-I matrix. In the Digitize quadrant, reasons where automation already exists may need more incremental goals than those where new functions are needed. Greater usage of an existing solution may be harder to achieve than creating a new solution. Targets in the Streamline quadrant can be harder to plan for, as they may depend on reductions in the time to do the process rather than on the volume of the requests. All of the Eliminate reasons, by definition, merit aggressive targets.

Most organizations don't have the resources to work on all issues at the same time. So it often makes sense to determine priorities for a subset of reasons in order to do the following:

- To focus attention and resources on some important areas
- To get some immediate results and overcome the skeptics
- To obtain immediate payback that will justify subsequent investments
- To allow greater investigation and analysis of problems and solutions that may take longer

The leadership team and owners should be able to nominate six to eight initial reasons as the top priority, since this number gives a range of priorities and usually involves several departments. Cost and volume alone may give an important view of the opportunity that exists and where priorities may be. However, customer impacts, such as related churn and customer satisfaction levels, may increase the urgency and/or payback for particular reasons and promote them up the list.

Priority-setting may need to be an iterative process. At early stages of this kind of analysis, the owners may not understand very much about the root causes of contact. They may consider a reason to be a priority only to realize that the solution is either costly or very hard to achieve. Other reasons may have less benefit but a greater certainty of payback. This kind of priority-setting can be facilitated by four-dimensional analysis that combines size, effort, risk, and customer impacts.

Step 4: Assess Solution Feasibility

The final step of Assign is to determine the feasibility of solutions for the priority reasons (and later all of the other customer contact reasons). For all reasons assigned to Eliminate, Simplify, and Digitize, the first part of this step is to conduct a deep-dive analysis to determine the root causes for these contacts. An excellent tool is the Ishikawa **fishbone diagram** to challenge the owner and other team members to break the underlying root causes into parts, as shown in figure 2.4.

Another method for root cause analysis is the **five whys** technique, which works particularly well for the Eliminate quadrant. This technique unpacks reasons and sub-reasons by asking, "Why does this occur?" at increased levels

FIGURE 2.4. Ishikawa Fishbone Diagram

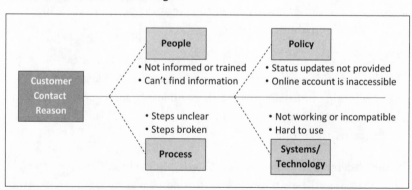

of detail. For example, for the reason "Where's my application for X?" the five whys technique might ask and answer the following questions:

1. "Why are customers asking where their applications are?"
   ○ Because we tell them it will be 5 days, when the service level is up to 10 days.
2. "Why do we say five days if the answer is longer?"
   ○ Because agents on the sales team think it sounds better.
3. "Why does it take more than five days?"
   ○ Because it sits in two different queues, each with a four-day turnaround.
4. "Why does it have a four-day turnaround?"
   ○ Because we have always done it that way.
5. "Why does it go to two different and sequential queues?"
   ○ Because the second process is used to check the first process.

Once the deep-dive analyses get going, the owner and **attack squads** can begin to estimate the contribution of each root cause. This will enable them to understand and quantify what will be needed to address each root cause and what the impact will be.

For all of the Digitize reasons, the owner and analysts could look at the problems in a different way. There may be a clear distinction between contact reasons that are already supported in some way by digital channels and those for which no self-service exists. Where digital options exist, the analysis needs to look at why these options are not being used more and how they could be used more. Where no digital function exists, the analysis should focus on whether it's feasible and cost effective to build a solution and which channel is best suited for customers to use.

Once the underlying root causes become clear across each of the V-I quadrants, feasibility analyses can assess the potential solutions, their costs, and their likelihood of success. This is a complex process. Some solutions are quite mechanical (e.g., "Change business rule A from X to Y"), while others require solutions such as the following:

- Reskilling the frontline staff and upgrading training
- Implementing incentives and marketing campaigns to enable customer adoption of the digital tools

- Reengineering the process(es)
- Replacing manual transcriptions and cutting-and-pasting with automation solutions such as **RPA (robotic process automation)**

In some cases, assessing the feasibility of solutions might start with a pilot or controlled test to ensure that the organization learns which approaches are working and which solutions might produce benefits across multiple reasons. Many organizations now use agile methodologies that look to roll out "low-spec" or **MVP (minimum viable product)** solutions before committing to major investments. The danger of these interim solutions is that they may not be complete enough to test the true outcome of full solution, but at least they can reduce risks.

As noted earlier, this is where a steering group or core team can help spot how solutions fit together. For example, it may be that new processes and training for the sales team can help tackle multiple reasons that have heavy downstream costs, such as "Why is my bill so high?" and "How do I access this function?"

Priority-setting and cost-benefit analyses are iterative because these actions influence each other. Some organizations complete a single iteration, while others revisit it frequently as we will discuss in chapter 8, "Learn."

HINTS AND TIPS

Ensure Committed Senior Sponsorship

Without a strong executive sponsor, such as the CEO or a direct report, and a committed leadership team, the organization will move in disparate directions at the same time—or worse, in no direction at all. This means that the path to being frictionless needs to be seen as one of the top priorities, if not the top priority, in the entire organization. That way it merits the attention, time, and investment that it deserves. If it's outside of the top five priorities, it probably won't get the funding or the resources needed.

Assemble the Right Cross-Disciplinary Team

Different skills are needed at different stages of Assign and Prioritize: customer service, marketing, and IT will obtain and apply the data from the Understand process to analyze root causes and solutions. This requires strong process, IT, and change-management skills to assist the teams that own the problems. Organizations that have succeeded in the Assign and Prioritize steps have assembled these core teams under a steering committee under the project sponsor.

Consider Customer *and* Cost Benefits

There is a risk that the Assign and Prioritize process can become an exercise in cost-cutting, particularly once the full and extended cost impacts are understood. Adding the CX and revenue dimensions can change this focus and help bring a more collective approach to customers across the business as departments like finance, IT, and product design that have little direct customer contact will gain greater clarity on the impacts they are having. It also helps these departments to understand the linkages among the functions and processes they control and customer outcomes like attrition and satisfaction.

Accept Iteration

There can be a temptation for organizations to want to jump into solutions and prioritize everything. The risk with that feet-first approach is that the scale of change becomes daunting, and initiatives can start to conflict. At the start of the process, it is important to set the expectation that this will need to be an iterative process. For example, it helps to recognize that initial priorities may change once the root causes and the feasibility of solutions are considered.

Don't Just "Go Big"

Another tendency is to focus only on the largest opportunities. It can help build momentum if the process also selects smaller opportunities that can be executed quickly to "get runs on the board." These smaller wins help sponsors see results from the process, provide wins to communicate to staff and shareholders, and help create capacity for the larger changes.

▬ SUMMARY

The Assign and Prioritize steps are critical actions for Frictionless Organizations because they place responsibility in the right hands and unite everyone toward a common purpose. There are many tactics for assigning responsibility, but they rarely work without committed sponsorship. Getting agreement on the ownership of contact reasons then leads to analysis of the real root causes and the feasibility of possible actions. The V-I framework helps determine what sorts of strategies apply, and using the data gathered in the Understand process helps drive priorities. The Assign and Prioritize steps can build momentum for an organization in reducing friction, but the real work involved in making improvements happen is explained in the chapters that follow.

ASSESS YOUR NEED TO ASSIGN AND PRIORITIZE

You need to do more to Assign and Prioritize if you answer no to any of these questions:

Q1. Do areas of the organization other than Customer Service agree that they own the contacts occurring in assisted channels?

Q2. Do all areas of the organization recognize that they must help reduce or simplify contacts to achieve other customer goals?

Q3. Has senior leadership made contact reduction, deflection, and simplification a top priority?

Q4. Has the organization agreed on priorities as to which contacts to tackle first?

Q5. Has the organization analyzed the root causes of contacts and worked out an appropriate strategy?

Q6. Do contact owners have a clear reason to act?

Q7. Have appropriate skills and resources been mobilized to tackle these problems?

ELIMINATE

3

Exterminate! Exterminate!

—The Daleks from *Dr. Who*

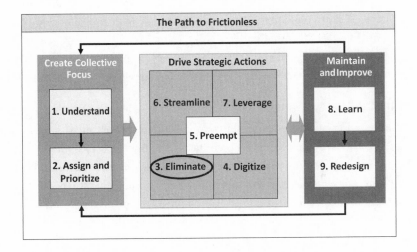

WHAT IS "ELIMINATE" AND WHY IS IT IMPORTANT?

Of all five of the frictionless strategic actions, Eliminate produces the most impact. "Eliminate-able" contacts are those that irritate customers and add cost and problems to an organization. Customers do not want to have to contact any business because their products or services are unsatisfactory, confusing, or delivered late. These contacts reveal the worst kinds of friction. They carry the greatest risk of escalation to expensive external complaint bodies, drive customers to defect, and produce negative reviews and word of mouth. As a result, Eliminate contacts are often labeled "dumb contacts" or "failure demand."

Eliminate contacts are often the most expensive because they are the most likely to require repairs, refunds, rework, and other expensive downstream activities. The total cost to address reasons tied to these Eliminate contacts can be 40% to 75% of all customer contacts. Among these downstream costs are the following:

- Researching what went wrong to determine the best resolution (often for billing reasons)
- Dispatching a technician to diagnose the symptoms, either at the customer's home or in the company's office, and then to fix or replace equipment
- Issuing refunds and credits
- Replacing parts or entire products or assemblies
- Engaging other departments to fix their mistakes

In insurance and other businesses, almost every contact following an initial logging of a claim represents an Eliminate opportunity. In theory, digital businesses should have no contacts, so almost every contact could be a candidate for elimination. Innovators such as Airbnb, Amazon, Uber, and Xero are set up as non-contact businesses and perceive the majority of contacts as subject to elimination. Of course, all four of these companies excel at providing Digitize solutions for self-service (discussed in chapter 4) on their websites or apps.

The Eliminate contacts also correlate with the worst customer metrics:

- High customer churn, often three to six times that of the average customer turnover rates
- Low resolution (the same as low FCR rates), because staff can't get to the bottom of the issue, which makes them the highest repeat contact generator
- The highest effort for customers who start dissatisfied and see every aspect of the contact as a form of complaint
- The highest rates of escalation
- The lowest satisfaction levels and the most number of negative customer sentiments
- Low STS, including cross- or upselling
- High frontline frustration, leading to attrition

Classic examples of Eliminate contact reasons include these:

- "Why is my bill wrong?"
- "Where's my stuff/claim/application/refund?"
- "Why is my bill so high?"
- "Why did you send me this?"
- "My product or service is broken, and I want a refund."
- "Why hasn't the technician arrived as scheduled?"
- "I don't understand X or Y."
- "You won't let me do Y."
- "Why didn't you get back to me as promised?"
- "I don't know how to do Z."

These reasons all represent different types of imperfections: faulty products, late services, bugs that have not been patched, or process mistakes. Even time delays (as seen with "Where's my stuff?" contacts) represent late delivery or poorly managed expectations and are fantastic opportunities to improve the upstream processes, raise satisfaction levels, and cut costs. That's why Eliminate contacts are the starting point of the five strategic actions. In the best scenarios, we've seen up to 80% of these problems removed with dramatic benefits. Companies looking to reduce friction have worked this out and have a much lower volume of these types of contacts. For example, electronics manufacturer Dyson has such intuitive and fault-proof products that they were able to close one of their complaint contact centers in the UK a few years ago. Everything just worked! Similarly, Apple's simple user interfaces and intuitive usage has reduced friction across the customer journey.

It's easy to identify these contacts when you start to classify them correctly, but their solutions may be challenging to deliver. It's hard enough to reengineer a broken process, redesign a product, reeducate an entire salesforce, or fix a badly broken billing system. It is harder still when the source of the problem represents an inherent criticism of someone or some part of the organization and can create a barrier to solutions. These barriers are more likely in cultures that protect themselves rather than find or admit fault. In any organization, the results of the analysis performed in the Understand step can come as an unwelcome surprise. The heads of marketing or sales, for example, may have been blissfully unaware of the problems that their teams or processes caused. When these issues surface, then, expect some denial and anger.

It's also worth remembering that customers who complain and comment may represent only a fraction of those who experience those problems. Some may leave—now or later—while others may badmouth the company and may have a large audience on social media. Some articles suggest that customers who do bother to complain may only represent the noisy minority, with the actual problem being much bigger than it appears: "Just one in 26 customers makes a complaint when they are unhappy. All the remainder churn without saying a word or providing customer feedback."[1]

The good news is that some of the root causes and associated solutions for these contacts will be very similar or even the same across multiple reasons. Therefore, attacking these root causes and designing their solutions will affect multiple contact reason types at the same time, or what we call **look for common** causes. They can also bring about radical simplification that puts a business in a much-improved position—and one that competitors struggle to match.

GOOD STORIES

Many Innovators have set themselves up to avoid frustrating contacts, and various organizations have pursued Eliminate as a core part of their strategy to renovate. Here are just a few examples:

Winnings Ways to Innovate

Buying white goods (e.g., refrigerators, dishwashers, washing machines) online seemed an unlikely success 15 years ago, since they have been sold, traditionally, in big-box retail formats where customers can compare devices, touch them, and ask for advice. Getting something delivered and installed when you wanted it, however, was always a problematic experience and one that most retailers outsourced and charged for. The Winnings business in Australia was, for many years, a leading white-goods wholesaler with no retail presence. When someone from the next generation of the founding family, John Winning, joined the organization, he asked the board if he could start an online business.

John had recognized that customers who wanted to replace broken appliances had a sense of urgency and often little time to shop around and visit showrooms, let alone hang around all day for delivery. They also didn't want to deal with getting rid of their old appliances. Appliances Online soon took off. The business model offered a much-improved experience versus going to a showroom:

- A large choice of products, with the option to do smart searches and comparisons, so customers could easily match their needs
- Phone and chat support, with agents who were experts in their category
- Competitive prices enabled by the lack of rent and no large commission-based sales teams
- Free next-day delivery in major cities, which met the urgency of customers replacing broken fridges or washing machines
- Delivery in defined windows of time, so customers could get back to work or be able to pick up their kids
- Free installation
- Delivery drivers who kept customers informed on the delivery approach
- Removal of old or broken appliances

The business was also fanatical about feedback and measuring CX; even the delivery drivers were rated on it.

This model effectively removed all the possible sources of complaint. Customers rarely if ever asked "Where is my X?" since the whole process was transparent to them, and updates were frequent. There was almost no time for anything to go wrong. Customers never called to complain about poor installation or a rude driver, and the advice they got on their products meant their expectations were well set. The net result is that Winnings spends very little on above-the-line marketing. Reputation, word of mouth, and social media tell their story. The business has been such a success that they have opened three other online brands for different market segments (e.g., bargain hunters prepared to buy a chipped or display refrigerator). Their logistics work so well that Winnings now offers this warehousing and delivery as a service to others. This is a great example of an Innovator designing processes to prevent failure demand and eliminate contacts.

Promotions Council

In the early days at Amazon, when each GM of the virtual stores (such as for books, music, or video) was aggressively building site visits and sales conversions, the customer service team detected that customers were calling or emailing to ask how sales promotions worked, whether expired promotions could be grandfathered, or whether certain promotions could be combined. After reviewing which promotions and products were the biggest culprits, customer service shared these insights with the GMs and recommended a promotions council that would meet weekly to review content for these promotions, sign off on the language used, and stagger the promotions or combine them. Given the strong customer obsession and ownership culture at Amazon, the GMs gave customer service final approval and veto power on the promotions that would go out to customers; it also helped that, every month, Amazon's CFO charged back the customer service costs for these and other reasons to the owners, including the store GMs, so they had a vested interest in reducing that "tax" on their budgets.

Uberizing Defects

Over the past four years, Uber has grown its revenues by four times but has been able to shrink its support staff by 25%, a huge improvement in CPX. One of the key ingredients for this success is the company's laser focus to eliminate defects, defined as situations where something goes wrong for the driver or rider (in Uber's original model) or for the delivery person and consumer (in UberEats). According to Uber's VP and global head of Community Relations, Troy Stevenson, the company has slashed the defect rate by 90% as a result. Among the solutions: (1) asking riders when they book a ride whether they are using the right credit card (e.g., a business card versus a personal one) to prevent subsequent contacts, and (2) ensuring the right items are in the consumer's UberEats order to avoid "Where's my X?" complaints.[2]

No Truck Rolls

Wave, a U.S.-based broadband cable provider, suffered call spikes in its technical support center after windstorms knocked out power to its rural customers. Some of these customers were using their properties for vacation homes and, when they arrived for the weekend, were frustrated to discover that their cable TV systems were down. After analyzing potential solutions to this problem, including upgrading the set-top boxes and modems, Wave came up with a brilliant and far less expensive solution: the company provided surge protectors to customers who had complained about power outages in the past and then used AI to determine other customers that might be similarly affected. These cheap but effective devices not only kept the cable TV running for its customers but also anything else the customer was able to plug into the power strip.

BAD STORIES

Unfortunately, most organizations have plenty of irritating contacts that they seem unable to assess or eliminate; instead, they cope with the demand, add customer service capacity and costs, and suffer a spiral of customer irritation and churn, as the following examples illustrate.

Where's My Delivery?

A major big-box retailer was late to the online retail party. Their big-box retail stores were such a success that they took time to set up an online channel with both home delivery and **click and collect**. They tried to follow perceived best practices, like notifying customers multiple times of upcoming deliveries. With some deliveries, they needed customers to be home and had a process to arrange a delivery window of a few hours, which included several email and text reminders leading up to the deliveries to ensure the customers were home. When they started to analyze their customer contacts, they were surprised that the top call reason to eliminate was "Why didn't my delivery show up?" Customers were clearly not happy, but the company initially reassured itself that it had notified the customers both a few days out and then the day before the delivery. The data on call reasons seemed to tell a different story. Why were so many customers calling in irate that their delivery had not shown up in the planned delivery window?

When they dug deeper on these contacts, the company discovered that in nearly all cases, they had already known that no delivery would occur before the customer called in. The customer care staff could see that the company's logistics team had rescheduled nearly all these deliveries, some-times days earlier. So why were customers still expecting the deliveries on the original schedule? The root cause analysis found that the emails and texts reminding customers about these deliveries had been set in motion when orders were initially placed and then were sent out regardless of sub-sequent scheduling disruptions. In other words, whenever the company needed to alter the schedule, no associated update was occurring in the mes-saging; customers were still being asked to be home during the original delivery window, even though the company had postponed or altered the delivery time in its internal systems. This represented a classic example of contacts that could be eliminated once the organization understood the dis-connects in its systems, processes, and customer communications.

Quality Is Release 2.1 or 2.2

Every software provider faces a balancing act between getting new soft-ware releases into the market quickly and spending the time and effort needed to ensure the product is truly bug-free. It's not an easy balance when customers are clamoring for new functionality or the sales team is eager to see revenue from new modules and features. One major accounting soft-ware provider appeared to get the balance wrong. Almost 20% of their contacts were related to new software releases in which customers found problems. When interviewed, some of the major customers commented that they never downloaded the first or second versions of any new releases (versions 1. 0 or 2.0) from this provider. Instead, they waited for version 2.1 or later because then they felt more confident that most of the bugs and problems would be ironed out. The customer support team lived in fear of major new releases and had to plan for more staff because there were always so many customer issues. In this case, the development and product teams didn't bear the pain as much as the frontline support staff who had to deal with the irate customers and then try to get the developers to fix the prob-lems: friction created by poor quality and testing processes.

Disconnect on New Connection

One fast-growing telecommunications retailer and internet service found that it was adding customer care and tech support staff at a faster rate than it was adding customers. Their initial analysis identified that customers were having to call on average 3.5 times for every new internet or mobile connection, a high level of friction for both the customer and company. Analysis also showed that 20% of new accounts closed within two months.

Their initial contact analysis showed that over 70% of contacts were irritating to the customer and to the company. Reasons included things like "My internet isn't working" or "I can't activate X" or "What is the status of my order?" They also had a very high rate of repeat contacts, at almost 40%. The analysis team looked upstream at the sales calls and found a complete disconnect between the sales conversations and the process that customers needed to get connected. The sales team gave incorrect advice like, "When your modem arrives, just plug it in," when, in fact, it would only work when an activation process was completed by the company and network provider. The sales team also set no expectations regarding the timing of post-sales processes and didn't set up customers with payment mechanisms, so many customers had to call again when they got their first bill.

The company began to realize that it had a very large percentage of demand that could be eliminated but only if it could change the sales conversation and provide greater information on the installation process. The high loss of new customers was based on their giving up on the process and seeking new providers. There was both a major overhead in these failed processes that drove almost half the calls in the service and tech support teams, and there was a loss of revenue, as 20% of these hard-won acquisitions were leaving.

HOW TO ELIMINATE

There are four key steps to enable the Eliminate strategy, with some iterative processes driven by this analysis, as shown in figure 3.1:

Step 1: Determine the Causes for This Contact Type

Customer contact reasons such as "Where is my order?" or "My bill is wrong" can have many root causes. The first task is to try to understand why these contacts occur. This starts with sampling numerous contacts (e.g., calls, email, chats) for this contact reason to pick up indicators based on what customers are saying during these interactions. It is also useful to

FIGURE 3.1. The Eliminate Approach

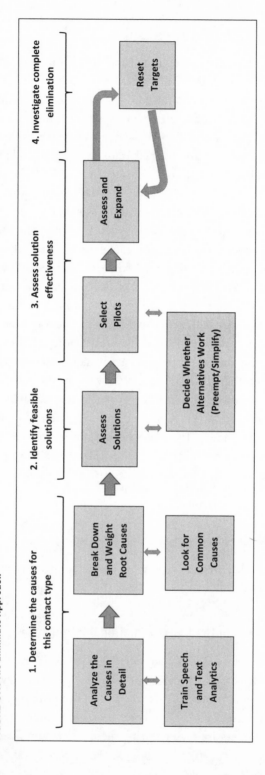

assess the methods that frontline staff use to fix the problems, because they can indicate the root causes. Another option is to ask frontline staff for their thoughts on the causes: as they fix the problems, they should figure out where they came from!

With data-mining techniques, organizations can now pull out tens of thousands of these contacts and interrogate them in smart ways, but it is hard for analytics tools to know what to look for. Where they add most value is in searching for common themes. For example, the analytics engine can pull out all "My bill is wrong" calls and emails and then look for a sub-set of causes. Feeding the themes to the analytics allows the technology to quantify and assess these more detailed problems. It's also valuable to look for common causes across contact types so that solutions get more bang for their buck. For example, bad sales processes may set up multiple problems down the track.

Sampling techniques, workshops with staff, and analytics can all be used as inputs to structured root cause analysis techniques, such as Ishikawa fish-bone diagrams and the five whys analysis introduced in chapter 2, "Assign and Prioritize." These root cause analyses help probe through causation chains to quantify the size of each cause, forcing the organization to under-stand the issues and get closer to solutions.

The Ishikawa technique can be refined to look at the problem through different dimensions, such as people, products/processes, and technology. Whichever technique is used, thinking through these dimensions is another reason to use a multidisciplined team to understand the problem. It is a natural tendency for anyone with a particular skill set to look for problems and solutions that fit their expertise. Multidisciplinary teams can challenge each other to scope the breadth of solutions required and identify a greater variety of fixes.

Step 2: Identify Feasible Solutions

Looking for feasible Eliminate solutions involves looking at breadth first, to identify a range of possibilities, and then looking at the cost benefits and combinations that work:

- **Consider a broad range of solutions and, for each, assess the extent to which the solution will fix the problem, regardless of cost.**

Understanding the impact of the solutions helps to weed out ones not worth considering, identify some that might work well in combination, and pinpoint others that are a complete fix. It is often worth considering the more fundamental question, "What would the world have to be like to eliminate this problem altogether?" That can be a stretch goal, but it often gets people thinking in a different way. Google uses this technique when they look for "10× solutions" (i.e., solutions 10 times better than today) and therefore have to consider more radical answers. Jim Collins calls it a **BHAG (big hairy audacious goal)**.[3]

- **Assess the associated cost benefits of solutions to understand the return on these investments.** Some solutions may already be underway from existing projects, while others may fix many problems and therefore yield multiple benefits. For example, redesigning a sales process and retraining sales staff to set up accounts better will fix more problems downstream. However, no retraining program is guaranteed to be 100% successful because some staff may still not get it right. Fixing software bugs or changing business rules may have a more controllable impact, in which case it is worth looking at multiple solutions. For example, it could be that simplified forms and tighter validation in a system may have a more controllable impact than training. It could be that a combination of solutions will be most effective and can be justified.

The return on these investments should include not just the direct costs (e.g., fewer phone calls, email messages, and chat sessions) but also the downstream costs and revenue impacts explained in the Understand analysis. For example, if this problem causes high volumes of complaints, or is associated with high levels of customer attrition, then the benefits will be far broader. The end goal of all this analysis is to find a range of solutions that more than pay for themselves and produce far fewer problems for the customer.

There may be situations where it doesn't seem feasible or isn't cost-effective to eliminate the problems. In these cases, there may be ways to mitigate the issue using Preempt tactics (explained in chapter 5), methods to Streamline the processes to reduce the effort for the customer (explained in chapter 6), or steps to promote Digitize solutions (explained in chapter 4). For example, some utility companies recognize when a bill is higher for a customer than they might expect. Bills that fall outside certain thresholds include letters warning the customer and giving them hints and tips about what to look for (Preempt), while other companies provide links to web portals where customers can check meter readings using texts and emails (Digitize). None of these solutions will eliminate the problem, but all of them help.

Step 3: Assess Solution Effectiveness

Testing Eliminate solutions is different than testing new product or software releases because with the former, the organization is already aware that something isn't working. Nevertheless, a pilot and testing approach may still be needed when the organization wants to test solution effectiveness or the success of a change. The process can be carried out by testing solutions first with frontline staff and then with a subset of customers. The types of problems and solutions should influence an appropriate testing regime. For example, solutions that require changes in staff or customer behavior may need more testing and fine-tuning than software patches. This **test and learn** approach can help refine solutions and get them to market faster by building momentum for these kinds of changes and helping organizations to test multiple solutions in parallel.

Step 4: Investigate Complete Elimination

When elimination momentum starts to build, it's often worth getting a cross-functional group back together to see if total elimination is possible for many of the problems (see BHAG) or if targets need to be reset. What may have been daunting in initial discussions, when the problems weren't well understood, can turn to positive momentum for change. Figure 3.1 shows an iterative loop in which targets are reset and then new solutions are considered. Once some ideas are proven, it is often possible to extend those ideas to other solutions or just to have greater confidence in what ideas will work.

An example of this **lateral thinking** after successful elimination came from a property maintenance business. They first worked out how to eliminate contacts related to late repair appointments by requiring each repair person to text the customer when they were less than an hour from that appointment. That was so successful in reducing the "Where's my repair?" friction that they started looking at all the other contact reasons related to repairs, such as "It's still not working" and even "You fixed the wrong thing." Each of these reasons needed different solutions, including using RPA, but the lateral thinking that had fixed the first problem soon found remedies for the others.

■ HINTS AND TIPS

There are three Eliminate strategies that have traditionally worked well in handling these classic Eliminate reasons: (1) "Where is my X?" (2) "My X is wrong," and either (3) "I've told you about X" or "Why didn't you fix X?"

The "Where Is My X?" Reason

"Where is my X?" problems are missed expectations and can occur in all industries, but they are most common in the delivery of orders or services with appointments (e.g., at-home care or requested trades). Solutions that have worked well are summarized in table 3.1.

The "My X Is Wrong" Problem

"My X is wrong" could be caused by an incorrect account setup, a misread form, or a wrong invoice. Innovators have an advantage in this area, because the root causes are built on digital processes with few paper forms or processes that can fail in this way, but all organizations face this customer frustration, as shown in table 3.2.

"I've Told You About X" or "Why Didn't You Fix X?"

Customers expect organizations to be **joined up** these days. If they tell a bank that their address has changed and they have a credit card branded by the same bank, then they expect that this new information will ripple across all of the organization's systems and departments as well as those of its partners. Similarly, if they ask for something to be fixed, they expect that to be a one-off problem, not a recurring one. Table 3.3 lays out solutions for this Eliminate reason.

TABLE 3.1. "Where Is My *X*?"

"Where Is My *X*?" Problems and Solutions	
Solution	**Example**
1. Deliver the same or next day	Delivering the same or next day reduces the tendency for customers to ask, "Where is my *X*?" It sounds simple, but the logistics and systems required to guarantee next-day delivery are challenging. Even Amazon doesn't offer this in all locations.
2. Shrink the process duration	Processes like insurance claims or loan applications can have many steps and take many days. Shrinking this end-to-end duration reduces the risk of mismanaging customer expectations. Another answer is to isolate exceptions and manage the customer's expectations of these in a different way or with greater levels of proactive contact.
3. Create a straight-through process	A straight-through process is one where the entered data goes straight into the required system. It is then processed immediately and can be enabled by RPA. This is cleaner and faster than any process that involves customer or staff completing paper forms that have to be checked, batched, and data-entered. The advent of more digital solutions for customers is more automation and upfront validation, so that cleaner work comes into the system. With RPA, there is less paperwork and less of a risk for errors and delays.
4. Set expectations on the outside and walk in "the customer's shoes"	Organizations will often say to a customer, "That will take 5 to 10 business days." First off, many customers hear the 5 but not the 10 and assume calendar not business days. Second, the time given may be for the internal process and may not account for postage and delivery time. The point is to think the process through from the customer's perspective, set the expectation "on the outside," and then beat it "on the inside." If it takes at most 10 days, and then 2 days to deliver, tell the customer, "That can be up to 12 days till you receive it."
5. Overcommunicate!	Amazon revolutionized order processing by sending updates at multiple stages of the process, such as when the order is received, when it leaves the warehouse, when it arrives in the depot, when it's ready for delivery, and so on. Keeping the customer in the loop moves from a reactive to a preemptive strategy.

SUMMARY

Eliminate contacts represent the worst kinds of friction. They are the best issues to start driving improvements because they are the most frustrating for customers and have the highest total costs. Eliminate strategies work best if the following are in place:

- Strong C-level direction and an agreed strategy to drive out failure demand and unnecessary customer cost
- A multidisciplined team capable of detailed root cause analyses spanning a range of solution disciplines
- Contact reason owners who are willing to take on the responsibility for root cause analysis, solution profiling, trialing, and rollout
- Analysis of related customer experience metrics, such as customer churn and first-contact resolution as well as contact volumes and costs
- Lateral thinking to consider how to create effective solutions and solve multiple problems in one go
- Targets that focus the entire organization on reaching the nirvana to eliminate the entire reason for each contact and, over time, all of the Eliminate reasons

TABLE 3.2. "My *X* Is Wrong"

"My *X* Is Wrong" Problems and Solutions	
Solution	Example
1. Bulletproof the process	Governments are moving away from paper forms (which are often incomplete or hard to read) and are using more digital forms that can be validated and checked for completeness and also fed "straight through" to the processing systems. Another bulletproofing process is checking key inputs. One smart bank has a team that uses software and smart people to check all mortgage applications before they go for approval. One European telco samples customer invoices before sending them out, often catching errors. It's worth the investment up front because it is cheaper to fix things at this stage than later.
2. Find the real culprits and give them a reason to change	Sales teams are often measured on sales performance and are not aware of their impact downstream. For instance, setting up accounts incorrectly may not impact their commissions or sales performance reviews. To correct this, some organizations use "quality-adjusted" sales incentives (rewards minus downstream costs or cancelations) to ensure sales teams do the process the correct way.
3. Shrink the promotions	Many of the "My *X* is wrong" reasons relate to promotional pricing that ends with the customer thinking that they are being charged the wrong amount. One U.S. telco shrank the number of promotions from 78 (they had no idea it was so many!) to under 10 and made sure to inform subscribers that their promotions were about to end, preventing sticker shock later.[1]

TABLE 3.3. "I've Told You About *X*"

"I've Told You About *X*" Problems and Solutions	
Solution	Example
1. Spot, measure, and empower snowball melting	Among the mechanisms for handling repeat contacts, described in the chapter "Understand," was the snowball process—a solution in which staff are given the time and authority to fix repeat work and are measured on it. The solution also includes a process that gives feedback to those who caused the problems in the first place.
2. Connect the business	Customers expect businesses to be joined up. If a customer has several relationships with a utility, they don't care that gas and electricity are on separate systems. If they communicate a change for one product, they expect it to apply to all products.
3. Provide process-timing transparency	Customers want their problem fixed or their change made. If they update details on a website, they expect it to be applied instantly or to be told when it will be. If it takes the company three days to load new addresses, then it's better to tell the customer than to have them be surprised.
4. Keep track	Some of the root causes for "I've told you about *X*" involve organizations failing to keep track of promises they've made to customers and, therefore, not delivering on them. Another common problem is when customers or their issues pass through multiple hands. It's often better to have a clear problem owner, along with a system that makes the outstanding issues and their timeliness visible to management.

ASSESS YOUR NEED TO ELIMINATE

You have the potential to Eliminate if you answer yes to any of these questions or don't know the answer:

Q1.   Do a large volume of contacts represent customer complaints?

Q2.   Do many customers contact you because your processes work slower than they expect?

Q3.   Do many of your customers call up and sound confused by your products, services, or self-service features?

Q4.   Do you have a higher rate of formal complaints per customer or account than others in your industry?

Q5. Are customers leaving after things don't work the way they expected?

Q6. Is there a high rate of repeat contact because customers aren't happy with how well their problems were solved?

Q7. Does your frontline staff take time away from handling contacts to try to investigate and solve customer issues?

THE REAL GENIUS OF THE COMPLAINTS
APP WAS THAT IT DIDN'T WORK.

KUDELKA.

DIGITIZE

4

> *Nothing important should ever be more than two clicks away.*
>
> —Steve Krug

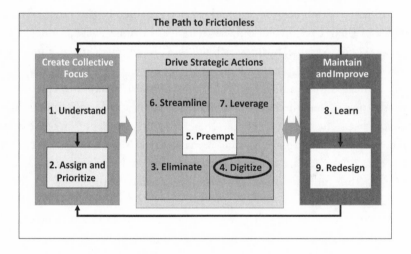

WHAT IS "DIGITIZE" AND WHY IS IT IMPORTANT?

Digitize is the second of the five strategic actions and typically covers simple transactions and information that customers want, rather than avoidable or preventable actions. Also known as automation or deflection, the Digitize solution typically offers the second biggest opportunity after Eliminate to reduce costs. Digitize actions can also improve the customer experience by offering self-service options that are convenient for customers and save them time.

Being able to decide when and where to interact is usually seen as a benefit by customers rather than an imposition, so self-service should be a positive experience for customers. However, surveys show that while "84%

of consumers are more willing to do business with companies that offer self-service . . . only 61% say these solutions are easy and convenient."[1] Therein lies the challenge to digitize! Customers expect self-service to work 100% of the time and be simple to use.

Digitizing is one of the differentiators for Innovators. Many Innovators have built their business models around customer apps or portals that are easy to use, while Renovators are often stuck with the legacy cost of physical networks, staffed interactions, and older websites and technologies. **Digital native** Innovators like Airbnb, Amazon, Netflix, N26, Uber, and Xero have been able to challenge incumbents through the lower cost and broad distribution of products and services enabled by digital channels. Some of them have revolutionized an industry through new products and services. For example, businesses like OLX, Realestate.com, Redfin, and Zillow have replaced real estate newspaper advertising with digital listings. These digital models provide consumers with access to the entire marketplace from their phone or desktop, with additional benefits like tailored searches by any criteria. They also offer any seller or real estate company extra information, such as market depth and sales history. The benefits of digital are not just cost, but also data, insight, and convenience. The combination of these benefits enables entirely new business models.

The customer contacts that organizations need to digitize are those that are valuable for customers, in that they need to perform routine queries or transactions. However, they are irritating to the company because they are routine in nature, do not produce any incremental revenues, and therefore appear on the lower-right quadrant of the V-I matrix (see chapter 2). Digitize contact reasons aren't associated with as much dissatisfaction as Eliminate reasons, but with customer need, and therefore drive less customer churn. However, if customers have no choice but to call or line up in the store for these simple transactions, they rate that as high effort and mark down the experience.

Classic examples of contact reasons that can be addressed by the Digitize action include the following:

- "What's my balance?"
- "When is my next payment due?"
- "I want to pay."

- "Where is the closest branch and when is it open?"
- "Do you have *X* in stock?"
- "I want to change my address/name/details/credit card."
- "How do I change my password?"
- "When will the technician arrive to fix *X*?"
- "I want to activate my new credit card."
- "I want to trade *X*."
- "I want to manage my portfolio."
- "I want to file a simple claim."

There are now many self-service options, and customers expect organizations to provide a variety of channels and solutions for transactional and information requests. These mechanisms must be intuitively usable and thus enable low-effort usage by customers. The latest self-service solutions, for example, are using AI to mimic human interaction through speech and text bots. It is getting harder for customers to know when they are dealing with a person and when automation is doing the job. AI-powered speech-based applications now have named personalities like Amazon's Alexa, Hey Google, and Apple's Siri. These personal assistants are widely used and have been embraced by many customers in their homes.

Surveys show that customers prefer using self-service for routine queries.[2] Lockdowns due to the COVID-19 pandemic boosted the use of self-service, as more customers shopped and transacted from home. Some surveys estimated this increase in use to be as high as 80% for some interactions.[3] In addition, the perception that elderly customers were adopting digital solutions at slower rates is now changing. At E.ON, Head of Customer and Market Insights Kristina Rodig says that the giant energy provider's elderly customers are using online channels much more than anticipated and that its younger customers, who are getting their own energy accommodations for the first time, are calling the company for help more.[4]

On the flip side, there are many examples of poorly designed Digitize and self-service offerings that have created more effort and increased customer frustration. The Understand analysis in chapter 2 should highlight where self-service is failing. Customer contact reasons for failure can take many forms, such as obvious statements like "I'm stuck," "This isn't easy for me," or "How does this work?" Problems also show up when customers continue to use assisted channels to ask questions that are available in self-service. We will address this dilemma later on in this chapter.

Common reasons why Digitize isn't effective include the following:

- Poor design that confuses customers or doesn't work well, often not tested on customers or customer-facing staff
- Use of company-speak or company-centered design instead of the customers' frame of reference
- Self-service options that are hard to find or a well-kept secret; it's best to place support or care links prominently on the home page **above the fold**, preferably on the upper right side
- Inconsistent answers or ways of working across channels
- Staff reluctance to promote self-service because they fear it will threaten their jobs, they don't know how well it works or what it can do, or they have metrics that indirectly discourage promotion
- Lack of measurement of how well the self-service does or doesn't work

In this chapter, we'll explore four overlapping approaches to Digitize. The first approach looks at ways to understand the flaws in current solutions. The second method looks at how to assess the opportunity for new digital answers, and the third describes ways to create usable, low-effort solutions. The last method also covers how to maximize customers' adoption of solutions.

GOOD STORIES

These good cases represent digital-native Innovators as well as Renovators that have implemented successful digital and automation strategies. They also provide examples of tactics that can be used to get greater customer usage of digital solutions.

Xeroing In

Wellington, New Zealand–based Xero aims to "simplify everyday business tasks" for small businesses, accounts, and bookkeepers"[5] and now has over 3 million customers around the world. The company's purpose is "to enable the small business economy to thrive through beautiful software, advice and connections." As a native cloud provider, Xero exemplifies how Innovators are frictionless and intend to remain so. They obsess about the ease of use of their products, recognizing that small businesses are time-poor and not experts in accounting.

Xero did recognize that customers would still need support. However, instead of offering an inbound phone or email channel, Xero promotes "digital support for a digital company" by offering answers to a wide range of queries in Xero Central, including 1,900 hours of video content. With 96% of the questions answered in this online portal, Xero then sets up outbound calls for the remaining 4%, assigning the most appropriate consultant to contact the customer within two hours. Xero Central also operates as a community platform where customers can share their questions or usage experiences with other customers in a "customer to customer," or **C2C**, format. Using **ML (machine learning)** and AI, Xero can also anticipate the next questions or issues raised in Xero Central by watching and comparing behavior with other customers.

According to Xero's chief customer officer, Rachael Powell, Xero wants their "customer experience to be outrageously positive" while recognizing that "the goalposts keep moving" and that "we need to anticipate what customers might need in the future." Xero is a great example of a company that has enabled help and support to be as simple as possible through digital means.[6]

Keeping Them Online—Not Up in Another Queue

Like many large B2C companies, United Airlines has been building and improving its online self-service capabilities. When Bryan Stoller arrived to become the global head of customer care and the senior customer experience executive, he and his team challenged themselves to address a new question. They switched from asking "What did our agents do right?" to "Why did our customers have to call us in the first place?"[7]

Their early insights showed that 50% of customers had either just recently been online or were online when they called. The customer service team then shared the contact reasons and volumes with their IT colleagues, which showed that their self-service was far from best in class (United's IT teams goal). The contacts-to-onboard ratio (a CPX metric) showed United that, over the years, they had trained their customers to call them for help rather than to use the website or app. They then worked hard during calls and through other marketing to convince customers that the calls were not needed. IT's work on the website produced a 25% increase in self-service containment, defined as customers who started in the channel and then completed their goal.

United's chatbot has also been successful, partly because they started with simple building blocks and worked up to add functionality as **containment rates** increased. The company also provided an escape hatch from the bot in each step to reassure customers that they wouldn't be stuck there. As a result, United Airlines appears to be well on its way to becoming more frictionless and embracing a culture that is more customer-centric.

Consolidated Online Support

Multiplayer game giant Blizzard Entertainment determined that its gamers (customers) were contacting the company for playing tips, including "How do I . . . ?" sorts of questions, often interrupting their playing and forcing Blizzard to add more capacity in its support operations. Moreover, this was threatening Blizzard's mission statement of being "dedicated to creating the most epic entertainment experiences . . . ever!"[8] After analyzing its customer contact reasons, the company determined that gamers had four to five siloed contact channels in which to seek information. Blizzard's SVP of Global Customer Services, Technologies, and Live Experiences, Todd Pawlowski, then convened a cross-functional team to attack this problem.

Blizzard held 33 town-hall-style meetings to help them understand what customers were looking for, along with the channels that they were using and not using. As a result, Blizzard delivered numerous new Digitize actions:

- Consolidate the multiple, but isolated, self-service channels into a single support portal to create one point of entry for the gamers. Blizzard consciously narrowed the channels to concentrate the right answers into one place.
- Replace its old knowledge articles for gamers with a **wiki** that its support team was able to update dynamically.
- Let gamers know when there were network outages that might affect their playing so that they didn't need to worry if the problem was on their end (a Preempt action).

- Offer a community-sourced solution (C2C) to address possible software bugs or common issues. This solution was in response to the simple how-to questions that periodically flooded the support team.

Over a five-year period, Blizzard's remarkable achievements included the following:

- Improving their CES, which was important, since customers who rated their gamer experience as being the lowest effort spent more
- Reducing its customer support team by 67%, while the number of games and gamers increased (hence an even better result in CPX terms)
- Changing the mix of problems that landed with the support teams, which meant they had to deal with more challenging problems and enjoyed handling them more than routine questions[9]

Pulling the Support Rabbits out of the Red Hat

U.S.-based Red Hat software is "the leading provider of enterprise open-source solutions."[10] The company's self-support website and customer portal have won numerous awards, including the Association of Support Professionals' award for best support website.[11] Using machine language and AI tools that profile 12 different customer **personas**, Red Hat has been able to provide targeted support online within these five tiers of automation:

Tier 0—A closed loop, with the issue resolved in the product itself
Tier 1—Red Hat Insights, a curated solution
Tier 2—Customer self-solved, using automated rules, trouble-shooting tools, labs, documents, and other solutions
Tier 3—Well-defined solutions
Tier 4—Individual support cases

According to Red Hat's Scott Froelich, who heads up Customer Experience and Engagement, the company's objective with its customer portal is to "Give back time to our customers" and "Reduce a ton of inbound call support."[12] Red Hat discovered a key insight to examine all **null** search results since they revealed gaps in the self-service content. Red Hat also used **design thinking** combined with an agile methodology in its self-service developments, starting with a concept that is storyboarded and then tested rapidly with many iterations.

The company measures its self-service using two metrics: NPS for overall relationship and CES to assess the transactions. Customers can highlight sections of the online documents with comments such as "This doesn't make sense to me," providing invaluable feedback to improve the content. The company is now trying to preempt customer problems and issues and move from reactive to proactive contact. This kind of thinking should maintain their reputation for great digitized support.

Vodafone Italy Wins Fans for Digicare

Vodafone Italy had rates of self-service success that they weren't happy with. Their call analysis showed that agents weren't promoting the available digital solutions because this had never been seen to be their role. If anything, productivity pressures pushed staff to underpromote self-service. Vodafone redesigned the call processes to build digital education and promotion into the calls in ways that helped the customer and made sense to the frontline agents. They deployed a range of tactics, including these:

- Educate agents to use a **DIWM (Do It with Me)** approach for transactions that customers would need regularly. Suggested wording included "Can I show you how to get that now?"
- Provide staff with text and emails that enabled them to send links to appropriate pages or parts of the self-service app, saying, "Can I text you the link now?"
- Train agents on all of the available services, giving them app and portal access, and then requiring them to use the features so they could tell customers, "Oh, I use that all the time—it's great!"
- Make it clear to agents when and when not to educate customers, rather than having them use a blanket approach. The QA (quality assurance) criteria for a good call recognized the distinction between contacts that needed further education and those that did not. This step was crucial since it showed agents that resolution of problems took precedence over promotion and had to be tailored to the situation.

The agents felt comfortable that the guidelines made sense. Their own use of the self-service made them more enthusiastic about its value and better able to help customers. Once the processes were rolled out, the company experienced significant benefits, including the following:

- Increased app use and a commensurate reduction in call volumes; within six months, the call-volume reduction more than offset the minor increase in handle time from the added education
- A higher NPS (by 4 percentage points) among customers who received education but didn't use the self-service
- A 16% improvement in NPS among customers who used the self-service once they were educated, and a halving of detractor rates among those who used the self-service

This story illustrates a "smart" and effective way to increase digital usage.

BAD STORIES

Is 80% a Failure or a Win?

One of the popular new interaction channels for customer contact is the chatbot, which is a type of software that can automate conversations and interact with people through messaging platforms. The best of these bots simulate human interaction and makes it hard for customers to tell whether they are dealing with a person or a robot. The attraction of chatbots is that they can displace anywhere from 10% to 40% of calls or chats from assisted channels. In big operations, payback from these investments can take only a few months.

One finance company created a chatbot for its self-service website. The target for the bot was 30% automation (and therefore 30% fewer assisted chats), which produced an attractive return on the investment. The company celebrated success when the chatbot was successful in handling 20% of its queries successfully. However, this meant that 80% of their customers tried and failed! The company was prepared to have 80% of customers fail for the return they obtained on the customers who were successful. Data also showed that many of the 80% who failed took longer in the assisted interactions that followed because they were suspicious of the outcomes.

This 80% failure rate may have been an acceptable outcome if those who had failed had done so quickly and with relatively little effort. However, there was also a risk that this failure would deter many customers from using chat in the future . This success-and-failure balancing act is very delicate. To understand the whole equation, it's important to understand whether . . .

- Contact durations and effort increase for the 80% who fail.
- There are other customer impacts, such as churn or reductions in revenue among the 80%.
- Customers who fail go public on social media and other forums, impacting the brand.

In this case, those other impacts were not calculated and may have impacted the return that the organization thinks they obtained.

The Rushed Promotion

An insurance business wanted their staff to promote the online portal to customers. They saw it as an important part of the call, with an opportunity to increase usage of the self-service solution. The company made "portal promotion" a quality-score criterion in their call QA process, where agents were assessed on a number of calls each month. In this QA assessment, agents were marked down if they had not promoted the portal, regardless of the call reason.

This blanket criterion didn't work well, as many agents would try to cram this "required" digital promotion into their wrap-up just as customers were trying to get off the phone. The agents used rushed statements, such as, "We also have an online option for customers to use if you follow the links from the website." Adding that statement ticked the quality box but didn't help customers understand what was available or encourage takeup. Worse still, agents would include this line even in inappropriate situations, such as when a customer was calling to complain or cancel a policy. The process was ineffective and annoying for customers and staff. This is a classic example of a one-size-fits-all digital promotion not being appropriately designed or tailored.

Make It Easy to Log On!

A large pension fund built a portal for customers to access their latest fund details, view their investments and performance, and update their contact information—in short, enabling them to handle all of the typical issues that customers want to handle themselves. But in the contact center, the biggest call reason was "I can't log on," closely followed by "My password doesn't work," which, together, accounted for nearly 10% of all calls!

Customers were clearly befuddled by the login and password process. Even the customer care staff seemed confused as to what was and wasn't a valid password and how to get things to work. It turned out that the "security police" in the company had insisted on an ultra-secure login process. The password had to be a minimum of 16 characters, and there were many rules covering what could and couldn't be included; for example, relevant words like *pension* could not be used. Worse still, these rules weren't easily accessed and weren't even explained to the customer care agents in training. It was almost as if the people who had created the security rules didn't want customers to get access at all. The Band-Aid fix was to ensure that staff had easy ways to explain the rules, but the long-term fix required a total rethinking of why these rules existed and how to reduce the unneeded friction.

HOW TO DIGITIZE

The approach to tackling Digitize splits into two streams, depending on existing capabilities: For Renovators, solutions often focus on improving and adding to existing self-service and digital tools and getting the customer base to adopt those solutions. For Innovators, the opportunity can vary from creating a brand-new solution that no business has ever created to refining an existing set of digital options, or in some cases completely rebuilding an initial "toe in the water" solution.

The methodology for "improving old" or for "building new" has many similarities, as figure 4.1 shows. In all scenarios, the organization has to do the following:

- Select the most appropriate self-service channel for the reason.
- Design and build appropriate customer experiences.
- Develop strategies that what will drive adoption.

FIGURE 4.1. The Digitize Approach

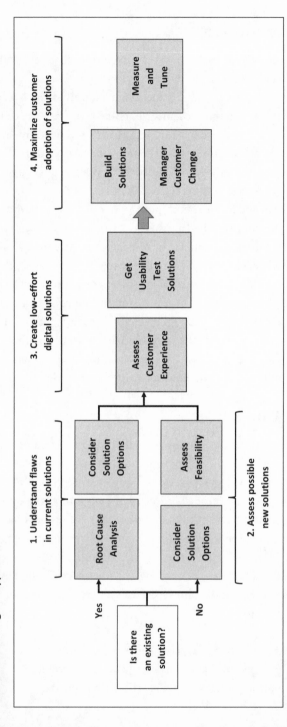

The need for adoption strategies varies widely. A government monopoly may be able to mandate the use of a digital solution. In contrast, a Renovator with a large customer base accustomed to existing channels may need to work far harder to change customer behavior. This is made even harder if an organization has already deployed digital and self-service solutions that have underwhelmed customers or that have failed.

The first steps, as shown in figure 4.1, are to understand what isn't working well in today's service or to assess what new solutions may been needed where none currently exist.

Understand Flaws in Current Solutions

Organizations whose customers have a choice of channels need to analyze why self-service isn't getting used as much as expected. In digital-only businesses, use of these solutions is unavoidable, but there may still be evidence that customers are getting stuck and turning to support mechanisms like chat or social media to "just get through" the experience. Organizations can size the opportunity for improvement by calculating the **take-up rate** of each self-service solution and then the containment rate of the existing solutions, which is equivalent to the percentage of customers who succeed in completing their needs in this channel.

The take-up rate of any channel is simply the number of people who complete the self-service process in that channel as a percentage of the total number who complete the process overall; for example, if 50 people complete a loan application using the website and 100 people complete it overall, including in assisted channels, then the take-up rate is 50%. The containment rate is more a measure of channel effectiveness. It is the percentage of those who try to use the channel and succeed.

It's harder than it sounds to amalgamate transactions and attempts across channels (i.e., to calculate take-up rates) and to have consistent naming of similar transactions across channels (see chapter 1, "Understand"). It's also difficult to calculate whether a customer has succeeded within an automated channel. For example, a customer may abandon an automated chat after some information is provided, but this could mean they received the information they needed or that they gave up; therefore, it's important to understand whether the customer then went on to seek the same information in other channels.

Take-up and containment rates can be low for many reasons:

- Poor usability or design of existing solutions
- Challenges logging into accounts
- Different answers in different channels that confuse the customer, either because the channels are not joined up or they are accessing different data
- Competing priorities (e.g., sales teams that try to keep customers in their channels)
- Inconsistent or limited customer education and promotion of self-service
- Self-service that was historically bad at some stage and put off customers as a result
- Customer fear and ignorance of digital solutions

These are all possible root causes that need to be assessed and understood in order to make Digitize work.

Getting to Root Causes of Poor Take-Up and Containment

One way to understand why customers either aren't using digital solutions or are struggling with them is to ask them. However, a quicker solution can be to mine what customers are saying when these digital solutions are referenced in staffed channels. Key comments often come in the **golden 30 seconds** at the opening of a chat thread or the start of an inbound call, when customers share their upstream experiences (e.g., "I tried to use the app, but . . ."). Other mechanisms that are effective at analyzing why solutions are failing include the following:

- Asking frontline staff what they hear when customers call for these services, because the problems roll down to them; however, you must also tap into the detailed feedback they receive from customers
- Using analytics tools that can extract a large number of specific inquiries that relate to the digital mechanisms and then isolating these for deeper analysis
- Querying social media sites where customers have commented on the company's self-service

- Reviewing free-format text responses in surveys where customers have been asked about their efforts in using digital tools
- Getting external experts to evaluate the design of a channel (e.g., an external usability expert who may be able to highlight issues with a website that the existing designers are unaware of)
- Holding workshops with customers who are not using the available digital solutions to determine whether they knew about the solutions and, if so, why they aren't using them
- Putting the current solution back through formal usability testing in a lab environment with customers; this step may have been missed if a business uses an agile-type methodology that rushes MVP to market

Assess Possible New Solutions

Once the problems behind low usage of digital and self-service channels are clear, the next task is to pick appropriate solutions to address them in order to increase Digitize success rates. This can range from a major makeover of a self-service channel to refreshing all advertising material or launching major education program using frontline staff. The root cause analysis should clarify the problems that need to be addressed by a revised solution so that an appropriate response can be designed. For example, one major telecommunications provider assessed how customers were getting access to self-service content and found the content hidden and hard to reach. That discovery produced a different solution than if the company had found the content didn't exist or wasn't understood by customers.

The Feasibility of New (or Changed) Solutions

There are now far more Digitize solutions to choose from, and organizations need to create identical options in multiple channels. Consider asking the following logical questions:

- In which channels do we need to add or change solutions?
- Do we need to add new channels, and, if so, how can we determine if they will be effective?
- Do we need the functionality replicated in multiple channels?
- Will the use of multiple channels increase take-up or just add cost?

This task might be simple if new functions and services can be easily added to existing portals or apps, especially if there was always a plan to add functions over time. It gets harder if portals and apps are already busy with customers struggling to find all the available functions or if the new function is more complex than those already deployed on that channel. This is where "horses for courses"[13] matters, and organizations need to consider whether the channel "suits" the interaction. Consider these examples:

- Web portals may be better suited than a smartphone-based app to capture complex information and lots of free-form text.
- Mobile apps may be ideal when photographs are needed to assist in the process (e.g., pictures of damages in a claims process).
- Video content may be a better way to explain complex procedures or product features than a static web page of text.
- Chatbots, IVRs, and speech bots are ideal for conveying simple information and capturing simple transactions.

The ubiquity and capability of smartphones has also evolved to change their implications for customers. A few years ago, if you needed customers to provide documentation, the only way they could do this was to fax it or send it using snail mail. Now, applications can use sophisticated phone cameras and AI technology to capture and recognize documents. For example, the Kohler plumbing-supply business deployed videos and photos from plumbers on-site to assist customers in finding the correct fittings. This has enabled the digitization of transactions that were previously thought impossible, as both customers and documents can be recognized, scanned, and accessed by humans or AI. The latest technologies are capable of recognizing passports and drivers' licenses and matching facial images. This kind of sophisticated matching and identification has enabled digital transactions that previously had to be done face-to-face.

The breadth and complexity of functions that are possible through web-based solutions is growing. Insurance claims, home loan applications, passport renewals, and tax returns are all complex forms of self-service that also used to require in-person contact. Even sensitive matters, like reporting children at risk or a harassment claim, can now be automated. Unassisted channels that offer the added benefit of anonymity may make it easier to report such sensitive issues, but they also exemplify the type of mechanism that needs parallel solutions; because while some customers may prefer a self-service solution in these cases, others will need the empathy and help that only a human can provide.

Create Low-Effort Integrated Digital Experiences

The emergence of more channels and increasing customer comfort with them (as shown by the success of many Innovator businesses that use only these new technologies) means that organizations need to design a "cross-channel" solution rather than create different solutions within each channel. This is harder than it sounds, because channels are often run by separate departments that have different goals. There are benefits, then, to tackling these needs with a team that has responsibility and understanding across channels. Such a group can look for an overall optimal solution and can recognize when a single channel will not be effective.

There are already many examples of solutions that span channels. One of the best-known is click and collect, in which digital orders are combined with retail store pickups. Target stores and Best Buy built very good examples of combining the benefits of these two channels, and many companies expanded these solutions through the COVID-19 crisis. Omnichannel experiences are also emerging in areas such as identity and security. In addition, many types of **co-browsing** software programs enable a phone- or chat-based agent to share information, videos, or presentations with a customer to convey complex scenarios or visual options. These mechanisms also enable signatures, photos, and other identity mechanisms and make physical contact less necessary.

Design Usable Self-Service

The best digital and self-service solutions require little help or assistance so that customers are happy to reuse them. There is a whole body of academic research, standards, and literature explaining how to make these channels work or how to assess them:

- Jakob Nielsen's definitive work on web usability was written over 20 years ago, and he has since written books on mobile usability as well.[14]

- There are global standards for IVR design that define which keys should be used for what, as well as what types of navigation are available.[15]
- There are also academic experts in universities that have IT faculties with varying degrees of specialization in self-service and digital tools.
- Website assessment tools allow an organization to self-assess against defined criteria.
- IVR assessment tools enable an organization to assess against logical criteria such as navigation, functionality, and call flow.
- Chatbot assessment tools assess against similar criteria.

With all of this available expertise and all of these well-defined processes, there is no excuse for poor designs that ignore common standards or proven design approaches.

A proven technique for self-service development involves usability testing, in which customers are asked to test versions of solutions in a controlled and observed environment. Usability labs emerged first in the 1990s but have become more common as many organizations look to exploit digital solutions. For example, the Australian Tax Office (ATO) created its own usability lab as digital tax returns and other processes became dominant. The lab is staffed with human-factors experts who observe and film customers using test versions of new or amended self-service solutions. This enables the ATO to refine solutions, create customer-centric language, and ensure customers can complete their goals unassisted.

Maximize Customer Adoption

The complexity and effort required to get customers to adopt and use digital solutions varies according to the industry, functions, and nature of the customer base. For example, as noted earlier, government institutions can, in theory, mandate the use of certain technologies or forms of self-service, where many industries can't. For example, many cities around the world have rolled out digital travel cards in their transport systems that have replaced tickets, and now these cards are being replaced by smartphone versions. The trend started with the Korean Upass, the Octopus card in Hong Kong, and the Oyster card in London; many cities have followed suit with stored value cards and then phone-enabled mechanisms.

Government bodies, recognizing that customers adopt at different rates, often left physical tickets in place for a considerable time after rolling out digital cards to allow time for their adoption. The card schemes used large marketing campaigns to educate the public. Staff were deployed at top-up machines to educate and help people adopt quickly and easily. New waves of marketing and customer education occurred as these organizations rolled out each new wave of capability (e.g., mobile-based versions).

These examples illustrate some of the key questions that any organization promoting new or changed self-service functions needs to consider:

- How do you create awareness of the function?
- What incentives or change strategy is in place to encourage adoption?
- How will customers be supported as they trial or use the functions?
- How will you measure adoption and when can you turn off the older mechanisms?

Companies are often in a different situation than government institutions because they are rarely in a monopoly market and cannot mandate the use of certain channels. This is an advantage that Innovators have over Renovators. A new entrant into an industry can be digital only, while Renovators have a legacy of older channels, including physical branches and contact centers. Renovators therefore have to work hard to create awareness and usage of new solutions. The must often use tactics such as these:

- Public advertising
- Direct marketing of new channels in "old" channels, like in IVR messages or on statements and letter inserts
- Promotion within the channel and on other web pages
- SMS and email marketing to the customer base
- Promotion by frontline staff
- Price incentives for using the new channel or price penalties for using nonpreferred channels
- Gradual withdrawal of channels (e.g., branch closures, reduced ATM networks)
- Bundling of new mechanisms as the only way of doing business (e.g., prepaid phones that offer only chat customer support)

The Role of Frontline Staff—Making Them Experts

It is still surprising how often organizations don't use their frontline support staff to promote and support new digital and self-service mechanisms. Unfortunately, organizations fail to recognize that it is not a natural act for frontline staff to promote self-service because of the following:

- Frontline staff may fear that digital take-up will remove their jobs.
- They may be ignorant about what the digital solutions can do.
- They may not be customers or users of these channels and therefore fear questions they can't answer.
- They may regularly hear about, and be forced to deal with, problems with the digital solutions, but know less about how often those solutions are effective.

These issues all need to be addressed for the front line to be effective as they promote and support new or improved digital solutions. Frontline staff need to be confident in the digital solutions and ideally be users themselves. They can only be experts if they have used the digital solutions and know exactly how they work. Note that the same applies to the organization's senior executives! The front line needs to be trained on when and how to promote digital tools effectively, and they need access to the appropriate materials and tools to help them support the Digitize strategy. For example, they could have texts and email formats with embedded links to key parts of the application using new forms of **augmented agent solutions**. That way, they can speed their support and properly promote apps or digital solutions with phrases like "Can I text you the link to that now?" These are the simple tricks that build confidence for the support staff and customers.

The greater the use of digital and other self-service channels means that frontline staff will perform simpler customer transactions less frequently. Staff also may have to transition from call handling to handling web chats to working in multiple channels. Therefore, the skills and channel capabilities of frontline staff need to evolve as customers take up these digital solutions.

Measurement and Improvement

Digital solutions are able to measure transaction use, page views, opens, clickthrough rates, customer effort, and feedback. Pilots and deployments of digital solutions are therefore able to assess their effectiveness and analyze where improvements are needed. A harder thing to measure is both the positive and negative impacts on other channels. Here are a few examples:

- Are new functions in an app generating new or different queries in the contact center? (For example, mobile banking applications created new customer queries like "What's this transaction?")
- Have new apps displaced transactions or created new ones?
- Which customers (segments, ages, personas, new vs. experienced, etc.) are using the Digitize solutions, and which ones are not?
- How do customers rate their experiences with digital mechanisms compared to other solutions?

The analyses suggested in chapter 1, "Understand," help an organization to track the positive and negative impacts of rolling out new digital solutions. For example, organizations should be able to track the impact of new applications on the volume of equivalent assisted transactions. This can become complicated, because help and support requests may also move from phone to chat or email as customers use different solutions. Effective measurement therefore becomes a multichannel problem that looks at the following:

- Usage rates in the digital channels
- Contact volumes in old support channels, such as inbound phone calls
- New contacts in new support channels (like chat) that may be attached to the new digital solutions

It is also essential to monitor customer experience metrics, such as churn, FCR, and NPS, to ensure that digital solutions improve these results.

HINTS AND TIPS

Remember the five following suggestions when implementing Digitize.

Know the Rules and Conventions

Each self-service channel has its own rules or standards that are familiar to users. In areas like web design, these are more conventions, while in channels like IVR, there are nationally and internationally published standards. One example is the use of "breadcrumbs" in web design, which are text trails that show users how they have navigated to a lower level. The following breadcrumbs are from an airline website:

Booking > Flight Selection > Travel Detail > Passengers > Payments

Breadcrumbs show users where they are and allow them to navigate backward up the path easily. They are a great navigation feature, and yet many sites just don't use them at all.

This idea in practice. IVRs should follow a set of proven design rules. For example, customers struggle to remember more than three options in any IVR menu. Ideally, the most frequently used options in any menu should come first, and each option should convey a single idea. If not, the customer is being asked to remember several things at once. For example, "For clothing, press 1; for household goods, press 2; for food, press 3" is a clear and easy design. In contrast, "For bread and meat, press 1; for vegetables, groceries, and pasta, press 2; for electrical and footwear, press 3" may shorten the menu, but the groupings are not related ideas, so customers will struggle to remember them. Even worse than unrelated prompts is when customers are offered too many choices (which is not uncommon).

Make It Easy to Adopt and Use; Make Its Design as Simple as Possible

It's amazing how complicated some companies make the registration process or the first user experience in a digital application. Becoming a self-service user should be simple—or better yet, totally frictionless. An ideal design allows any customer to log in to the web application automatically without registering (or to be remembered without having to log back on to the site). The idea that portals or apps need separate identifiers and passwords is just a convention that should be challenged. Even if customers can input their email addresses or mobile numbers as their usernames, most organizations already know this information, meaning it can be input for them.

You will know you've achieved a good, simple digital design when these hallmarks are present:

- There's plenty of white space.
- The order of data capture makes sense.
- Fields that can be prefilled (because the organization knows the user) are prefilled.
- The organization asks only for what is needed.

This idea in practice. Apple, Google, and Microsoft try to make it easy for end users. The latest Windows operating system, Apple's IOS, and certain parts of Google help customers by remembering and defaulting passwords so that users don't have to remember the idiosyncrasies of different sites, although this is really a workaround for the complexity of many registration processes.

Borrow Tricks from the Innovators

One of the reasons some Innovators have been so successful is that they provide extra reasons to use their sites. For example, in theory, Uber doesn't need to show a user the approaching car on a map. Using a simple countdown clock would have still been more informative than with the typical taxi company. However, having the visual of the approaching car puts the customer in control and prevents cancelations and "Where is my X?" requests. Thinking of how you can offer the user more than the bare minimum in the digital app can raise reputation and usage levels.

This idea in practice. Amazon was the first Innovator to offer customers recommendations with their famous "Readers who liked this, also liked. . . ." This was one of the first uses of data mining and **predictive analytics**, and it created loyalty, drove revenue, and has been hard for others to emulate, even 23 years later.

The Overlap of Digitize and Preempt

Digital solutions don't have to consist of apps and portals. An automated solution can also be an automated preemptive message. A great example is the telco that sends text messages warning customers when they are approaching the limits of their plan. This is a form of preemption but also automation.

This idea in practice. Some utilities automatically include more bill detail and explanation when a bill is higher than the norm. This is a form of preempt, but it is enabled by automation and algorithms.

Make Everyone Use the App

It helps build momentum and understanding if all executives, managers, and frontline staff have to register and use all of the Digitize tools. This will increase their appreciation for the customer journey and help them see any need for improvement.

This idea in practice. A credit card company changed its approach to phone sales so that the sales team mirrored the online application rather than the old paper one. As the sales team began using the online platform all day, every day, they became familiar with how the system worked and how to help customers better.

Have Clear Goals for Adoption and Clear Ownership of These Goals

It is important not only to be crystal clear with staff regarding the level of adoption needed to get a return on investment but also to have a plan to achieve that level of adoption. Further, there needs to be executive-level ownership of the Digitize improvements, and often these are product or customer-segment owners, not the IT shop. Business ownership ensures connections with product and service design and reduces further errors or confusion.

This idea in practice. When a bank decided to invest in a chatbot, they set out a clear goal that it had to displace over 40% of assisted contacts from the chat channel. This forced the design team to include sufficient scope and functionality to achieve this level of automation. The project was put under the control of the director of customer service, who owned the budget for support. The project achieved just over that target (41% of assisted chat) but might have fallen short if the goals hadn't been clear.

▰▰ SUMMARY

The Digitize strategic action can be one of the most powerful ingredients in becoming frictionless. Automating simple queries and providing robust answers in multiple channels can satisfy customers and remove demand from assisted channels. Done correctly, Digitize is seamless and easy; however, if done poorly, Digitize can create friction and drive poor customer experiences. To enable success, there is a body of methodology, academic research, and expertise that can help organizations get this right. Good design and usability are now a science, not an art. The growth in channels provides more opportunities but means that channels need to be considered in an integrated and consistent way. Fortunately, there are plenty of great examples that demonstrate how to increase containment rates and satisfy customers.

ASSESS YOUR NEED TO DIGITIZE

You have the potential to Digitize further if you answer yes to any of these questions or don't know the answer:

Q1. Do your competitors have better self-service and digital solutions than you do (and your customers tell you so)?

Q2. Do you find that you don't understand or measure the rate of containment of customers who attempt to use current digital solutions?

Q3. Do your customers often call up or chat with straightforward transactional or informational requests?

Q4. Have you invested in digital and self-service solutions but feel frustrated that customers don't often use them?

Q5. Do you find that your frontline staff don't promote self-service as much as you would like?

Q6. Do many of your assisted contacts relate to problems in self-service channels, such as "I can't log on"?

Q7. Do your customers provide negative feedback on your self-service and digital solutions?

Q8. Do your customers say, "Why isn't your self-service as easy to use as Amazon's?"

TEXTING MARY THAT HER FLIGHT HAD BEEN CANCELLED 15 TIMES DID NOT MAKE HER 15 TIMES MORE SATISFIED.....

PREEMPT

> *In life, as in chess, forethought wins.*
>
> —Charles Buxton

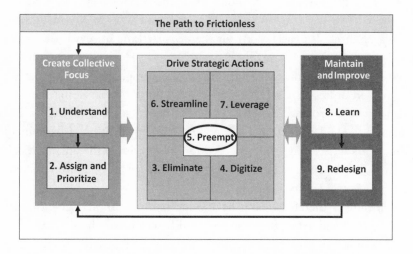

WHAT IS "PREEMPT" AND WHY IS IT IMPORTANT?

Preempt is the third of the five strategic actions and it represents a very different approach to how customers interact with organizations. Preempt is about moving the organization from reacting to customer issues and problems to being proactive to prevent the need for customer contacts. Preemptive actions reduce friction because they reassure customers that the organization is looking out for them and serving the customers' interests. Eliminate actions stop irritating impacts and hopefully fix them "once and for all," and Digitize actions automate routine transactional needs. In contrast, Preemptive actions recognize that things do go wrong and that situations change but that organizations can anticipate these changes and reach out to customers to warn or inform them. For example, while Eliminate actions prevent a customer from ordering something that was never in stock, a Preemptive action notifies the customer that delays somewhere in the process will make an order late and thereby reposition the customer's expectations.

To some extent, Preempt can overlap and assist with all of the other actions (Eliminate, Digitize, Simplify, and Leverage), which is why it is shown bordering the other four strategies in the overall schematic. Often, executing the other actions may be more complex and take longer than a preemptive strategy, so this can be an interim solution. For example, a company may get many calls if orders are frequently delivered beyond the promised two-day window. It could look at two ways to eliminate these contacts: reset all expectations for the delivery time or revisit the entire logistics and delivery chain. These two solutions are hard, time-consuming, and expensive. A temporary preemptive strategy might help manage expectations on orders that go over the two-day mark by messaging the customer whenever it occurs. That may help, but it isn't a complete fix and does not get rid of customer disappointment. In addition, a permanent Preempt strategy may still be needed for events outside the organization's control, like bad weather even after the logistics are fixed, to keep customers from getting nasty surprises.

Preempt is therefore about having mechanisms to manage customer expectations and needs. It also suggests a different approach to manage current or potential problems proactively rather than reactively. It requires a deliberate mindset for a business to ask these three critical questions:

- "What could go wrong here, and how can we manage it?"
- "If we can't always meet customers' expectations, how can we help them?"
- "What will customers want to know before they ask us?"

Frictionless Organizations think in this proactive way. They not only preempt issues of their making, but they also guide and influence customer behaviors for their own good. For example, a telco using Preempt will suggest when a customer might need to upgrade or **downgrade** a plan that consistently doesn't meet their data needs. A frictionless company would rather have customers on the right product than receive higher fees or charges from customers on the wrong product (sometimes called "toxic revenues"). They recognize that lower short-term revenue from a happy customer produces better long-term returns than short-term overcharges.

Over the last 20 years, capabilities to enable Preemptive actions have increased significantly. SMS, text, mobile apps, portals, messaging in many forms, automated calls, and emails all represent cheap, fast, and simple ways to alert customers compared with old methods like sending letters or making calls to the customer. Other mechanisms are also now available, such as community forums and proactive software updates. Analytics and AI enable organizations to understand much more about customer behavior and trends, enabling smarter and better targeted interventions.

Situations Where Preempt Applies

There are many situations where proactive Preempt strategies are nearly always applicable, illustrated by these eight categories:

- Customer expectations need to be managed, particularly when an agreed-upon timetable can't be met (e.g., delayed flights or deliveries).
- Events or issues that impact the customer are known to some of them but not to all of them (e.g., software bugs or system faults).
- Long-running processes have variable timetables that customers want to track or understand (e.g., insurance claims, loan applications, or job applications).
- Customers need prompting or reminding of future events (e.g., appointment reminders).
- Customers could make mistakes or be impacted (e.g., warnings of missed car services or plans about to expire).
- Customer actions could put them at an advantage (e.g., preregistration for tickets for in-demand events or early health interventions).
- Customers may be out of date on how the business operates (e.g., new hours, new terms and conditions, new locations and new offers).
- Organizations can help customers achieve positive outcomes (e.g., in areas like health and wealth management).

Well-executed Preempt strategies do more than just prevent contact; they also demonstrate respect for customers and their time. They show that the organization is concerned about their customers and values their time and efforts. Preemptive strategies put customers in control of their time and, if done well, build loyalty. They also save time and money, since a 20-cent text costs far less than an eight-minute "Where is my X?" phone call. Preemptive strategies can therefore be a win-win for both the customer and the organization.

The proposed approach to use Preempt intervention has three stages:

1. **Decide what to preempt.** Look at which issues lend themselves well to preemptive strategies, and consider whether there are unpredictable situations that the organization must prepare for.
2. **Select the best Preempt mechanisms.** Work out which mechanisms will be timely and effective, whether one or more mechanisms will be needed, and how these mechanisms can be used in combination.
3. **Increase the success of the Preempt mechanisms.** Refine the messages and mechanisms used.

The benefits of Preempt are both reduced costs and increased customer loyalty. Informing customers quickly about situations will prevent inbound contacts and related complaints and therefore reduce costs. Showing a genuine concern for things that impact the customer will drive loyalty and advocacy. As some examples will show, Innovators go further and are willing to forgo revenue rather than create disappointment (e.g., allowing a customer to cancel an order that can't be delivered before Christmas). Using many Preempt solutions will build a customer-focused mindset in an organization.

GOOD STORIES

National Care Preemption

Two Australian government programs represent excellent Preempt strategies to deal with breast cancer and bowel cancer, two of the most frequent and lethal cancers. The Australian government designed a Preempt program to ensure frequent screening, which enables earlier intervention that saves lives. All Australians are sent bowel-testing kits every two years from age 50. They don't have to complete the test, but over 42%[1] of them do, even though it involves sampling and storing feces in a complex and unpleasant procedure. Australian women are invited to a free breast cancer screening every two years, and 54% take up this test.

Both programs have contributed to reduced rates of cancer deaths in Australia: breast cancer fatality rates fell from over 17% in the 1980s to below 10% today, with early identification and treatment being a major contributor; likewise, bowel cancer fell from 35% to well under 20% today.[2] These programs illustrate the benefits of a well-defined Preempt strategy. Bowel and breast cancer testing are unpleasant procedures, but well-designed processes and great education and promotion have made the programs a success.

Outage Information Mechanisms

In a broadband and media business like Renovator Cable One, outages will occur. Unfortunately, outages frustrate the customer who wants to stream a documentary or manage their business, and they generate avalanche levels of contact as they also do for electric utilities. Cable One has employed the Preempt action by populating websites and IVRs with outage information as soon as possible. Their network operations center notifies customers using multiple mechanisms (text and email) if any outage occurs. They'd rather customers find out quickly than have to deal with calls that overwhelm their support centers. Field techs can also update the status of the network, and customers can opt in to various notifications systems. These are all excellent and useful Preempt systems. In a similar way, most of the electricity distribution companies in Australia provide outage information through multiple mechanisms such as websites, text notifications, and email. Blizzard Entertainment, a software business, points to its outage notices as one of the key reasons its contacts per gamer have dropped so dramatically over the past five years.

Vodafone Relaxes Credit in a Crisis

During the COVID-19 lockdown, all of the Vodafone markets (country operations) came under stress from serving customers who worked from home. Many of these subscribers also lost their jobs, and in some countries without safety nets, they suffered a big drop in income levels. By closely tracking reason codes like "I cannot pay now and want to set up a payment plan" and identifying at-risk customers (using **big data** and predictive analytics), Vodafone markets created a series of preemptive messages to reassure customers that they would have more time to pay their invoices. In some cases, they also automatically placed certain customers on a payment plan. Customers were surprised and delighted, Vodafone experienced fewer contacts for these payment reasons, and customers have remained loyal. Many other companies also relaxed their credit strategies through the COVID-19 crisis, including power utilities and insurance companies that reduced premiums during or after the lockdowns.

Tesla Goes the Extra Miles

Tesla's electric vehicle division has put into place a wide range of Preempt actions to reduce "range anxiety" and prevent its customers from spending time in the service shop. Because of the company's always-on telemetry that monitors battery usage and remaining charge, Tesla emails or texts customers when their car's battery falls below 5%, alerting them to charge as soon as possible.

Tesla also takes one-off actions to help customers in need. During Hurricane Irma, in the U.S. state of Florida in 2017, Tesla "unlocked" additional battery power for customers fleeing the huge storm. Many customers had 60-kw models but actually had a 75-kw battery in their car. The 60-kw model was cheaper, but Tesla thought buyers might upgrade later. When one customer reached out and asked for the extra range to escape the storm, Tesla realized that many customers needed this extra range and remotely unlocked the extra 15 kw for all drivers fleeing the storm. This "preemptive" unlock won Tesla great kudos for literally going the extra miles![3]

Tesla now demonstrates other preemptive characteristics, partly in response to complaints that it was getting harder to book appointments in their service centers (even though this is needed far less often for electric vehicles). The head of automotive, Jerome Gullen, quoted a familiar mantra: "For us, best service is no service. So, we spent a lot of efforts trying to improve the quality and the reliability of our cars. In the last two years the frequency of service visits are reduced by one-third, so customers have to come less frequently into service, which is really the goal—no service." Tesla made two other changes: they increased the number of potential mobile services so that 40% of services were done at a customer's home, then increased the functionality of the app so that it could notify the customer of the need for service and help book an appointment, a great example of preemptive care.[4]

The Best Delivery of Delivery

Amazon has defined and led the way in demonstrating how to manage customer expectations through the processes of online order and delivery. The mechanisms pioneered by Amazon are now common in many online retail businesses. Early on in the late 1990s, Amazon started to send order and shipping confirmations via email immediately after various steps in the order-fulfillment process, such as at the point of shipping from a warehouse or leaving a depot. Amazon still provides a range of updates at different stages of the order and shipping process and offers a range of alerts in case of shipping delays, including identical alerts from its drop shippers (who deliver directly to Amazon customers) and from its warehouse deliveries.

Many shipping and delivery businesses, such as FedEx and UPS, now also allow order tracking and alerts, and there has been a tight handshake between online retailers and the delivery companies they use. Many other businesses have copied aspects of Amazon's notifications to manage their customer expectations. Some companies use similar messaging in long-running processes like insurance claims or mortgage applications to keep the customer in the loop.

BAD STORIES

Many organizations have the potential to analyze usage and other data in order to adopt preemptive strategies, but they choose not to do so. Some organizations don't even bother to collect these data. Many are also happy to blame weather events or other issues rather than help customers deal with disruption, even if it is outside the organization's control.

Whose Software Is It Anyway?

There are software companies that think they are being preemptive by releasing new operating system versions, but they often do so in very inconvenient ways for their customers. For example, some will inform users that updates will be installed upon their computer powering down but not warn users of the delays or lost bookmarks when the machine powers back up. Sometimes it can take several minutes to install updates, but users are not warned of the process or told how long they should allow for it. This can be very frustrating if users have an urgent task to complete when they restart. It would be so simple to warn the user of the likely impact with a message like, "When restarting your machine, you may need an extra five minutes to reconfigure."

Previous mechanisms for updates used to take control of the machine and force a power down after a countdown period. The users had almost no choice but to stop using the machine for a software update that may not have been urgent for that user. It is a delicate balancing act between offering the best protected software and taking control of a device in situations that only the end user can know. A frictionless company would place more control in the hands of the end user and make the reasons for the updates clear.

Missed Deliveries

One of the leading UK-based daily newspapers delivers to the United States, and its weekend edition is particularly popular. On occasion, the weekend paper is delayed, but the paper never sends any alerts to its subscribers. Instead, the customer can extend the subscription only if they call to report the missed delivery and do so before its East Coast contact center closes; there is no email option or opportunity to register a "missed delivery" in the customer's online account, and there is no way for the paper to process a refund. The customer service agent always reminds the customer that the online version is available, but sometimes holding the physical paper is what weekends are all about. Too much friction!

'Air-Raising Experience

Airlines have become better at providing preemptive contact for weather events (e.g., warning passengers via texts or emails about flight schedule disruptions so that they can make alternative plans). However, it's when the really bad weather events hit that other preemptive strategies come to the fore. The Sydney-Melbourne air route is the third-busiest domestic route in the world. In 2019 bad storms forced the closure of the Sydney airport on a busy Thursday afternoon, leaving thousands of passengers stranded. One of the two major airlines acted in a preemptive manner and booked hotels for all out-of-town frequent flyers to save them the angst. The other major airline was slow to inform passengers of the airport closure. By the time passengers were told that they were stuck, the other airline had scooped up most of the available hotel accommodations.

The sudden rise in demand for hotel beds and a very limited remaining supply sent prices skyrocketing. All of the second airline's out-of-town passengers were on their own, scrambling for accommodations and trying to negotiate revised itineraries for the next day. Passengers paid up to 200% of the normal hotel price out of pocket while having their plans disrupted. In effect, the preemptive strategies of one airline created a bad experience for the passengers of their competitor. One looked caring and organized at a time of customer need, while the other left their customers in the lurch and appeared to not have any kind of plan for such an event. This illustrates the value of anticipating possible problems and having Preempt strategies ready to go.

Is This Text from You?

Recent legislation in Australia meant that pension funds had to contact many customers with low balances to allow them to opt in or opt out of product options such as life insurance. Many funds notified customers using text messages as well as email and letters. They did the right thing by using multiple channels to try to get the customer's attention; however, one fund worded the text so badly that many customers called in thinking it was some form of fraud. The contact center was flooded with calls, many of which started with questions like, "Is this text from you?" The wording of the text didn't explain who was sending the message, why, or what was required from the customer. Worse still, it had wording similar to known fraud attempts like, "Your fund savings will be sent to the tax office."

The wording was so limited that customers feared the links provided would take them to some rogue site that put them at risk. It appeared that the company never tested how customers would react and used terminology that customers didn't understand. It was an attempt to Preempt that backfired, and it resulted in the flood of calls that the contact center had originally hoped to avoid and which they struggled to answer in a reasonable time.

HOW TO PREEMPT

Figure 5.1 shows a series of three steps that organizations can take to determine what to preempt, how to preempt, and how to improve the effectiveness of Preempt interventions.

Decide When and What to Preempt

Preempt is used to complement the other four strategic actions. It can work in five ways:

- As a *temporary alternative* to other actions like Eliminate and Digitize (e.g., providing information proactively while other solutions are being built and deployed)
- As a more cost-effective solution that achieves a *partial outcome* but may be more cost-effective than other actions

- As the only *answer to unavoidable situations*
- As an effective way to *manage a process*
- As an effective way to *manage the customer relationship*

Each of these ways requires different thinking and analysis. All of the Eliminate or Digitize contact reasons on the Value-Irritant matrix need to be assessed to see if a Preempt solution could work as *a temporary alternative* or *a partial outcome*. Delays that cause customers to call are an obvious place to look, since proactive updates to customers may prevent customer contacts, disappointment, or churn. Preempt mechanisms are great ways to keep customers informed and reset expectations. Preempt solutions also work well for Streamline contacts where many customers are impacted but have not yet found the problem, such as for software bugs, product faults, or network outages.

Frictionless Organizations have mass-notification mechanisms ready to go when *unavoidable situations* occur. They have recognized that they can't be perfect, but they try to minimize the impact of these imperfections. If they fall behind on shipping products or detect a fault, they notify customers and try to reset expectations. They also work on preempting the problems and may follow risk-averse solutions like piloting new products to iron out problems before they impact all customers.

Frictionless Organizations also take the time to consider how they may help customers, even in situations outside their control, such as in extreme weather events or when experiencing problems with suppliers or third parties. It takes a different mindset for an organization to sit down and consider, "What could go wrong here and how can we help the customer in those situations?" For example, some airlines now send out warning messages as soon as 24 hours before a flight when extreme weather events are forecast that might impact schedules. They know they can't control the event but have recognized a responsibility to help customers prepare or make alterative plans. The more forward-thinking utilities have prepared for how they will notify customers during extreme weather events and outages.

The fourth area of thinking is around expectations management across *long-running processes*. This could be, for example, a complex insurance claim or passport application. Frictionless Organizations try to provide as many proactive updates as possible to keep the customer informed and to

FIGURE 5.1. The Preempt Approach

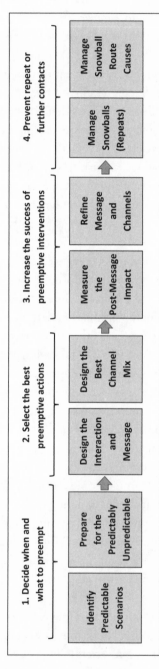

TABLE 5.1. Preemptive Message Examples

Industry	Mechanisms	Benefit for the Organization and the Customer
Health and services	Appointment reminders and warnings such as day-before confirmations ("Reply *Y* to attend your *X*") and day-of reminders.	Fewer missed appointments. Clear wait lists, keeping capacity full.
Delivery services	Multistage reminders of impending deliveries or pickups.	Fewer wasted truck rolls. The customer is in control and has more time.
Health insurance	Free checkups for ancillary services, such as optical and dental. Gym membership and exercise gear subsidies.	More expensive treatments like root canals are prevented by early intervention. General fitness prevents other health costs.
Telco and broadband	Usage-level warnings on plans with limits (e.g., "You are at 80% of your plan maximum, and it's only 50% of the way through the month.")	Allows upgrades for customers to avoid penalty rates or cut back usage.

prevent status queries. For example, a loan application process might inform the customer of stages like document receipt, assessment completion, and final approval. This thinking might also include using outbound communication to inform the customer if any delays occur or any exception conditions are hit that would extend the process. These organizations constantly challenge themselves by asking, "What would keep me informed if I were the customer?"

Examples of these types of messages are shown in table 5.1.

The *management of customer relationships* requires a different approach to analyze how customers are using products and services. This can make great use of analytics to assess situations such as the following:

- Which customers are on the wrong product or service for their needs and would benefit from an upgrade or downgrade?
- Which customers have risks that might need to be managed (e.g., possible fraud)?
- Which customers should be rewarded for loyalty?
- Which customers may be experiencing some form of difficulty that the company could help with?

This analysis needs to look beyond short-term customer profitability because it may well be the most profitable situation to leave the customer on the current product or service, and not notify them. Alternatively, Frictionless Organizations recognize the long-term benefit of showing a customer how to save by spending less. They may also give discounts if they recognize that customers haven't received the full value from their products. The best example of this is when telco and broadband providers offer to downgrade or upgrade customers to products that suit their usage patterns rather than charge them for services they don't need. Not many organizations do this, since most of them prefer to take the penalty fees and extra margins. However, this can leave the customer vulnerable to better offers from competitors.

A pension business gave a different example of this preemptive behavior. They completed analysis of the age profile, balances, and portfolio profiles of all their customers. Then they reached out to customers who they believed were on investment profiles (e.g., high risk or low risk) that didn't match their stage in life and accumulated assets. They didn't force the customers to change investment profiles, but they did suggest the alternatives and rationale. They left the customer in control, but they showed that they had the best interest of the customer in mind.

Select the Best Preemptive Solutions

Solution design for Preempt requires the right message, the right mechanism and channel, and the right way to assist the customer. There are different levels of complexity:

- The simplest preemptive actions merely provide information such as the status of a process or a reminder of an upcoming appointment.
- Slightly more complex is information that may lead to an action or choice for a customer (e.g., "To confirm your appointment, reply yes").
- More complex are solutions where customers have a range of action choices, and this may need a more complex dialogue or set of controls to confirm a choice.
- Last, some preemptions may invite the customer to make contact, as this is the only way to resolve an issue. For example, if a customer is being warned of a fraud, they may need a call to unlock an account or confirm transaction activity. Table 5.2 shows examples of each.

TABLE 5.2. Types of Preempt Solutions

Type	Example	Design Impact
Information only	"We have received your email."	A simple message, usually in one channel.
Information and confirmation	"Your appointment is in 48 hours. Do you wish to proceed?"	Simple two-way automation and simple responses like, "Send Y." Allow for all responses.
Information and choice	"You have exceeded your limit. Do you wish to upgrade, stay on this plan, or have a temporary upgrade?"	More confirmation required of each action. Likely need to link to additional information to help customer confirm.
Information and conversation prompt	"We think your privacy may have been breached. Please click here to talk to us."	Channel links that make it easy to get the contact to the appropriate staff.

Next, it's important to find the right trigger and timing for each proactive intervention and then calculate the appropriate time lag. For example, for known delayed flights, the airline might want to text the passenger immediately and follow up with their preferred second channel—perhaps, a voice message. Other preemptive strategies may need to provide a warning X days before an event, while others need to be notified only after the fact. The organization must also consider whether alerts are sent too often to be sure that they will still be effective. They may saturate the customer with messages that they learn to ignore or miss the boat on the required actions. Some countries such as Turkey now limit the number of text messages that organizations can send to their customers per year, so it is critical to sort out which Preempt messages will have the greatest impact.

Customers can now easily block texts, emails, and phone calls, so it's important to reach out with a compelling message that the customer will want to receive. Some organizations now allow customers control of their notifications. For example, stored-value transport cards may offer the customer a choice of how to be notified about their balance falling to a certain level and what dollar trigger point to use.

The structure of the wording and format of messages is also critical. Unfortunately, fraud and spam are increasing so that customers are more wary of the messages they receive; therefore, messages to customers need to be credentialized and explained. The customer needs to know and trust that the message is genuine. The reason and actions must also be clear, and it can help to have links to other information that adds detail or confirms the identity of the organization that sent the message. Testing the wording and format of messages reaching many customers can help an organization ensure that the wording will be understood by customers. Thinking through the language and wording that customers will understand and avoiding jargon makes these strategies more effective.

Channel Choice and Mix

Selecting the most effective Preempt tool or channel that fits each reason is critical, but some organizations may have limited choices. They may not have all of the contact details for customers or they may have opt-in strategies that need to be invoked before some channels can be used. The channels available include synchronous or **asynchronous text messaging**, SMS, email, alerts on apps or in customer portals, IVR scripting, automated calls, chatbots, outbound phone calls, or old-fashioned snail-mail letters. It's important to think through whether multiple channels will be needed and ways that the channels can work together. An organization may consider that a message is so important that multiple channels should be used in parallel. This works better if the messages can acknowledge that they are linked (e.g., "This message has also been sent to your mobile phone"). Messages designed to prompt action or further contact in another channel need to be simple, with links and buttons that enable customers to talk to someone or send the requisite information. If a message is important enough, the organization may just want conformation of receipt. Thinking through the two-way nature of the dialogue is another part of the right preemptive design.

Increase the Success of Preempt Tools and Approaches

One advantage of Preempt as an action is that it is usually in the organization's control. Because they are taking action rather than reacting, they can often adopt a more experimental approach. This allows them to fine-tune messages and the mechanisms used. For example, they can send a text message to a limited number of customers to assess the reaction. They can also stagger messages that will provoke action so that they are ready to respond.

To increase the success of Preempt actions, organizations need to measure and report post-alert contact rates in different ways. For example, preemptive actions that produce a response can be easily measured by their response rate. Preemptive actions that prevent contact may be measured by the contacts that remain. Organizations may be able to measure opening an email or acknowledging a message on an app, but they can't measure whether a customer opens a letter.

The ability to measure an alert or preemptive message may dictate whether this channel is effective or not. For example, when testing a new message, an organization may ask for an acknowledgment merely as a measurement tool, even if this acknowledgment isn't really needed. This will help determine right away (literally within minutes after dispatching the message) whether or not the Preemptive strategy engaged the customer. The organization may also need to measure negative reactions to the strategy, such as subsequent calls to assisted channels including unexpected reactions (e.g., customers asking "What is this message?" or resentment that they were interrupted).

When results are below target or customers complain about the Preempt message, the organization will then need to consider how to do the following:

- Modify the Preempt tools and channels to reduce the rates of unwanted contact.
- Adjust messaging to make it clearer or reduce fears and concerns.
- Provide more choice and control.
- Readminister the pilot and/or gauge success carefully.
- Reset targets.
- Repeat the experiment!

Prevent Repeat or Further Contacts

Another category in Preempt is melting snowballs, as described in the Understand chapter. Every organization knows that resolving problems or answering questions in the first contact is an essential ingredient to satisfy

FIGURE 5.2. AHT for First-Time Versus Subsequent Contacts

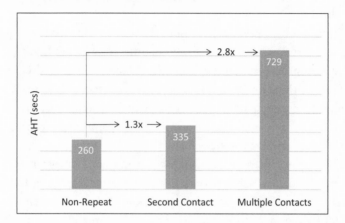

customers. Achieving an FCR of 80% to 90% still means that 10% to 20% of the contacts are not resolved the first time. Figure 5.2 shows the extended duration in **Average Handle Time (AHT)** of repeat contacts in a typical operation.[5]

The main way to prevent snowballs is to resolve the issue the first time. Part of the reason to analyze repeats, as described in the Understand chapter, is to enable organizations to assess why resolution wasn't achieved. Every repeat represents nonresolution and therefore enables analysis of the causes. The reasons for repeats may include the following:

- Agents fail to resolve issues because of lack of training or poor behavior.
- Processes don't allow resolution, because staff aren't allowed to execute them fully or processes aren't available
- Customers are confused by apparent resolutions that aren't well explained.
- Processes are not resolved in the time frame that customers expect (in which case, time frames either need to be reduced or expectations need to be reset).

This is where the analytical techniques described in the Understand chapter can come into their own, to report levels of repeats and resolution by contact type. However, analyzing why this resolution isn't achieved often requires more manual techniques, including listening to calls, holding workshops with frontline staff, following processes across the business (such as in the classic *Harvard Business Review* article "Staple Yourself to an Order"[6]), using speech and text analytics, and conducting more detailed customer research. The solutions can vary from coaching and training individuals and processes to redesigning end-to-end processes.

One reason that many organizations fail to resolve contacts the first time is that they have separated taking a request or inquiry from the process requested. The idea is that taking the call should be separate from the more complex data processing or calculations that may follow. A common example is that a phone-based team receives a claim but other areas process the claim. The temptation to move processing to cheaper back-office or offshore locations has exaggerated this trend.

A way to tackle this is "back-to-front" reengineering. Through this mechanism, all handoffs to other areas are analyzed for processes that could be resolved quickly by the agent. New forms of automation like RPA may assist by making these processes easier for frontline staff. The latest technologies therefore add to the potential for greater FCR, because the time-consuming back-office work is now automated. This puts long, complex processes at the fingertips of frontline staff and thereby enables resolution.

The second preemptive mechanism is to ensure that if staff do receive a second contact, they are in a position to sort out the problem once and for all. There are many mechanisms that organizations can use to achieve higher levels of resolution to melt snowballs:

- Knowledge systems that are easy to search and can be updated in real time as new problems emerge (e.g., as a Wiki)
- Measurement systems that let frontline employees take more time to resolve repeat contacts
- Skill structures and routing mechanisms that match highly skilled or tenured employees with the tougher issues and repeat contacts
- Feedback and coaching for the frontline staff member who failed to resolve the initial problem
- Measurement that makes visible who is solving or causing repeat contacts

FIGURE 5.3. Solvers versus Repeat Creators

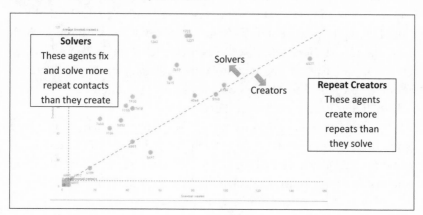

Figure 5.3 shows an example report: agents in the upper left melted more snowballs than they created (the "solvers"), versus the lower-right agents who started more snowballs than they melted (the "creators").[7] Creating a grid of this sort can provide an organization with valuable insights, such as how solvers are able to perform at such a high level and whether training or knowledge access needs to change.

HINTS AND TIPS

Six techniques look at every aspect of Preempt, from channel selection to timing and language choice.

Use Multiple Tailored Channels

To appeal to the widest range of customers and get their attention, Preempt solutions need to use multiple channels and use them in complementary and integrated ways. Today this includes techniques like the following:

- Acknowledging that messages have been sent in multiple channels (e.g., "You may also receive an email with the same message.")
- Providing links to other channels within messages (e.g., a website link in a text message)

- Making outbound calls, leaving messages, and providing the customer with other channel options

This idea in practice. Text messages today are mostly received on smartphones, where customers can follow links and get more information. Banks sending warnings about fraud risks provide links to information and to the customer's online login. The banks offer links to call centers for more information, and realizing that they need to differentiate their messages from fraudsters and scammers, they may quote a masked part of an account number, useless by itself, but sufficient to be confident that it is your bank (e.g., "This message is in regards to your account number ending in *XXXX*.").

Messages That Are Concise, Complete, and in Customer Language

Customers are far more likely to act when messages are concise, complete, and in their language. To create such messages, organizations have to put themselves in customers' shoes. For example, rather than use a formal product name, the company might want to use the common name for the account type that customers use. Good short messages tend to focus on the "what and when," with little information about "why and how" because those need a conversation.

This idea in practice. Notifying a customer to collect a package at the local post office reminds them to bring the correct identification. This avoids a wasted or frustrating visit. Good medical appointment reminders include time, location, and everything else you will need. In COVID-19 times, reminders also included all safety-related requirements.

Obsess about the Timing

It seems like a good idea to reach out ahead of events to warn and help the customer, but as Bob Hope once said, "Timing is everything."[8] Too far ahead of time, customers will feel annoyed and hassled. Too close to an event, and the prompt may be ineffective. Timing is something that organizations can experiment with to see what works best.

This idea in practice. A major insurance company prompts a customer two months prior to renewal to ensure their details are up to date. This is the gentlest of reminders in a product that can be almost frictionless because it may need no contact all year. This reminder helps the company engage with the customer before a critical renewal event. Likewise, a broadband provider has different trigger points in a monthly payment cycle. The messages typically link usage-level warnings to the stage of the month. They won't tell you if you are 50% through the plan halfway through the month. However, they will warn you if you are 70% through the quota halfway through the month or 90% through with 10 days remaining. The nature of these warnings is all about timing combined with various limits.

Communication Needs to Be Two-Way

Organizations can get lazy and use text, email, and messaging as a form of one-way communication. "No reply" type email addresses or "Do not respond" messages show this lack of willingness to have a dialogue. It takes only a little more effort to allow some form of confirmation or to provide links that allow conversation. It's much more polite to enable a two-way conversation than to make it hard for the customer.

This idea in practice. Good appointment reminders enable a positive affirmation response. Many dentists or surgeons now invite customers to "Type *Y* or say yes" to confirm. They may even have a process to follow up with those who haven't confirmed. **Two-way text messaging** allows customers to request alternative dates or to pose questions and thus establish a dialogue with the organization.

Allow Customer Control

In many situations, customers need to be given control to propose, or at least to approve, how they receive preemptive contacts and what they receive. Most companies encourage their customers to tailor profiles and channels, accessing their profile to select mechanisms to be used for different reminders and statements. Some even allow customers to dictate the thresholds (e.g., "Remind me when my balance is X.").

This idea in practice. The simplest example of this kind of tailoring is the dental surgery center that offers customers a choice of reminder mechanisms. As you make an appointment, they ask if you'd like an email, text, or phone call reminder. They even offer the oldest reminder of all: a handwritten appointment card. Similarly, a major public transport card offers the customer a choice of how, and at what level, they will receive reminders of their balance. This lets every customer tailor their profile.

Walk in the Customers' Shoes

When an organization sends customers a prompt such as, "We've received your X and will complete it in Y business days," they assume that they will have it in their hands at that time. They may not take the time to calculate what "business days" means, let alone allow for extra time in the mail. If you "staple yourself to the order," you might discover that it goes to the mailroom, relies on snail mail for a further period, and may then go through multiple departments, each of which allows a certain number of business days more. Customers hate waiting and will fill that void with many contacts to check status, clearly adding friction.

This idea in practice. The best organizations set expectations on the outside and then beat them on the inside. One company walked itself through the process and realized that mail-based delivery was adding uncertainty to the process. It changed its process to always use email as the outward send mechanism so it could control when customers received their information.

▬ SUMMARY

Preempt complements and reinforces the other four actions, either by providing welcomed alerts and updates for customers before they realize that something has gone awry or by reminding them to make contact when it is needed. This gives control back to the customer and saves unwanted contacts and unpleasant surprises. It can also encourage customers into actions that the organization wants. Making Preempt work is tricky, but it is well worth the effort to determine what to preempt, how to preempt, and how to increase the success of Preempt tools and approaches.

Preemptive actions will produce a significant cost reduction despite the investments needed. Channel choices are now plentiful and almost instant, making Preempt far cheaper and more feasible than having to handle contacts in assisted channels. However, customers don't want to be swamped, and regulators are looking to control how these channels are used to prevent spamming and abuse. Therefore, preemption has to be used wisely and with restraint. Every message or email is an interruption or intrusion on the customer and should be treated carefully.

When done well, customers will notice the outreach and the attention, and it will please them when Preempt strategies are offered in their interest. Customers do not need to make as many contacts, but they will recognize when an organization is trying to help them save time or use products cost effectively. They will "vote with their pocketbook" and reward organizations that are easy to work with and collaborate with them through disciplined and well-organized preemptive interventions.

ASSESS YOUR NEED TO PREEMPT

You will need to practice more Preempt activities if you answer yes to any of these questions:

Q1. Do events happen periodically that cause customers to call but that your business could have told the customer about earlier?

Q2. Do things go wrong that you could warn customers about?

Q3. Do you need to reset customer expectations about process timing on occasion?

Q4. Do you have the potential to help customers get more value from your products or services?

Q5. Could you do more to warn customers of possible events that will cost them more or disadvantage them in some way?

Q6. Do customers frequently contact you to find out the status of a process or an order?

Q7. Do your customers miss appointments, renewals, or other time-based events?

Q8. Could you prevent customers from making contact or leaving if only you could tell them about X?

Q9. Do your competitors have lower rates of contact because they keep customers better informed?

STREAMLINE

If you define the problem correctly, you almost have the solution.

—Steve Jobs

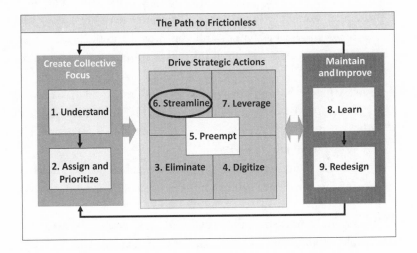

WHAT IS "STREAMLINE" AND WHY IS IT IMPORTANT?

Streamline actions should be assigned to those contact reasons that are irritating to the customer but valuable to the organization. In fact, this contradiction—between the customer's perception of the contact and the organization's—is at the heart of what makes Streamline complex; it represents a risk to customer relationships, begging the question, "Are these reasons really valuable for the organization?" In many organizations, we find that groupthink develops that convinces everyone that they value these contacts, when in fact they may value only a subset of them. At times, then, the Streamline action ought to be considered a "hot potato" that moves as quickly as possible to the Eliminate action.

On the surface, any reason that irritates customers should be eliminated, but there are five special cases in which the Streamline action is appropriate:

- **The first (or early) problem instance.** The organization has never seen the problem before and needs information to start to assess deeper root causes to Eliminate, using Streamline as a temporary action.
- **The need for contact or other information.** Action or information is needed from customers that will enable the organization to better serve them (e.g., data that allows a company to tailor services and products to a customer). This becomes a delicate juggling act between the customer's and the organization's best interests. Some forms of customer feedback and customer profiling fit in this category.
- **"Last Chance Saloon" instances.** The organization has only one more opportunity to fix an issue for a particular customer before escalations or other negative consequences occur (e.g., legal action, escalation to a regulatory body).
- **Outbound contacts.** The organization reaches out to **silent sufferers** who have never contacted them for help or who no longer bother.
- **A temporary fix.** Streamline is used as an alternative strategy (1) if feasible Eliminate or Digitize options don't exist or will take a prohibitively long time, or (2) for Leverage reasons. In some ways, this is using Streamline as a secondary or suboptimal solution when other solutions are too costly, time-consuming, or impractical.

Streamline versus Eliminate

The volume of contacts needing Streamline actions is typically lower than that associated with the other four strategic actions (Eliminate, Digitize, Preempt, and Leverage), but the handling and downstream costs of these contacts can be just as high as those needing to be addressed by Eliminate. That's because the customer experience involved in contact reasons needing to be streamlined is, by definition, irritating—and this experience leads to high customer churn and low advocacy. Many of these contacts resemble complaints and impose on customers' time, so they do not represent opportunities for further sales. The best an organization can do is to make the interactions as painless as possible, with Eliminate as the longer-term goal.

Many reasons that are best addressed by Streamline arise when the organization needs to hear from the customer. Consider the following examples:

- "My power is out" (and the organization is unaware).
- "The network is down" (and, again, the organization is unaware).
- "I can't connect my new device to the network" (when the organization has not yet tested or vetted this new device).
- "I have a complaint."
- "I am encountering intermittent problems."
- "I got an error message that I can't define."

The Streamline action also includes contacts that the organization initiates with the customer. Here are examples:

- "Please tell us about X."
- "We need this information to refine our service to you."
- "For compliance or risk reasons, we need X from you."
- "We haven't heard from you, so please tell us what you think about X."

Many Streamline reasons are linked to new product launches, updated policy statements, or surprising or new events and problems. In effect, they are instances in which the customers become the eyes and ears of the organization. Innovators tap into these customer perceptions through innovative and low-cost rating systems (e.g., Uber riders rating drivers, eBay customers rating sellers, Airbnb guests rating properties and hosts). Streamline contacts can also be caused by outside forces, such as storms or other natural disasters, or deep-seated faults or bugs, where something isn't working properly or at all. For other instances, customers may be combining new services or products with existing ones, essentially testing compatibility for an organization.

The Actions

The Streamline actions fall into four streams. The first two streams try to prevent "more of the same" or further escalation of a problem. These actions can stop an issue from affecting more of the customer base (e.g., outage notifications, bug fixes) or keep a potential complaint from turning into a worse problem (see the section about "snowballs" in chapter 5); as such, they sometimes overlap with Preempt approaches.

The second two streams work to simplify the actions that customers have to take. This might include removing or combining processes, reducing steps within processes, or providing clearer instructions to customers. It might also involve automating some or all of the customer interaction, to give customers choice and flexibility.

GOOD STORIES

Following you will find several good cases showing how organizations have been able to Streamline.

Nike's Avid Runners

Athletic shoe and clothing manufacturer Nike is well known for its "Just Do It" ad campaigns. Their products have a wide range of use, and major athletic stars wear and promote their gear. In the mid-2000s, Nike began to get phone calls from some of its avid runners, who opened with questions such as, "I have run six marathons on the flats, but in a few months, I'll be running my first marathon at altitude. Will my Nike X shoe hold up to the wear and tear?" Even though Nike's customer service representatives might have been joggers or runners themselves, and Nike provided a voluminous amount of product detail about it shoes, these questions challenged the agents to provide the right responses to these customers.

As is typical of Nike, the company decided to flip things around so that whenever its call-routing system or customer service reps detected that avid runners were on the line, Nike routed them to the shoe engineers at its world headquarters in Beaverton, Oregon. Not only were the shoe engineers able to provide precise and useful answers to these avid runners' questions, but they also learned a great deal about what these elite athletes needed. As a result, Nike was able to invent an entirely new category of shoes for them called Flyknit, which gave the feeling of wearing a comfortable sock on top of a durable base.[1]

Simplification in this case came from applying the right level of expertise to these customers. The calls would have been harder to answer for others at Nike, but for shoe engineers, they were simple—and provided valuable input and feedback.

Vodafone Romania to the Rescue

There is no handbook for managing business through a pandemic, but like many other companies early in COVID-19, Vodafone's Romania market met the challenge head-on. When subscribers to its broadband services complained of slow speeds while also seeking extra time to pay higher bills, Vodafone's customer operations team quickly mobilized network, billing, and product managers. Contacts related to slow speeds were irritating to customers but useful in providing feedback to Vodafone; on the other hand, contacts by customers seeking payment delays could be seen as valuable to both parties, as customers wanted more time and Vodafone had an opportunity to manage debt.

Ana Paraschivoiu led a cross-functional team that found clear patterns for these two contact types: (1) everyone was locked down and stressing the network, especially during specific hours of the day, and (2) while many workers had some sort of social support, others were unable to afford what had become an essential service. So instead of viewing "My Broadband is slow" as an Eliminate reason, Vodafone Romania combined it with the bill-payment-delay requests and created new products and a new billing category to support customers. In effect, the Streamline answer was a new product and process design to handle these situations differently. As a result, the company also created loyal customers through the pandemic and managed the potential risk of bad debt.

Stop the Products!

Soon after Amazon instituted the e-commerce industry's first fully automated product-returns function on the website, offering nine reasons the customer might want to return the item (such as "I just don't want it anymore"), one of the reasons that customers were reporting caught Amazon product managers' eyes: "The product is defective." Even before examining the product in question, Amazon took the bold step of removing it from the Available status until it could be examined to confirm whether it was defective. In essence, these product managers argued, "Why should we continue to offer something that might result in every one of our customers finding a problem?"

Amazon immediately sent an automated alert to the manufacturer and distributor, advising them that the product would be on hold until the reported contact reason could be verified. The manufacturer howled, but Amazon stood its ground. They made it clear that this would be their process: Once the product was returned, they would test it. If it was, in fact, defective, they would send another message to the manufacturer alerting them. If the product worked properly, they would quickly restore it for sale on the website and, again, update the manufacturer. Later, Amazon adopted this process for all "defective" contact reasons, refining its algorithm so that after a second customer signaled that any given item was defective, the company would remove it for sale from the website.

This Amazon response epitomizes the textbook "First Fault Is Valuable" strategy, taking any fault seriously and choosing to put revenue on hold rather than risk several bad customer experiences. Indeed, Amazon takes the first two defect contacts to heart, doing their best to eliminate the need for further contacts until the product is proven.

Outage of This World

For energy businesses, a network fault can cause an avalanche of call volumes since every impacted customer wants to report the problem and insists on knowing when it will be fixed. This is a good case of the first few contacts being valuable but all subsequent contacts being irritating—for all parties.

Network provider CitiPower & Powercor has many regional customers with power lines impacted by storms, lightning strikes, and fallen trees. Once alerted to an outage, the company goes to work to update an outage page on its website with useful information such as which areas they believe are impacted and the likely time for restoration of power. They also capture SMS and email addresses from customers who can get updates on these situations if they opt in. A few years ago, they also provided customers with a free app that shows current outages and their likely durations. All of these responses allow customers to stay informed while reducing the number of assisted contacts. The advantage of apps is that they are on mobile phones, independent of the power network, so customers can check if the provider is aware of an outage before they place a call. These are great examples of using the Digitize and Preempt strategies to work on a Streamline problem.

The Complaints Threat

In many industries in Australia, such as utilities, telecom, banking, and insurance, customers can take problems that a company hasn't sorted out to an industry ombudsman, who then handles the complaint and charges the company for it. Therefore, it makes sense for organizations there to try to prevent these escalations.

One of Australia's leading utilities, AGL, managed to reduce external complaints through a variety of mechanisms that, in effect, streamlined the types of problems that might escalate to the ombudsman. First, the organization set up a **tiered service model** in which harder problems were funneled to experienced staff—problems that included, importantly, recent calls (described further in chapter 9). In addition, these staff members handled all complaints or threats of complaint. They not only had more skill and experience to solve these kinds of problems, but they were also given extra discretion, such as the authority to provide refunds or fix bills.

To streamline the process for the customer, this group could also take problems offline. This allowed them to investigate and solve problems and then get back to the customer without keeping the customer on the phone. Although it would have been even better if these problems hadn't occurred and the customers hadn't needed to make contact, AGL at least recognized the problems and created an appropriate model to solve them. At one stage, AGL had the lowest rate of external complaints of any large utility, and this model had much to do with it.

▮ BAD STORIES

Complaints Should Be Different

A wealth management business had staffed the complaints team with brand-new recruits. This group was new not only to the industry but also to its arcane systems and processes, and therefore not well qualified to handle complaints. That inexperience was bad enough, but to get complaints resolved, they needed other departments to investigate, correct, and act on problems. In these other functions, the complaints were placed in queues behind many other types of work. Therefore, a first-time problem would carry the same priority as a customer's third or fourth attempt to fix an issue. This meant that many complaints escalated to the industry watch-dog who then passed an even more severe and costly complaint back to the organization.

This is the antithesis of streamlining the process. Complaints passed through several pairs of hands and took longer than first-time inquiries to address. The complaints team was less qualified and had no greater authority than a normal customer service rep: They didn't analyze sys-temic issues, since they barely had time to report the volume and reasons for complaints. Rather than treating complaints as customer insights into what was broken, the organization understaffed the whole process and added costs while further annoying customers.

A large U.S.-based airline suffered the same fate when it decided to out-source lost baggage inquiries and claims to an outsourcer based in India. These were probably among the most demanding contacts from the carrier's passengers, eager to retrieve their luggage or obtain compensation. Not only did the company task frontline staff who had rarely flown, so that they couldn't empathize with customers, but they also told the staff to hew to tight concession limits or "Call us again" when they had no immediate answer. In short order, the carrier returned this critical function to its stateside staff.

Deadly Denial

A few years ago, a major vehicle manufacturer had a big problem. A few customers around the world complained that they had sudden cut-outs by engines at various speeds. For over three years, the company denied there was an issue. Eventually, in Australia, a passenger died and a coronial inquiry identified that there was indeed a fault. Within months the com-pany announced a recall to repair all of the impacted models sold over a two-year period, with all costs covered, but by then it had been over three years since the first incident. The product recall was very expensive, as the company had to bear high service costs and replace various parts.

This was the opposite of the Amazon approach. While Amazon withdrew a product after only one or two faults, this company initially denied that there was any issue, presumably to avoid the recall costs. This eventually led to at least one fatality, a forced recall and repair, and some loss of reputation. The sad thing was that the company managed to keep the issue surprisingly quiet. In fact, it later suffered more reputational damage by faking its emissions-reduction tests than it had burying and denying this dangerous product fault. For some reason, the media made a greater fuss about rigged emissions tests than about lethal car parts.

HOW TO STREAMLINE

There are four alternative strategies to Streamline, as shown in figure 6.1.

Streamline actions are different from other strategic actions in that they consist of four independent paths, depending on the type of contact. These four paths are driven by the four key questions, and although they vary, they also have something in common: each path combines a Streamline action with some form of Eliminate thinking. We'll work through these paths next.

Prevent Many of the Same

If you are dealing with a contact reason that is the first of many possible contacts for this reason, then your process must consider how to quickly extract the detail required to work out the remedial actions. In other words, you must ask, "How can we get the need quickly?" For the customer, there may be a sense of urgency (e.g., a service outage) or a need to understand how a situation can be repaired (e.g., a faulty product or bug), but the organization's need is different. If notified of an outage or a faulty product, for example, the organization may need details like when the outage occurred, how the product was being used, or whether the failure or outage is intermittent or constant. A power network going down on a stormy and cold winter night will produce different questions than an outage on a calm summer's day.

In all cases, the organization needs to consider how it can get to the root cause of the issue and try to solve it before it affects customers en masse—regardless of whether the solution is as simple as rolling out a repair crew

FIGURE 6.1. How to Streamline

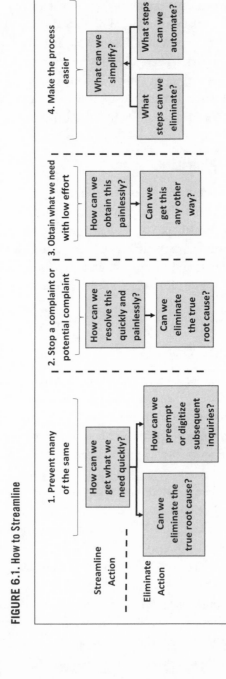

for a downed power cable or whether it's more complex, such as requiring that a faulty or intermittently faulty product be tested. The Amazon case, with the organization's rapid product withdrawal, demonstrates the lengths they were prepared to go to prevent other customers from having poor experiences. Conversely, the bad stories indicate that some companies care less about poor experiences where revenue is at stake. It can be that even internal product owners and managers can go into denial about faults and issues. Making them listen to or answer the complaints is often an excellent way to break down that denial. There is nothing more effective than having experienced customer service managers and product experts listen to recorded calls, comb through emails or text exchanges, and review social sites in order to develop a mutual understanding.

The Streamline strategy also includes elements of Preempt and Eliminate. For example, some utilities launch straight into Preempt strategies after a problem notification just to prevent others from having to make contact. Many utilities publish outage maps on their websites and text customers in the region before those customers get a chance to call. Others have smart software that recognizes when customers from the impacted area are calling and play them a targeted message. Likewise, food producers often launch product warnings, and software developers may try and patch a problem or release a workaround.

Once a problem is understood, the root cause analyses described in chapter 3 also apply here. Solutions may not be easy. A faulty product may need an examination of manufacturing and design processes that take a while to fix. A software bug could stem from its design or programming or from weak testing processes. The complexities of getting to the real root cause make it likely that shorter-term Preemption and crisis management is needed.

Stop a Complaint or Potential Complaint

Many organizations see complaints as irritating and therefore target their elimination. However, as noted earlier, others recognize that "every complaint is a gift."[2] Customers are taking the time to give critical feedback in a situation they aren't happy about. It is ironic that many organizations invest so much in asking customers for feedback through surveys and market research but very little in mining their complaints for recurring themes and problems. Often companies have a complaints team and process, but many team managers don't have the resources, time, or power to investigate root causes and solve the deeper issues.

The first Streamline step to take in response to complaints is to ask, "How can we resolve this quickly and painlessly?" The best complaint teams include experienced and empowered staff who have the knowledge and tools to solve the problem. A good example of this, introduced earlier, is Amazon's snowball process, which empowers agents to "melt" repeat calls or problems. This was a great tactic to prevent escalations to third or fourth contacts and external parties. Amazon also had a cherished program called Flipping the Turtle: Amazon likened irate customers to turtles on their shells, unable to turn themselves over to seek food or water. Whenever a customer service rep encountered an irate customer, they took as much time as necessary to resolve the issue and to ensure that the customer was satisfied, hence flipping the turtle. Further, if Amazon noticed that that a formerly irate customer purchased another item, that customer was deemed a CPR—Customer Permanently Retained.

To be effective, complaints teams first need the knowledge to assess the validity of the complaint and then they need to understand how to fix it. Customer-centric organizations like Costco, Nordstrom, or Trek Bikes assume the customer is right and do not put them through hoops to prove that a product is faulty or an order incorrect. Conversely, organizations that are primarily financially driven add friction by making customers prove the product's fault or provide copious information about the problem.

Effective complaint processes also streamline by having rapid access and support from other areas. For example, they may need other teams to provide same-day turnaround of any corrections or a rapid refund from finance. A simplified complaints process will therefore need fast-tracking, waiving normal business rules and timetables.

The second step in complaint handling is an Eliminate process to surface and attack the root causes. In the case of complaints, this means doing the following:

- Aggregating similar complaints, which is dependent on consistent classification and investigation
- Linking complaints to related contacts—the complaints may be the tip of the iceberg, but this same problem may be driving many irritating contacts that don't surface as formal complaints

- Looking outside the organization for social media and other commentary that may indicate a wider problem
- Getting those who handle the process to workshop the causes

This is a similar process to the Understand methods described in chapter 1. In the case of complaints, the organization is trying to understand the breadth of the problem in order to set priorities for improvements. For example, a complaint caused by one bad phone call with a single agent who provided the wrong information is different from a series of complaints and contacts caused by the whole workforce not being trained correctly. The latter might mean a complete revamp of training in that area, while the former would require the coaching of one individual.

A more proactive stance is for the organization to analyze and try to help those who have experienced the issue but haven't made contact. Identifying and assuaging these silent sufferers has proven to be extremely valuable, as many studies show that a only small percentage of customers encountering the same problems contact the organization. One found that 96% of unhappy customers don't bother to complain, and 91% simply leave and never come back.[3] As a result, a large percentage of customers might well be on their way to canceling their contracts or taking their business elsewhere. Thus, it is very useful to harness big data and predictive analytics to identify silent sufferers and to produce an appropriate campaign to reach out to them; and using some of the Preempt techniques can be particularly helpful.

Obtain What You Need with Low Effort

The third Streamline strategy relates to an organization getting the information it needs from the customer, including feedback or information for marketing, compliance, and other departments. Many companies think that they can subject customers to frequent surveys or ones that are long and complex. The obsession with tracking scores such as NPS to provide sentiment measurements seems to have generated a whole industry of survey tools and methods. Very few organizations have simplified feedback to its maximum extent, which is to give customers a single open-ended prompt like "Please tell us what you think" or "How could we have made this easier for you?" Rating scales and numeric feedback are there to "keep score," but free-format questions are there for true feedback.

These open-ended questions are actually quite simple to produce and leverage. They give customers more freedom and force the organization to listen and analyze the responses. The latest generation of text- and speech-analysis tools now make open-ended and free-format responses easier to analyze, enabling an organization to find patterns and themes. Meanwhile, scorekeeping and boxing the customer into complex surveys, which should be used sparingly, has become the norm. As a result, it is no surprise that survey response rates are falling and customers are suffering from survey fatigue.[4]

Where the company needs information for marketing, legal, or compliance, the Streamline mindset is also important to minimize effort for the customer. Identification is the most common area where organizations are forced to gather and check information, with limited benefit for the customer (although it can be argued that it is for everyone's security and protection). Technology that makes this identification process easier is very mature but unfortunately underutilized; take, for example, **CLI (caller line identification)** or **ANI (automatic number identification)**, where technology can pick up a caller's phone number and match it to customer detail records. Other solutions include biometric identification, like voice prints, facial recognition, or fingerprints. Phone manufacturers have educated a generation of customers to use these technologies, but they are not yet permeating general business and government processes.

Reducing effort via Streamline also means considering whether there are other ways to obtain needed information. When Amazon first created Dropdown 1-Click ordering profiles, they demonstrated this thinking. The original 1-Click locked in one address and payment method; Dropdown 1-Click gave customers a choice of different addresses and payment methods to use for their orders (e.g., send to address X and pay using card Y). This saved data entry for the customer. When launching Dropdown 1-Click, Amazon trawled the transaction history of each customer to find previously used combinations and **autopopulated** the list, enabling customers to edit if needed. This is a great example of using automation to streamline, removing the effort for those customers for whom more information is needed.

Streamline thinking of this kind could be used for all requests sent to their customers. Most organizations send blank forms and then ask customers to enter their details, many of which are already known. But

Frictionless Organizations prefill forms for customers. They keep the imposition on the customer to the bare minimum and do the same on online forms and web pages that they can prepopulate.

Make the Process Easier

The last Streamline strategy applies to those contacts for which other actions, like Eliminate, aren't possible or will take too much time. Streamlining a process can almost use a microcosm of all of the five strategic actions, but it applies to the steps within a process rather than to its root causes or drivers—in other words to Eliminate or Digitize steps, or Preempt them. If that isn't possible, then perhaps the step can be simplified. Last, for remaining processes, the organization needs to offer the customer choice and guidance in the process. This Streamline method is shown in figure 6.2.

Eliminate Effort

To eliminate effort means to determine where the customer is encountering roadblocks or friction with the process and then to reduce that effort. This can mean prefilling screens and forms, cutting forms down to the bare minimum, or not asking for information that the organization already knows. It can also mean going to extra lengths to link systems or look up external data.

Eliminating effort often means isolating exceptions rather than putting every customer through the same treatment. For example, in a mortgage application, only customers close to a bank's lending limits may need to provide extra documents to prove their income and credit-worthiness.

Isolating exceptions can make a big difference in process design. For example, many organizations require frontline staff to identify customers before they perform an action. This adds time and effort to the process, so

FIGURE 6.2. Within-Process Streamlining

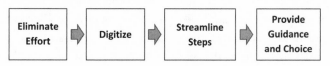

it should be done only when necessary. Yet many organizations apply rigorous identity checks to customers paying a bill. Who fraudulently pays bills for other customers? It is harder to train staff to use a more variable process, but it saves time and effort all around.

Reduce Effort through Automation

Reducing effort and automating parts of a process may also go together. A number of countries have simplified the passport application process by digitizing it, accepting photographs rather than physical copies of some documents, and no longer requiring attendance at a passport office. Likewise, a number of companies have set up processes to enable digital document scanning, authentication, and validation to streamline processes: insurance businesses are starting to use digital photos of damaged items to reduce customer effort for small claims, and utilities are accepting photos of meters as "self-reads" to simplify bill correction. Government offices can also automate COVID-19 vaccination records by making them available on apps instead of requiring citizens to dig out dog-eared vaccination cards.

Streamline Steps

Streamlining interactions involves making sure that the right resources and thinking are applied to a process. Consider some organizations' tendencies to push the burden of proof for a problem onto the customer (e.g., "Please send us a copy of a bank statement to prove the payment occurred" or "You need to send us the 26-character serial number to confirm that we sold you this product"). Streamlining this process trusts the customer's version of events and takes the problem offline to save the customer's time and resolve the issue more quickly, putting the customer to work only where all internal investigations fail. An effective complaints process also keeps the customer informed and pulls out all the stops for rapid resolution and customer recovery.

Streamlined steps also provide customers with choice (e.g., channel or timing) and with guidance through any complexities of a process. A good customer survey is an example of this. If an organization is conducting a survey that does need complicated information from customers, then they should make this clear at the outset, saying, for example, "This will take five minutes and involve 10 questions." Expectations then need to be managed throughout. A survey with multiple pages, for instance, should show the customer's progress (e.g., "You are on page 3 of 7") and offer reassurance ("We will save your responses if you cannot complete them during this session"). This gives control of the effort to the customer.

Guidance also involves giving help and support. Today this takes many forms, such as video guides, worked examples, frequently asked questions, chatbots for process support, and in-form explanations such as help fields. The important thing is to recognize that a process is, in some ways, an imposition on the customer and then to make it as painless as possible.

HINTS AND TIPS

The hints and tips for taking Streamline actions cover five ideas.

Isolate Exceptions

Designing a process that isolates exceptions is different from designing one in which all customers and scenarios are treated the same. Isolating the exceptions involves these elements:

- Recognizing the exceptions
- Having an upfront triage process
- Thinking through what can be made easier for the normal customer and what additions are needed for the exceptions
- Focusing on the skills and knowledge needed for the exceptions

This idea in practice. Many general insurance businesses have simplified claims processes for small claims or for claims where detailed checking and proof are less valuable. During major storms or floods, some insurers send out assessment teams to fast-track claims in the impacted areas, recognizing that these are unique events and that customers need support.

Throw the House at Complaints

In some organizations, complaints teams are populated with the most knowledgeable and skilled staff who recognize these complaints as valuable insights. It makes sense to overinvest in these teams and their learning processes. Sadly, complaints teams and processes in many organizations seem like afterthoughts.

This idea in practice. An Australian bank put one of their most dynamic GMs in charge of complaints. She raised the profile of the function across the whole bank and promoted it as the source of continuous improvement. The executive team had to listen to complaints and discuss their implications. Complaints were analyzed for common root causes, and the whole organization mobilized to identify more complaints rather than hide issues. It changed the entire culture of the bank to one where it was okay to share and admit issues rather than to hide or suppress them.

Ask the Front Line before the Customer

Many organizations seek feedback from customers but don't tap the staff who deal with them all the time. The frontline teams on chats, on calls, or in shops get feedback all the time and are closer to the customer than those in the head office.

This idea in practice. A rapidly growing broadband business holds a monthly forum with staff to make suggestions on how their customer service app should be improved. The staff are also users of the application and hear feedback from customers. They are ideally placed to assist with design suggestions.

Employ Smart Design

Designing process and user experience is a skill, just as systems architecture design is a skill. Good process designers have all kinds of tricks and techniques that others may not. To streamline processes, then, apply those who have the capabilities and help them facilitate the design with those who know the products and systems well.

This idea in practice. The complaints team in a company was overwhelmed and underskilled. A lead process designer redesigned the whole end-to-end process, creating the following capabilities:

- A receipting function to triage the complaints better and to provide immediate feedback, including a time frame, to the customer

- The authority to enable the complaints team to handle more complaints without help
- The ability to fast-track complaints as work items to other teams, making them top priority
- Analyses to look for recurring themes and to report complaint drivers to the areas that created them
- A monthly complaint forum, with better reporting and analysis to work on systemic issues

The net result was falling complaint volumes, reduced complaint expenses, and a reduction in the size of the complaints team over time.

Use Analytics

Speech and text analytics can be used to predict and spot problems. Where one agent may think a complaint is a unique situation, analytics can go to work to look for similar issues and then warn of more comprehensive problems. Predictive analytics can also be used to comprehend the scope of the problem and begin to lay out possible root causes. Analytics can also trigger alerts in near real time to support Preempt actions (e.g., background analysis can update websites with outage information or give warnings to staff or customers).

This idea in practice. One company used AI and machine learning to find patterns and links between complaints and other related contacts to warn of the true scope of an issue. The analytics mechanism was trained to pull out related reasons to show whether a complaint was a one-off issue or the tip of an iceberg. This same company used a combination of analytics and **smart routing** technology to predict when customers were in a likely complaint or repair scenario, with calls routed to more experienced agents to prevent them from turning into full-blown complaints.

▓▓▓ SUMMARY

Streamline can be the most difficult strategic action because it can include elements of eliminating, digitizing, and being preemptive. It also addresses scenarios such as mass customer impacts and individual issues that may escalate to external complaint bodies. It is different because it also includes information that the organization wants from customers rather than requests that customers make or transactions they want. Because these interactions are irritating to customers and valuable to the organization, they should be challenged at three levels, based on whether . . .

- This reason can be thought about differently and can be eliminated or digitized.
- It can be restructured for most customers, even if some will still need to make contact.
- The interactions themselves can be reengineered to be more streamlined.

Last, it's important always to remember that these interactions are still irritating to customers, so don't get seduced into trying to exploit the interactions in some way. Pare them back to the bare minimum.

ASSESS YOUR NEED TO STREAMLINE

You have the potential to Streamline if you answer yes to any of these questions or don't know the answer:

Q1. Do events occur in and around your business that overwhelm the contact centers, impacting a large customer base?

Q2. Do many of your interactions seem to escalate to formal complaint mechanisms?

Q3. Do you ask for customer feedback and find it takes at least five minutes of the customer's time?

Q4. Do you use most of your customer feedback to keep score rather than to drive improvement?

Q5. Is the response rate of feedback falling?

Q6. When customers make contact, is much of the process driven by regulation and compliance?

Q7. Do you need feedback from a few customers about issues, but you end up getting it from hundreds or thousands?

Q8. Are several departments asking customers for information, and it becomes a long and complex process?

Q9. Are all your forms blank, with nothing prepopulated?

LEVERAGE

7

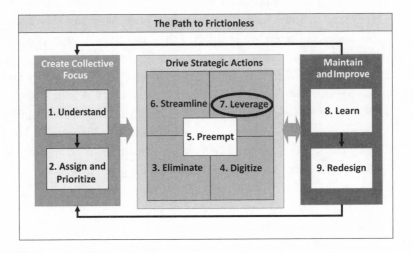

WHAT IS "LEVERAGE" AND WHY IS IT IMPORTANT?

The final strategic action is Leverage, and it addresses reasons that are valuable to the customer and valuable for the organization. By definition, every organization wants more Leverage contacts, should invest time in them, and may want to increase their frequency. Customers don't see these contacts as friction because they value them, and the organization knows that these interactions are often key to revenue, retention, and relationship-building with the customer.

Some of these reasons represent **moments of truth**[1] for the customer, such as hardship or the start of a complex insurance claim. As such, both the customer and the organization should be prepared to invest time in these interactions to get successful outcomes. For the organization, there is significant potential return from these contacts through increased revenue, cost containment, and/or reputation preservation. Therefore, organizations should be prepared to invest in technology solutions, extend interaction times, and dedicate their best staff to contacts with these reasons.

There are two steps to executing the Leverage strategic action:

1. **Determine which contact reasons and which customers are to be treated as Leverage interactions.** Understand and Assign may have led to an initial allocation of some contact reasons to leverage, but those contact reasons alone may not be sufficient justification for Leverage treatment. Making decisions about those contacts can be further complicated by the value of the customer, the contact channel, and the customers' circumstances.

2. **Figure out how to deliver the experiences that the customer and the organization want.** This is where Leverage differs from the other four strategic actions (Eliminate, Digitize, Preempt, and Simplify) because there is no intent to displace or reduce these interactions. Here the focus is about how to make the most of the interaction and achieve all the outcomes that the organization and customer are seeking.

As for the first step, it's complicated to identify Leverage reasons because they have four distinct dimensions:

- **Type of contact**. For example, "I want to cancel" may be a Leverage contact, but "What's the status of my cancelation?" usually requires Eliminate, Digitize, or Preempt.
- **Channel**. The same contact reason may be seen as an irritant by the organization in one channel but not in another channel. For example, some organizations want more interactions using chat and messaging and now see certain interactions as irritants if they come by phone. Some organizations offer different channels to different groups of customers, so this becomes quite a complex decision-making process.
- **Customers and their value**. High-value customers may be given premium service levels that enable them to contact the organization for any reason via any channel. In contrast, low-value customers may be restricted in the channels they use and for certain interactions (e.g.,

they may be expected to purchase and cancel via digital channels only). The how-to section of this chapter will describe some of the complexities of determining customer value.

- **Situational urgency and impact**. There may be times when an interaction becomes more valuable to the organization and customer. For example, if a customer fears potential fraud on a credit card, their bank may want to receive immediate notification and to talk to the customer to ensure risks are managed. In contrast, if a customer damages or breaks a card, digital channels may be best since there is no risk of financial loss.

Analyzing contact reasons, channels, customers, and impacts is a complex process, and it might lead some organizations to leverage a combination that other organizations decide to digitize. Different markets or regions might assign different strategic actions to the same combination based on maturity levels, the trade-off between revenues and costs, and the available staff. It is not easy to separate particular groups of customers or to divert certain reasons to certain channels, leading organizations to apply one-size-fits-all solutions, such as sending all customers to a save team, even though they would prefer to apply that treatment only to the most profitable customers. They might not want to retain the bottom 20% of customers at all, but their processes and systems don't enable rapid differentiation.

What Experiences Are Needed for Leverage Contacts?

The second step of Leverage is to design and deliver effective experiences that meet the organization's and customer's objectives for these reasons. This is a problem that can require design and implementation across a variety of operating model dimensions, such as well-designed processes, the use of appropriate technology, and the allocation or equipping of staff suited to the nature of these contacts. When the reasons being addressed are critical to revenue and reputation, most organizations are prepared to invest more in the design and delivery of effective interactions.

For Leverage contacts, it is also important to understand why they occur. For example, if customers are asking to leave, what issues and problems brought them to that point? Leverage contacts can also have addressable root causes that need analysis, and the how-to section covers that approach.

What Are Typical Leverage Reasons?

In general, contact reasons to address with Leverage are those that can produce significant financial or relationship impacts, falling into five likely themes:

- Contacts that have the potential to produce greater revenues, including new sales or sales extensions:
    - "Tell me about your new products."
    - "Can I extend my membership (or lease)?"
- Contacts related to debt or credit risk, sometimes as a result of customer hardship:
    - "Can I get on a payment plan?"
    - "I've lost my job. How can I keep X?"
- Contacts that may require preserving the relationship, such as saving a customer who is requesting cancelation, price-matching for a customer to counter competitor offers, or **rightsizing** the customer to a more appropriate product:
    - "I need to cancel my account."
    - "This plan is too expensive for me. Is there anything else?"
- Contacts that alert the business to a possible fraud or reputation risk:
    - "There is something strange on my account."
    - "Did you send me this?"
    - "My card may be stolen."
- Contacts that initiate expensive, long, and complex processes:
    - "I want to make a claim on my income protection insurance."
    - "I was in a bad car accident."
    - "We need to restructure our business with you" (e.g., a B2B situation).

▮ GOOD STORIES

There are many good examples where organizations have invested in delivering excellent experiences when dealing with Leverage contact reasons. All of these stories manage to strike a balance among cost, customer experience, and revenue outcomes.

Leveraging Sales to the Max

The Royal Automobile Club of Victoria (RACV) is an example of a mutual fund that has grown in breadth and depth despite, or perhaps because of, competition from listed businesses. Each state in Australia has a similar member-based organization that provides roadside assistance services and insurance products; RACV also offers lifestyle and resort options. Its insurance business had a specialist sales team to leverage inquiries from members and non-members looking for insurance products. The business was looking for ways to improve its sales conversion rate and the value of sales. They followed a textbook approach with these three steps:

1. They analyzed current calls and the call-handling process, revealing which conversations were frustrating for customers and for the RACV (e.g., customers would get deep into a conversation and then reject a quote because it was too high). Few customers selected the extended product features, and frontline staff seemed frustrated and disengaged by the process they had to follow.
2. They redesigned the process by balancing the customer experience with the desired business outcomes of high sales conversion and throughput. The revised processes turned the conversation inside out: RACV provided the customer with a low, competitive quote as quickly as possible and then "earned the right" to offer extended features for the product. Staff were excited when they were trained on the new process.
3. They conducted a short pilot that led to an immediate step change in sales conversion.

These changes improved product margin with shorter conversations with fewer discounts. RACV saw a significant rise in the sales of higher-value products, and since the process was quicker, the sales team had more capacity. The customer reaction was also positive. In post-contact surveys, there was a 7-percentage-point improvement in customer satisfaction after the new process. Presented to the board as one of the most successful projects of the year, this project saw an overall gain in sales, margin, and sales productivity of over 40%.

Online-to-Independent Dealer

Trek Bikes makes some of the most popular recreational and competitive bicycles in the world. Like many other successful manufacturers, Trek had built a loyal independent dealer network over the years to sell and service its range of bikes and associated gear. When Trek decided to go direct to consumer (DTC), however, the company faced a dilemma: How could they build an even better relationship with its riders but not alienate its loyal dealer network? Trek took a novel approach to this dilemma. When the company designed its online product search and sales feature (using Digitize), it required customers to pick up their assembled and tuned bikes at nearby dealer shops (using Leverage). This multi-action, omnichannel strategy recognized that the post-sale activity represented an opportunity for dealers to develop relationships with customers, offer them accessories and clothing, and set them up with services and maintenance. Far from upsetting its retailers, Trek managed to pull off its online-to-dealer strategy to great success and has now opened its own branded shops without upsetting its traditional dealer network. In effect, Trek put the fulfillment stage of the sales process into the dealers' hands.

Making the Claim

Automobile claims, especially those involving personal injury, represent some of the most sensitive and fraught cases for customers—and too often, there is considerable friction involved in the claims process. One of the many reasons USAA Insurance enjoys the highest customer loyalty of any U.S. property and casualty insurer (its NPS is in the high 80s, and its number one reason for churn is death, not going to another company) is the ease of its claims experience. Using a combination of online tools (Digitize) and well-timed outbound calls with USAA members (Leverage), the company keeps members informed throughout the complex claims process. As with all claims, USAA needs to know details about the location, timing, and situation. By enabling a member to upload photos (of the auto accident and damages to the involved vehicles) and to provide detailed maps showing the situation that led to the accident, USAA is able to analyze the data offline. After that, USAA arranges for a conference call with the member to confirm details and discuss options. USAA then keeps the member informed of claim details in its online portal, inviting the member via text message or email, whichever channel the member requests. This Preempt tool also reduces the urge for USAA members to call the company with "What's the status?" questions. USAA balances and stages each of the strategic actions during the claims process, using Leverage for the most sensitive moments for the member.

Value-Add Conversations

Vodafone Portugal believed that there was greater potential to have value-add conversations on certain contacts. The marketing analysis team had already assessed which additional products were suited to customers. Some initial research also showed that customers were actually more satisfied after calls in which additional offers were well explained and matched, even when they didn't take up the offer.

The contact center conducted further analysis to assess which calls really were in the Leverage quadrant. They recognized that attempting product conversations on Eliminate reasons was a waste of time. Their analysis of current calls showed that around 20% of them fell in the Leverage quadrant. They then worked with frontline staff to design these conversations. That produced another interesting finding: staff didn't want to be constrained by just one marketing offer in a conversation; instead, they wanted to be empowered to pick from several options.

As a result, their design of Leverage conversations included trigger statements that staff could look for before initiating conversations. This meant the conversations were targeted to customer needs. New conversation guides also helped staff explain product options and benefits, gave them ideas for handling objections, and offered other tips that helped them to be well prepared for any negativity and to offer better explanations. The company trained several pilot teams in this new way to handle Leverage calls. The results were quite remarkable. The pilot team made 6 times more offers than with the old process, producing 10 times as many new products or changed-product sales. Better still, tNPS increased with the new process.

Far from being "Do you want fries with that?" conversations, the new Vodafone Portugal offers and explanations were made at appropriate times. The company was elated with the associated revenue gains, and staff benefited through aligned and increased commissions, a good example of a triple win (for the organization, customer, and staff) achieved through designing Leverage calls that would benefit all parties.

■ BAD STORIES

Falling down the Cracks

The major earthquake in Canterbury, New Zealand, in 2010–11 left many homes unlivable and created more than 650,000 insurance claims valued at NZ$21 billion. Insurance customers needed support so that they could get on with rebuilding their homes and lives. Some companies responded well, sending extra assessment staff to Canterbury or waiving some of their normal rules to enable claims to be fast-tracked. Unfortunately, that wasn't a universal story. Over the next few years, stories emerged of customers still in dispute with their insurance companies over their claims. They had been unable to proceed with rebuilding their homes or buying new homes because of delays and disputes in the claims process and the complexity over deciding whether they should be allowed to rebuild in quake-ravaged areas.

Rather than being flexible and responsive to a clear Leverage need, one or two insurers seemed intent on making the claims process as long and drawn out as possible. This led to newspaper and TV reports exposing these companies. Several ended up in claims tribunals, which extended the process further. The problem became so bad that the New Zealand government stepped in with extra quake support and proceeded with major legislative reform to prevent these situations in the future. Even as late as 2019, however—eight years after the earthquake hit—the NZ Insurance Council reported 1,100 claims still incomplete. Unfortunately, there was limited publicity naming and blaming these companies, so they remain in business today.

Channel Trapping

There are times when certain channels are ineffective at handling contact complexity. For example, many organizations are using email less or have stopped it completely because it can produce drawn out and ineffective interactions.

In one instance, a business utility client was trying to get a new meter installed to support a new site. This is an example of a Leverage contact, as it represents extended business for the utility and is important for the customer. The business customer emailed the request, including the site details, and attached forms for the associated process. Twenty-six email messages and two months later, the meter installation was still not arranged or complete. The customer was very frustrated at the process and at being unable to rent out the premises.

The emails were handled by up to four different staff members in the utility, all of whom could see the whole sequence if they looked hard enough. However, at no point did an agent call the customer or seek to switch to a more direct and complete way of communicating. Neither was there a clear directive to resolve the contact by phone, which no doubt would have been a more effective mechanism.

Order Taking

A small telco offered competitive plans for mobile and broadband and had a smart strategy to target regional and rural customers who wanted an onshore sales and service experience. Many customers would call the sales team with clear Leverage statements like "I think I want this plan" or "How do I sign up?" These calls landed in the laps of the sales staff, who easily converted over 40% of the calls. Unfortunately, though, a poor sales process produced terrible post-sales experiences. The company averaged over three service calls for each new plan sold, and it lost over one-fifth of those new sales within three months from disappointed customers.

A detailed Understand study showed why the company saw these outcomes: the sales agents did a poor job of listening to the customer's needs. If a customer asked for a product, the agents gave them that product without checking the customer's requirements. The sales reps also knew little about the post-sales processes. They didn't explain how and when the customer would get connected or set them up to pay bills in an efficient way. The sales reps merely took the orders. Customers, therefore, called in later, confused about connection speeds, the connection process, and why they were being billed for certain features or products. Many downstream contacts could have been avoided had the sales team explained the process and set expectations up front. These were Leverage contacts handled with a bare-minimum approach that delivered poor outcomes.

▓ HOW TO LEVERAGE

As shown in figure 7.1, the Leverage strategic action first considers which interactions to leverage, for which customers, and then it looks to design and deliver appropriate Leverage experiences.

Determine When, How, and to Whom the Leverage Strategy Applies (Customer Cohort, Problem, Situation, and Channel)

It is not easy to determine which contact reasons should be given Leverage and treatment, especially when also considering different customer segments in different circumstances. This becomes a multidimensional problem once organizations offer numerous contacts channels that vary in cost and effectiveness for different contact categories. A good way to start this analysis, though, is by considering (1) the type of contact (e.g., revenue generation, service, risk, or fraud mitigation) and (2) the value of the customer.

For any contact reason, there is usually a healthy debate as to whether Leverage or Digitize is the most appropriate strategy. For example, for "I want to learn more about your new products," a digital Innovator might decide to steer all customers to the web first before talking with them, while an older-style Renovator might prefer to split customer segments and take their most valuable customers into the assisted channel while the rest remain in digital channels.

Most organizations segment their customers by current or potential value.[2] Leverage considers whether the organization wants to treat these segments differently and, if so, what that would mean in terms of what channels are offered, what differentiations should be made, and whether frontline staff should be deployed to handle these interactions. For example, airlines might offer separate phone numbers for premium frequent flyers to connect to a special service team composed of the most experienced staff, while referring the mass market directly to websites and chat.

Even where differentiation is desirable, an organization still needs to ask whether it *can* apply different treatments or whether doing so would just be too hard and complicated. Most organizations have to apply broad-brush approaches to this problem because they can't easily distinguish between different customer segments and needs "on the fly."

FIGURE 7.1. Leverage Approach

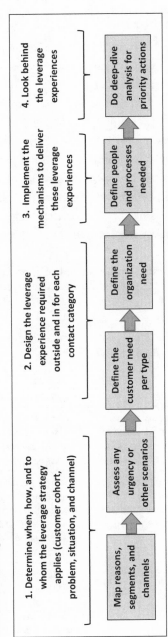

An organization should also recognize the relationship between the value of customers and the cost it is willing to pay to provide various channels. The value of the different customer segments will determine which channels the organization may be able to offer profitably for different types of interactions. Low-value customer segments may only be profitable if they aren't handled by assisted contact channels, even for Leverage interactions like sales opportunities. For example, prepaid mobile customers (usually a lower-value segment) may only get access to automated sales and service channels such as apps.

One way to simplify this multidimensional problem is to use a matrix of three "buckets" of typical customer interactions: Joining, Maintaining, and Leaving. This helps paint the broad strategy; then the organization can add more detail to the contact reasons in each stage. In table 7.1, the Digitize opportunities are shown in plain text and the Leverage opportunities in bold italics.

This matrix illustrates the potential mix of Leverage tactics in those instances when an organization wants to offer assisted contact versus digital

TABLE 7.1. Example Segment Strategy: When to Leverage or Digitize
Leverage = *Bold italics*; Digitize = Plain text

Customer Segment	Joining	Maintaining	Leaving (Cancel/Save)
Gold: Highest lifetime value	*Phone and message-based sales team, but customer can choose any channel* including digital.	*Phone and message based. Customer can choose any channel* including digital.	*Dedicated saves team. Proactive save and preventative saves.*
Silver: The profitable majority	*Phone-based sales or digital sign-up. Customer can choose which channel.*	Mostly digital and app based with phone-based support and escalation. *Chat and voice available for urgent reasons.*	*Combination of digital saves with some use of an assisted save channel. Recommend down-sell options.*
Bronze: Marginal lifetime value	Digital sign-up only.	Customer limited to mobile app, web portal, and chatbot. *Escalation to assisted support only in exceptional circumstances.*	Customer can leave using digital channels.

strategies for lower-value customers and interaction types. In this scenario, the organization is prepared to invest in the Silver segment to initiate the relationship and preserve it, but routine maintenance is handled by a digital strategy, except for urgent reasons. The Gold segment can choose between assisted channels or digital self-service. Their higher value means that the organization views all contacts with this segment as being leverageable.

Many banks follow a strategy similar to this. For their highest-value private-banking segment, they offer a one-to-one relationship with a personal banker and a bevy of wealth managers. These bankers handle all of the customer's needs, including routine maintenance transactions. In effect, the bank sees all interactions with these customers as valuable and worthy of this Leverage treatment. In contrast, a customer with a simple checking account might have a limit on which transactions they can complete in branches or by phone. Some banks even charge for interactions over a certain limit. Since most banks now offer online banking and mobile phone apps, they expect the majority of customers to use them for routine transactions.

It can be oversimplistic to look purely at the economics of the customer relationship to determine how a particular contact should be treated. For example, a customer in difficult circumstances may need hand-holding regardless of their value to the organization. The urgency and need of the customer can change the importance of the issue for the organization. Even routine transactions, like bank withdrawals or mobile phone-balance top-ups, can start to incur a reputational risk if the organization doesn't handle them efficiently and effectively when the customer is in a difficult position. For example, in weather-related crises, many organizations offer additional help and support. During these crises, banks waive overdraft rules, and utilities extend payment terms. This happened during the bad Australian forest (bush) fires of 2019–20 and in the wildfires in Portugal and on the West Coast of the United States. Many organizations offered extra support to their customers financially and through special help and support lines that bypassed normal queues and treatments. This is a good illustration of customer urgency outweighing other issues. Regardless of whether organizations do this merely because it is the right thing to do or because of the possible reputational benefits, the outcomes are still positive.

Design the Leverage Experience Required Outside and Inside for Each Contact Category

Customer contact reasons that require the Leverage strategy tend to be more complex by nature than routine transactions. They are also more complex contacts that involve getting simple information, which are addressed with Digitize actions, or ones that can be eliminated or preempted. Leverage interactions are often the hardest interactions to manage well and thus need effective experience design both for the customer and the organization. Interactions with a revenue element, such as new sales, upsells, and saves, often also face regulatory scrutiny in some industries. Consumer law may protect customers from aggressive selling, misleading sales, or overly aggressive retention tactics.

Saves and cancel transactions illustrate a delicate balance between customer and organizational needs. Customers calling to cancel an account want the interaction to be quick and painless; they want to be in and out as fast as possible. By contrast, the organization is often looking to save the customer and retain the revenue. Many organizations use deceptive practices when customers attempt to cancel their contract, telling the customer they will be sent to the cancelation team when they are actually sent to a special "save team," whose performance is measured on their save rates. A well-designed save conversation recognizes this balance of needs. The save team may be able to repair a problem that has led to a cancel request or match a competitor offer, but they should also be good at understanding why a customer wants to leave and stop trying to save customers who are clearly in no mood for an extended conversation.

Hardship conversations are also a juggling act. If a customer can't pay a bill or can no longer afford a product or service, the organization should balance their financial exposure to this customer with other factors, such as reputational risk. In most countries, utilities like electricity and water are seen as essential services, so organizations have to offer hardship schemes that balance trying to get payments in the door with customers' needs, including distressing circumstances. Information and history about the customer can help. If this is the first time a customer has sought relief, it's very different from a customer who never pays on time. However, even the chronic late payer may have extenuating circumstances. These conversations have to be well structured and must be handled by frontline staff who have information at their fingertips and a range of options to apply.

Complex claims issues are another illustration of the need for well-designed conversations. At the start of a claims process, customers may be in trying circumstances (e.g., damage to their home or car, an illness, or personal bodily injury). However, the insurer is trying to move the customer down a certain path to control the cost and duration of the claim. In many situations, the customer's and the organization's need are aligned. Getting the right treatment early can help the customer recover faster and contain claim costs. There are also benefits to advising the customer in the right way, which should align with the organization's need to contain the cost of the claim. The claims conversation needs to have a well-defined process so that staff can explain the process and advise the customer appropriately. There are many systems that can assist with this kind of conversation. For example, well-designed knowledge tools, especially with AI and machine learning, can help the claims agent identify the customer's medical condition and recommend appropriate treatment paths.

Implement the Mechanisms to Deliver Leverage Experiences

To help deliver the Leverage experiences they want, organizations typically draw on combinations of people, technology, and processes. We explore each of these areas next.

- **People.** It is one thing to design the experience for Leverage contacts, but it is quite another to execute it—and execution is critical. A key part of the execution is assigning the appropriate individuals to handle these contacts. That might be as simple as getting the customer to the hand-picked and specially trained hardship team. In areas like sales, however, or for higher-value customers, it might be better to match the best skilled or tenured agent with the customer.

    Larger organizations, in particular, may have the luxury of matching agents to customers via several new methods, such as assigning certain frontline staff members to particular customer **personas**. To do this, they classify certain needs and characteristics of customers into definable groups that help clarify the way they should be treated. If done correctly, this can help the frontline agents handling the

contacts to recognize the broad needs of those groups and ways they
generally want to be treated. If interacting with a customer who fits
the "Information Seeker" persona, a staff member knows to tailor
the conversation to provide lots of explanation; but if speaking to a
"Bargain Hunter," they know to simply inform the customer of the
best offer available as quickly as possible. Further, matching staff
members with customers who share their attributes can help staff
empathize and better serve their needs. As organizations get access
to increased amounts of data about customers, their ability to classify and tailor the experiences should increase.

One large BPO claimed good results from attempting demographic matching of customers to their sales and service team.
Wherever they could, they tried to route calls from customers to
agents with a similar demographic profile that took age, marital
status, and family status into consideration. The organization had
sufficient scale to achieve this level of matching 60% of the time and
compared the revenue results of matched calls versus unmatched
calls. They reported increased revenue of 45% per call on a combination of sales and service calls.

- **Technology.** Technology can play an important role for Leverage
reasons (e.g., with hardship or saves), making it important for staff
to have a well-analyzed history of clients' prior relationships. The best
technology solutions, such as augmented agent technologies, recommend offers to make or other actions to take. In save environments,
technology may suggest alternative products that the customer can
afford (e.g., a lower price plan) or put a limit on the discounts or offers
that frontline staff can give a customer (also called down-selling or,
more accurately, rightsizing).

Technology can play an important role in augmenting Leverage
experiences. **Real-time speech analytics** (analytics that assess a
conversation as it occurs in real time using AI and machine learning)
can enhance frontline skills. These augmented agent services can
analyze the customer's history to match them to alternative or additional products and services or serve up relevant knowledge articles
and comparisons. In a save situation for a telecommunications company, the technology can analyze all aspects of the customer's phone
and data history to recommend alternative products that may fit their

spend and behavior profile. This agent augmentation technology can suggest a range of products and even help the agent predict future bills, likely savings, and future purchases. In a hardship scenario, technology can calculate different payment profiles and plans and even suggest questions that the agent should ask to diagnose information that is important for the process. Some companies are even using technology to make individual offers tailored to a customer rather than making offers based on broad product groupings.

- **Processes.** Well-designed processes become critical in Leverage interactions. In sales conversations, for example, the frontline staff need to be able to execute a range of effective processes, including the following:
  - ○ Build rapport with prospects and customers and listen to their spoken and unspoken needs.
  - ○ Probe for and diagnose needs for those products and services.
  - ○ Match needs to products.
  - ○ Tailor the offer.
  - ○ Overcome objections and obstacles.
  - ○ Convince and close.

  Some staff will perform these tasks instinctively, but each of these sub-processes can also be defined, trained, and coached. Complex processes like claims can also be broken down and documented so that staff can be taught the best sequence of questions to ask to get to a good claims outcome.

Leverage execution requires this combination of people, technologies, and processes working in harmony to get outcomes that the organization and customer both want to achieve.

Look Behind the Leverage Experiences

While Leverage reasons are, in theory, ones that the organization wants to handle, some of the reasons are worthy of further analysis. That's because Leverage contacts may also provide important insights into the organization's core processes, pricing, and products. For example, if a customer asks to cancel, this may be the culmination of many failed processes—or it could be that the customer was sold the wrong product initially, has had a series of poor experiences, and/or received a more compelling offer from a competitor.

Many Leverage reasons require deeper root cause investigation to understand what is driving them. This process might identify that many customers are equally affected and could be handled preemptively. The examples that follow illustrate potential analyses of cancelations, hardships, and contacts with fraud potential.

Example 1: Cancelation mining. One large utility analyzed its calls to cancel service and realized that a competitor was bringing aggressive pricing to the market. However, they also noted that their offers had a limited benefit period. They equipped their saves team to educate customers about this short-lived benefit and worked up examples to show that their product was as cost-effective in the medium term. This helped lift their saves rate.

Example 2: Learning from hardship. One company recognized that they could learn from hardship-related inquiries. They went right back to the process by which they had acquired customers to analyze whether certain campaigns and processes had attracted customers who were more likely to end up in debt and hardship. They recognized that discount offer campaigns, which ran at certain times of the year in certain geographies, had a far higher propensity for those in hardship. They also had to balance this analysis to see if the ratio of profitable customers emerged.

Example 3: Preemptive fraud warning. Banks that experience potential fraud and customer scams now look to mine these contacts so they can build in early warning systems for their customers. One credit card company alerted their customers about potential credit card fraud from taxi companies. They had spotted a trend in which their customers would see many similar but fake deductions on their cards from taxi suppliers; these deductions would resemble their prior fares. The difference was that the fraudulent transactions had rounded amounts like $64, where most legitimate transactions were rarely rounded. In this way, the bank was able to monitor for these transactions and warn customers before the fraud mounted to large amounts.

HINTS AND TIPS

The hints and tips for Leverage cover a broad range, from sales, to fraud and risk, to saving customers.

Provide Choices for Sales and Save Conversations

It is always a good strategy to offer customers choices so that they have control over their product-related decisions. A UK bank discovered this when the first digital sales solutions it created made a single recommendation to customers. Many of them walked away not trusting this apparent fait accompli. They reworked the solution to offer choices and got a much better result.

This idea in practice. A self-service web-based solution allowed customers to specify their needs for white goods. Even where the technology could have recommended only one product to the customer, the solution was designed to present at least three options so that the customer could choose. It did flag the possible best pick but allowed the customer to choose and provided a link to assisted support where needed. The application is now the best-selling white-goods website on the market.

Integrate Channels to Make It Easy for Customers

Leverage contacts are often lengthy and complex. Using a mix of channels can help customers make decisions in their own time and put them in control while making the process easier. That can mean using text and email messages to explain the organization's processes to the customer or, if needed, creating a "trialogue" among the customer, the sales agent, and a digital sales platform.

This idea in practice. Customers often report motor accidents while they are in no position to remember details or even write them down. Many claims processes now use text and email to get the customer the information they will need, such as claim reference numbers, useful process details, and even links to videos and guides to help them. Having that information on their phone means the customer can easily reference it while dropping off a car at a repair shop.

Balance Trust and Risk for Hardship and Fraud Conversations

Hardship conversations (and some claims conversations) often require organizations to trust their customers' information. This can be a delicate balancing act for an organization that may also be concerned about fraud or payment evasion. It's hard for customers to admit to situations like being laid off, so this also has to be taken on trust. The savings in paperwork and effort, however, often outweighs any financial exposure.

This idea in practice. An energy utility changed its hardship process so that they could now accept certain information with few questions asked. They realized that customers very rarely lied about scenarios like being recently bereaved or unemployed, so they decided to take this information on trust: no death certificates, no intrusive need for government proof. The process was quicker and, when monitored, produced no change in the ratios of bad debt. In other words, they were right to trust the customers in these circumstances. It was a quicker process and less intrusive.

Value the Customer's History in Key Transactions

Organizations hope for lengthy relationships and loyalty, and in certain situations, customers expect this loyalty to be acknowledged and rewarded. While it's quite difficult to design processes in such a way that they flex to the length and value of these relationships, customers do often say, "I've been with you for a long time" so it's not unusual for a 30-year customer to expect at least acknowledgment if not also forgiveness or greater leniency and flexibility in payment terms.

This idea in practice. Pilots at a well-known international airline went on strike. Their main competitor recognized a one-off opportunity to impress their rival's most valuable customers with the benefits of a frequent flyer program: they threw open lounges and preferred seating to any of this competitor's customers who had the equivalent status. In effect, they "status-matched," offering frequent flyer benefits for one year to customers who came from their competitor and booked flights even after the strike ended. This showed customers that they valued frequent flyers and would welcome their business. This helped increase their market share of the most valuable customers.

▉ SUMMARY

Leverage enables the organization to move from cost containment and customer experience improvements to revenue enhancement, customer retention, and investment in long-term relationships. Deciding which interactions to address with the Leverage action is a complex and multi-dimensional process; it's also a challenge to work out how to design and execute Leverage experiences successfully. Deciding what to leverage requires calculating long-term customer value and channel strategy and then analyzing what level of differentiation is possible. Building Leverage interactions needs careful design in terms of who handles the contacts, how the technology enables and supports them, and how the processes work. Frictionless companies design Leverage interactions that demonstrate an understanding of what makes them easy, providing choice, demonstrating when to trust customers, and conveying how to esteem lasting and valuable relationships.

ASSESS YOUR NEED TO LEVERAGE

You have the potential to deliver Leverage better if you answer yes to any of these questions or don't know the answer:

Q1. Do you force customers to use the same channels for sales and key service interactions, regardless of their value to your business?

Q2. Have you found that you haven't analyzed which interactions make it likely that your customers will leave?

Q3. Do you invest the same effort in retaining a low-value customer as you do a high-value customer?

Q4. Are your prospects a very different demographic than your sales team?

Q5. Have your sales conversion rates changed very little over a long time, and/or do you think many opportunities are wasted?

Q6. Is your industry under increased scrutiny for how it handles sensitive issues like appropriate sales or customer hardship?

Q7. Do you have one or two processes in your business, such as claims or product applications, that drive a large proportion of cost?

Q8. Do your most valuable customers deal with the same staff as your least valuable customers?

Q9. Do you find that you can't differentiate between high-value and low-value customers?

LEARN

8

Look for what's not there.

—Harry Bosch

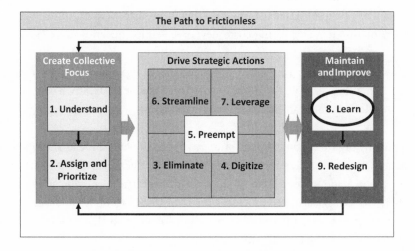

WHAT IS "LEARN" AND WHY IS IT IMPORTANT?

Learn actions enable organizations to know what their prospects and their customers are experiencing and what they think about the organization's processes, policies, products, and services in a continuous improvement loop. Learn also provides the insights and data to guide customer-related improvements and helps the organization to invest in the right tools and systems at the right time. It provides the key measurement of how well improvements are working and who should be held accountable. Just as the Understand step obtains a first pass of data to reveal friction, the Learn step makes this an ongoing endeavor by selecting and integrating different mechanisms and tracking continuously. Learn feeds decision-making and informs those who own the issues. It shows a business where friction exists, who is accountable to remove the friction, and how to track improvements.

The right combination of Learn mechanisms will achieve the following five results:

- Produce continuous data on the customer experience and indicators of friction.
- Yield insight across the whole of the business and all channels so that there are no blind spots.
- Provide qualitative information that helps inform quantitative information (e.g., by asking customers open-ended questions like "Why?" or "Why not?").
- Limit the effort required by customers to provide information and therefore exploit the information that a business already has.
- Make accountability clear across the business.

In any organization, responsibilities will change over time as staff members change roles and structures evolve. An effective Learn process enables the right leaders to be held to account despite these moves, adds, and changes. The governance processes for Learn need to be frequent enough that the business is in control but not too frequent so that reporting and meetings limit the capacity to improve.

Learn requires these four actions:

- Design the right mechanisms to keep track of customer needs and opportunities to improve.
- Integrate Learn mechanisms and attack the issues.
- Make ownership stick.
- Build the Learn rhythm.

Each is discussed in more detail in the how-to section of this chapter. In effect, Learn builds on the ideas described in the Understand, and Assign and Prioritize chapters but moves from a one-off instance of analysis and allocating responsibility to continuous analysis, allocation, and action.

Why Is Learn Important?

Learn provides the data and insight needed to drive improvement and hold the right managers to account. Learn-related data and insights drive the initiatives that will deliver cost and revenue goals, thereby directing expenditure and maximizing the return on improvement investments. Learn helps to keep the organization accountable when factors change, and it connects the organization more closely to its customers. Without the data and insights from Learn, or with narrow or poor data, an organization is, in effect, flying blind.

Why Is Learn Hard?

It is not easy to Learn. First off, it's hard to select the right data mechanisms, and then it's even harder to integrate the data. For example, the reason customers experience clumsy and intrusive surveys is that these tools and data are often separated from information the organization already knows about them. The tools used to track contacts and contact history are often separate from those for surveys and feedback. Second, scorekeeping can become an end in itself, with the goal of getting feedback pushed aside. As a result, Learn processes can become more about measurement than improvement.

Another obstacle to success is getting busy executives to focus on these problems. A well-sponsored workshop to "assign and prioritize" might have obtained temporary attention by senior business leaders, but that is different from telling executives that reducing friction is a permanent responsibility and a goal that they will be measured on constantly. Learn's goals require a much greater commitment by leadership than those of Assign and Prioritize.

▮▮▮ GOOD STORIES

Airbnb's Video Epiphany

From its early days, when Airbnb's cofounders donned headsets as the original Customer Service agents, the company has tracked host and guest experience in order to learn the needs of both customer types. Over the years,

Airbnb has improved its host and guest survey techniques. In order to make its Learn capabilities more impactful, Airbnb's Community Support VOC programs lead, Desiree Madison-Biggs, expanded the technical solution to include video messaging. This process encourages customers to upload video messaging about their experiences, whether positive or terrible.[1] This has compelled the Airbnb product and service owners to address negative issues raised and to fix them, thereby creating a virtuous closed loop. The company also forwards positive reviews and comments to frontline staff.

Another Learn response was the company's ability to track what happened after guests declared, "I will never use Airbnb again." These situations were analyzed in greater depth, and subsequent bookings from these customers were probed in more depth to find and apply broad improvements. The combination of surveys, video logs, and predictive analytics created "a treasure trove of improvement potential for our support organization" according to Madison-Biggs.

E.ON's Customer Insights for Development

For many years Germany-based energy giant E.ON has been using a desktop tool for its agents called **WOCAS** (what our customers are saying) to augment its agent contact coding system, and it has revealed numerous insights not contained in the agent contact reporting. In Germany, E.ON's customers receive only one bill per year for their energy usage, which produces the potential for dispute and defection to a competitor if the actual usage is lower than prepayments. Using feedback from the WOCAS tool and insights from predictive analytics (for example, examining family or lifestyle changes, including moving to another location), E.ON has been able to encourage its customers to implement automatic meter readers and to check their usage in their online portal. The changes included encouraging customers to call the company if they had questions. The company's annual invoice also meant that, after it signed up new customers, E.ON didn't hear from them. While that looked attractive (fewer initial contacts), it was also a churn risk. E.ON built a range of outbound contacts to check in with the new users, especially younger customers living in their first flat or home.

Using the insights gathered from frontline staff via the WOCAS tool, E.ON is able to analyze weekly (or more frequently) small trends in customer contact reason codes, passing concerns or needs to its development team. It then kicks into a **top-issues management** process to dig into root causes. According to E.ON's head of Customer and Market Insights, Kristina Rodig, as a result of WOCAS's insights and these integrated processes, E.ON has managed to reduce its CPX (contacts per subscriber) by 40% while enjoying churn rates that are less than half of their competitors'. Interestingly, E.ON's older customers have embraced the company's online and self-service tools much more than anticipated, again in response to using WOCAS's insights.[2]

Vodafone's Fine-Tuning

As part of its global strategy to improve customer experience and reduce unnecessary contacts, Vodafone has been using a Pareto report called **Skyline** that includes historical, recent, and target contact rates (CPX) by reason code, plus several KPIs measuring customer experience. Each market (country) reports the same reason codes using a standard taxonomy that mirrors the customer journey. Each reason code has a clear business owner in each country. The reason code owners decide on what target actions to take (e.g., Eliminate, Digitize) and are required to describe their progress toward those targets and to work with colleagues to produce improvements.

These Learn processes have helped Vodafone spot opportunities across the world and deal with dramatic change. Vodafone has been able to compare and contrast results very quickly across markets, sharing improvements or challenges, according to Vodafone's global senior manager for Service and Digital Transformation, Kim Hiltz.[3] These results have included creating an all-digital product as well as plans to accommodate new customer usage patterns when working from home. Vodafone was able to learn quickly and then use the data to fine-tune solutions. Consistency of measurement helped compare behaviors and issues across markets, which, in turn, helped leverage investments and learning globally.

Uber's Focus on Apps, Ratings, and Defect Rates

Part of Uber's innovative approach is that riders, drivers, food deliverers, and consumers use its app for bookings, changes, and self-service. The company has also built in ratings and feedback functions to measure all four parties. This measurement philosophy has helped create a culture of customer focus, with drivers often offering mints and bottles of water because they want to get high ratings. Uber cars are usually also far cleaner than a typical taxi. Further, passenger behavior is driven by a need to score well.

This feedback helps Uber improve its internal processes and systems. Uber has been able to reduce its defect rate by 90% over the last four years, according to Troy Stevens, Uber's VP and global head of Community Operations. He stresses, "The best customer experience is one that doesn't have to happen."[4] For its food delivery service, Uber has added a Missing Items feature on its app after analyzing why customers were reporting that their orders were incomplete. Uber then digitized the function to make "problem repair fast and simple." For the rideshare service, Uber added a Cancel Ride option to the app that automatically dispatches another driver for the customer who sees that their original driver is not coming or is too far away. These and many other features have reduced friction for customers and for Uber.

The company also uses scores and app interactions to drive improvement in other departments. Stevens added, "Community Operations has become a really good partner with our tech team in order to create an operational metric for the tech-development groups. They provide the tech team with a flavor of what the customer experience feels like, or VOC real-world examples." In this way, Uber is able to respond to customer needs very quickly.

Red Hat's CX-360

Like most organizations, Red Hat had many sources of customer insights initiated and managed by different functions or departments. That was until, according to Megan Jones, Red Hat's director of Customer Experience Programs, the company was prompted by a drive to "Be more customer-centric." At that point, Red Hat collapsed these sources into an integrated 360^0 view across 16 touchpoints, spanning from the first interaction to renewal.[5] By defining several of these touchpoints as "moments of truth" with the company's Lifecycle marketing team, Red Hat added 13 surveys to 3 existing surveys and fashioned a visual dashboard and sentiment models, by which sales reps could quickly obtain a clear picture of customers' pain points. Using clearly presented color-coded results in coxcomb reports (similar to pie charts but scaled more dynamically), together with NPS open-ended comments in word clouds, Red Hat's CX 360^0 has enabled its product and sales teams to learn, at a glance, what matters to its customers, how the company is addressing their needs, and which emerging needs require attention across the company. This has also led to the popular Red Hat Learning Community, where resellers, integrators, and corporate customers of its **PaaS** tools share with each other.[6]

BAD STORIES

The bad stories for Learn illustrate common issues. Many organizations invest in apparent Learn mechanisms that don't work, while others seem to expect customers to do all the work. Some companies fail to integrate the data and insights they have, producing isolated islands of information. Finally, other companies have become obsessed with measurement but don't seem to act on it.

Flying Blind by Loading the Survey Dice

You know it's going to be a bad experience when an airline introduces its survey with "This will take between 10 and 15 minutes of your time." Yet, several airlines still do this. The rest of the survey process then continues to impose on customers in a variety of ways. The first questions ask the customer what the airline already knows:

- "How did you book this flight?"
- "How often do you travel?"
- "Did you use the lounge?"

That is frustrating for customers, as they can tell the airline has been lazy. After all, the airline has already pulled certain data and passed it over to the research house to initiate the survey. They know the customer flew on a particular flight or they wouldn't be asking! It's not much more effort to extract other data the organization has about the customer and the booking, and yet one particular airline prefers to put the customer to work.

Their survey's 15 pages of questions are all heavily structured around topics that the airline thinks it needs to know, like the food and beverage

experience or the boarding procedure. Only one question, the last one, con-
tains a free-format text box where the customer can provide feedback on
what interests or bothers them. It's as though the airline thinks it already
knows what all the issues might be and isn't really open to listening to other
feedback. If the airline really wanted feedback, then why not ask only the
open-ended questions?

This survey format is frustrating enough, but there is one more catch.
This airline only conducts these surveys when their flights run on time.
When flights are delayed, they give customers no opportunity to critique
or give feedback. Talk about flying blind! When delays occur, airlines
and the service experiences they provide are really put to the test, but this
airline doesn't want to know how it handles those critical situations. It
wants to load the dice toward positive experiences. The executives of the
organization may not be aware how much the airline is missing out on
the feedback it really needs. It is going through the Learn motions but
failing to listen properly, subjecting the customer to frustrating, unnecessary effort.

Ignoring a Golden Opportunity

A fast-growing SaaS provider conducted quarterly NPS surveys with its
business customers and dutifully summarized the average scores for that
time period, comparing them with the previous quarter. However, even
though the organization knew that a nettlesome percentage of its customers scored 0, 1, or 2 (**deep detractors**), they rarely reached out to those customers to ask the salient questions "Why?" and "What can we do to fix
the situation?" Instead, they patted themselves on the back for minuscule
improvements in overall NPS while shirking the opportunity to learn from
customers who gave them low scores.

A major bank also underreached with its NPS strategy. They got survey
responses from 4% of their customers, but supervisors and team leaders
had to follow up with the deep detractors. When the contact center
manager was asked why they only surveyed 4%, management responded
that the frontline leadership "wouldn't be able to cope" with finding more
detractors. In other words, it was better not to know than have to do
something about it—a sad "head in the sand" approach to Learn.

Fees for No Service Lead to Industry Shame

The financial advice industry in Australia has been besieged with scandals dating back to the 1990s. Most newsworthy were rogue financial advisors who pocketed hefty fees by recommending products that didn't suit their customers. These and other scandals led to increased regulation. One wave of legislation, the Future of Financial Advice (FOFA), tried to make sure that advisors were correctly engaged by their clients and working in their clients' best interest. When that also failed to fix the issues, the government called for a banking and wealth-management public inquiry, a Royal Commission, which exposed further rogue behavior.

The biggest scandal in the inquiry uncovered major wealth-management businesses that had charged thousands of clients for advice when none had been given. In some cases, companies were continuing to charge customers who had died. The "fees-for-no-service" scandal caused the downfall of the CEOs and chairmen of some of these companies. This public horror occurred because these organizations had failed to learn from these situations. Some were aware that they were charging money for nothing but kept doing it. Other companies failed to have the measurement and controls in place. This was a good example of an industry that had refused to learn.

▇ HOW TO LEARN

Learn requires four actions, as shown in figure 8.1.

Design the Right Learn Mechanisms

There are myriad Learn mechanisms that collect different types of VOC, some providing rich quantitative data and others yielding more qualitative data with different insights. These Learn mechanisms are divided into three groups that (1) quantify friction; (2) collect rich stories and suggestions that may provide commentary on products and processes or enable a drill-down on particular issues; and (3) enable the connection of executives, management, and staff with customers.

FIGURE 8.1. The Learn Approach

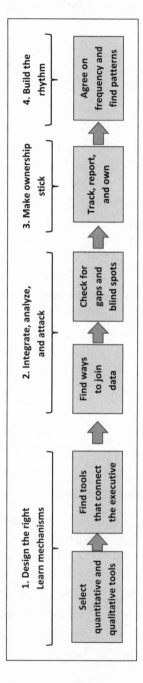

Group 1: Quantify Friction

The mechanisms in table 8.1 can be used to track the quantity of friction continuously, with analytics as the most refined and complete way to do this. As noted in the Understand chapter, cruder mechanisms, such as QA sampling or agent contact coding, can also be used, but they are harder to verify or smaller in sample size.

Group 2: Rich Qualitative Insights

The mechanisms in table 8.2 include traditional customer research and focus groups, both covered earlier. The following mechanisms are alternatives to that form of research; they have more data points and at a fraction of the cost.

Group 3: Connection of Executives, Management, and
Staff with Customers

The mechanisms in table 8.3 are used to keep executives and management in touch with customers by immersing them into customers' experiences. For Renovators, where management may have become separated from customers, these tools can become the necessary "shock and awe" to reconnect them to customers' reality.

Organizations need to use mechanisms from each of the three groups to detect and reduce friction. The mechanisms that span the most interactions (e.g., data-mining all contacts) provide the best breadth of analysis. However, the qualitative techniques are better for deep-diving into specific issues and bringing a direct customer voice to the table. The connection mechanisms are more useful for keeping executives and management engaged about what really affects customers.

Unfortunately, customer surveys have become the dominant form of customer feedback measurement. Surveys have a place and a purpose, but many are used in biased or loaded ways, and others are used to keep score rather than to obtain real feedback and insights. You can tell it is score-keeping if a survey includes measurements and ratings on scales from 0 to 10 or from 1 to 5 but don't allow free-format feedback. If organizations want feedback, they need only to ask an open question like "Please tell us what you think." The old U.S. truckers' decal, "How's my driving?," is a good example of this. It won't keep score, but it will provide feedback that is often very frank, specific, and actionable.

Table 8.1. Mechanisms That Quantify Friction

Mechanism	How It Works	How It Is Used
Speech and text analytics of all customer contacts	Analyzes sales and service calls, emails, chats, and messages using a consistent analytics framework to report what is driving contact (see chapter 1, "Understand")	▪ Keeping a constant watch on what drives contact ▪ Quantifying the volumes and costs of customer contact reasons ▪ Measuring improvements
CPX (*X* = the driver of contacts such orders shipped) overall and by reason	Measures the rate of contacts and whether a company is getting harder or easier to deal with (see chapter 1, "Understand")	▪ Measuring "customer effort" ▪ Yielding deeper analysis, including analysis of which reasons are most frustrating ▪ Tracking results of process or other changes ▪ Scorekeeping
CES—evaluating how much effort it takes a customer to achieve a goal during every interaction with a company	Can be based on customer survey or imputed as a composite of contact rates, durations, and other factors that show how much effort is being imposed on the customer	▪ Revealing areas of potential improvement ▪ Leading process breakdowns to be actionable by product and process ▪ Placing the managers and executives "in the shoes of the customer"
Repeat contact analysis	Uses analytics to show how often customers are having to make contact about the same or related issues, either within or across channels (see the "Understand" and "Preempt" chapters, especially the resolution-tracking topic in "Understand")	▪ Highlighting processes that are not working well and that need improvement (e.g., through training, knowledge, how-to guides) ▪ Building performance management programs from frontline staff up through site leaders and different enterprises including BPOs
Volume and effort analysis of key processes, such as repair visits, faults, or repairs	Identifies key processes that reflect failures and problems and highlight their volumes and workload	▪ Understanding faulty products and processes ▪ Ensuring that changes are moving the needles in the right directions

Table 8.2. Richer Qualitative Insights

Mechanism	How It Works	How It Is Used
Frontline inquiry	Asks staff, "What are our customers saying?" (WOCAS) and "How often are they saying it?"	■ Identifying new needs or problems ■ Enabling drill-down by researching when these issues occur
Social media monitoring	Obtains feedback from social media sites on your products and services. Some companies offer scraping services to aggregate this for you.	■ Analyzing feedback that your products and services are receiving in the public domain ■ Providing early indicators ■ Intervening, where allowed, to address concerns
Customer exit process	Visits with or interviews former customers to figure out what went wrong. (This sounds easy, but many former customers won't be willing to share much!)	■ Understanding issues and problems or customer offers that were serious enough to tip customers over the edge ■ Applying these lessons to similarly situated customers who might churn as well
Customer observation	Watches how your customers use your products and services in their own environments. Merge observations with those in usability environments, if necessary.	■ Understanding the customer perspective and frame of reference ■ Grounding designers and product owners in customer reality
Mystery shopping	Samples your products and customers' experiences in a structured manner, either by engaging specialists or using your own staff	■ Demonstrating what customers actually experience and providing rich feedback and frequent · monitoring ■ Showing managers how much friction their products or services are causing
"Staple yourself to an order" or happy/ unhappy path analysis	Follows an order or other long and complex procedure through all processes. Happy path has no friction; unhappy path analysis flags what can go wrong.	■ Demonstrating the large number of steps and possible roadblocks ■ Quantifying failures
Customer journey mapping	Shows all aspects of the end-to-end journey of customers, from marketing, onboarding, and usage through renewal, continuation, or account closing	■ Bringing all departments together to get traction on action and change ■ Revealing even more friction (e.g., delays or lack of updates; see chapter 5, "Preempt")

(continued)

Table 8.2. Richer Qualitative Insights *continued*

Mechanism	How It Works	How It Is Used
Customer feedback surveys	Asks, at the simplest level, How did we do?" and then uses analytics to mine responses. Many companies use this as score-keeping instead with complex multiquestion surveys.	▪ Enriching data if requests are simple and/or use a free format (open fields)
Null search analysis	Mines every time when customers ask for something that has no "hit" on websites or in requests of sales teams	▪ Indicating future product or service needs
Customer panels or communities	Uses a group of customers in constant contact to review products or services (e.g., website self-service look and feel)	▪ Prompting ongoing two-way communications and, as close as possible, unvarnished feedback and recommendations

Much of the investment in surveys could be more profitably directed toward analyzing the data that organizations already have or could easily collect. It's unfortunate that many businesses are spending a great deal of their money and customer effort administering surveys and analyzing them when they could invest in mining the insights available from the thousands of customer interactions they have already had. All that most organizations need is a central repository of customer contact data and the ability to tap into that repository with key words, customer profiles, or personas.

Integrate, Analyze, and Attack

Most organizations already have some of these mechanisms from which to learn, so it is essential to integrate them and to spot obvious gaps. Here's a method for analyzing and assessing your ability to learn:

▪ Document all of the mechanisms used for customer voices and feedback today in your business (see the three groups previously mentioned).
▪ Record how frequently each voice is collected, the approximate volume collected, who initiates the contact, and which channels are used.

Table 8.3. Connection Mechanisms

Mechanism	How It Works	How It Is Used
Management monitoring or "back to the floor"	Requires executives to spend one day a month, or a week at a time, working as or with frontline staff in retail shops or handling calls or chats	▪ Grounding executives in the issues that customers and frontline staff face
New-hires start in service and vice versa	Schedules every person who joins the organization to spend time in customer service, and all service staff work in other areas such as in the fulfillment center, in billing or credit (e.g., in a utility), or in ride-alongs with field technicians	▪ Creating broader awareness of how departments need to collaborate ▪ Establishing useful links between and among departments
Customer days [where everyone talks to customers]	Mobilizes the entire organization to talk to a customer on a given day or week (very useful for Renovators)	▪ Forcing connections with customers across the business to gather hundreds of stories ▪ Finding crisp ways to collect insights as customers are experiencing them
"Worst call" playlist	Sets up sessions for executives, either together or on their own, to listen to 10 calls a month that represent complaints or bad experiences	▪ Helping all departments understand the issues they cause
Customer stories	Obtains and widely publishes stories of success and failure (e.g., Trek and Nordstrom)	▪ Educating staff to address/ reduce friction ▪ Showing "what good looks like" ▪ Creating a culture of help and support ▪ Granting permission for frontline staff to take initiative and "do the right thing" for customers

- Record uses of these data, including their frequency, the receivers, and the ways they are presented to potential users (e.g., push alerts, portals, attachments, PowerPoint reports, etc.).
- Document stories of how these customer voices have been used across the organization and how they have changed the organization. This can also take the form of an impact score. You may find these

stories are limited. If this becomes a massive exercise, that is good news, as it suggests change is occurring.

- Share those reports and stories broadly and widely within the organization as well as with prospective customers, investors, and other stakeholders.

This documentation will provide an overview of what exists and how it is used. It will be important to examine (1) frequency, where data exists but is episodic; (2) scope, where some channels or products aren't covered; (3) quality, where there is limited insight from the data; and (4) action, where data seem to be useful but no one does anything with it. Symptoms of the latter include negative feedback of different types or poor scores that produce no outcome.

Links in the Chain

The best mechanisms complement one another. For example, contact analytics provides constant data, monitoring, and quantification based on all the contacts that are occurring. Ideally, in central **data lakes**, it also links to research and feedback on particular issues. For example, complaints and frontline feedback should be classified in such a way that they can also be connected with contact reasons. When organizations can start to link these mechanisms, they are in a better position to quantify the benefits of investment and track the impact of actions. This means using common causes and classifications across customer complaints; repeat contacts; social media commentary; and the plethora of phone calls, email messages, chats, and other channels. For example, it helps that certain calls, emails, chats, and posts all relate to the problem of "Product X doesn't work."

Once all of these mechanisms and voices are properly linked, organizations can start to turn off some of the redundant mechanisms. It's far better to have 3 to 5 Learn mechanisms used in an integrated way than 10 mechanisms used ineffectively and in a way that delivers no action.

Mind the Gap

There are key questions to check if your Learn mechanisms are complete. Any of them can be an indicator that you may have gaps to close.

- Do you have data to track the reasons customers need to contact you, which reports continuously and shows you new and emerging trends?
- Is the information telling you about what customers think of your products, services, and processes so that you can refine them?
- Does it take a long time to get detailed information on customers' perspectives or to find root causes of issues?
- Is the data you are getting driving improvement and change?
- Are some products and services outside the scope of the information you are receiving?
- Are you surprised by negative feedback, such as complaints that weren't represented earlier?
- Do you appear to be getting different and contradictory feedback from different mechanisms?

Because there are now so many contact channels, it is critical to get a broad view across all of them and to understand their interplay and where gaps exist in Learn mechanisms. For example, call rates (CPX) may be dropping, but an organization needs to know if those contacts have shifted to other channels like web chat, email, or messaging. The Digitize and self-service channels also need to report their effectiveness in order to answer these three key questions:

- Are customers completing more transactions, or are they getting stuck or navigating excessively?
- Are all of the possible elements of friction and dissatisfaction being captured?
- How are these data changing?

Make Ownership Stick

The Assign and Prioritize chapter introduced the idea that issues and problems need to have unique owners across the organization. Some organizations have developed sophisticated mechanisms to maintain ownership. At Amazon, the customer service team developed a complex Pareto reporting mechanism nicknamed Skyline that engaged owners with their assigned customer contact reasons weekly and held them to account. The Skyline report provided a succinct visualization of customer contact reasons and their trends and goals (see figure 1.5 for a simplified version) relative to business growth because everything was normalized in terms of CPX or contacts per order. This reporting format has since been used by organizations all over the world.

This type of reporting becomes more useful when there is consistency across divisions, markets, and countries rather than allowing each one to have its own taxonomy. This consistency allows benchmarking and the exchange of solutions. It works better still when there is a standardized framework for creating actions, assigning owners, and agreeing upon targets. The larger the organization, the more that standard mechanisms like this can help create visibility and accountability across the business.

Accountability works best when the organization puts the following practices into place:

- The CEO or most senior sponsor holds their executive team to account. If executives are assigned a category to own, they are forced to understand the reasons and trends, especially if they have to explain these trends to the CEO each month. Ignorance looks bad if the CEO is asking questions, so senior sponsorship and interest forces owners to get involved.
- Costs are reversed to each owner so that they bear the financial impact that they caused. This includes not just the cost of the staff handling contacts but all of the costs related to fixing the problems (e.g., refunds, repairs, truck rolls, and product returns, as described in the Understand chapter).
- The metrics are front and center in the organization's goals and targets. Ownership means executives have related targets. Many organizations have made satisfaction, NPS, or CES goals that are collective and individual. Using contact rates or CPX can create collective targets that are easier to measure and understand and have clear accountabilities. For example, the head of finance might be held accountable for contacts like "Where's my refund?" while the head of field operations might own "Where's my repair technician?"
- The organization has enough data and analysis capability to get "under the hood" of the trends and changes. Owners of different categories will get very frustrated if deeper dives don't help them explain trends for which they are accountable.

This same style of Skyline reporting can be applied to many other VOC data types, including complaints, customer satisfaction, NPS, and CES. Linking contact categories to these other VOC measures makes them easier to break down (e.g., NPS and churn by reason).

Build the Learn Rhythm

In dynamic, changing businesses like Innovators or Renovators, the leadership team usually meets once or twice each week to review these customer contact reports, while a more stable organization might need to meet only monthly. The Skyline report referenced earlier has some key features that help to establish the right rhythm by capturing and picturing the following for each reason:

- Microtrends over four- to six-week periods
- Comparisons to "this time last year" and to seasonal peaks
- Recent variations, highs, and lows
- Tracking against targets and goals

This type of reporting makes it easier for C-level executives to review progress and direct resources to accelerate changes or new investments.

Findings Patterns

The essence of the Learn strategy is to find patterns quickly and then to figure out how to apply them to remove friction. That might sound easy, but Learn requires the capacity and capability to sort through many data sources and mechanisms and to pull out the relevant stories. Four techniques help find these patterns:

- **Create common linkages among data types by using the same classification scheme or taxonomy.** For example, calls, chats, messages, emails, repeat contacts, complaints, and customer feedback can all be coded the same way, with the same reasons. As a result, analyzing and reporting reasons such as "Why is my bill so high?" can include the following:
  - The volume and rate of contacts in each channel and across channels

- The number and rate of repeat contacts
- Customer satisfaction scores, NPS, and CES
- The amount of customer effort
- The workload to handle the reason
- Downstream costs to resolve the reason
- The volume of related complaints
- Other feedback received

All of this together provides a complete picture of the impacts of this reason.

- **Teach the analytics tools what patterns to find.** These machines are much more useful once shown language patterns, including variations in accents or expressions. As explained in the Understand chapter, product vendors may claim that tools can find all the patterns, but the tools will find them faster when shown where to look.

- **Track the success rates of the analytics to find matches and then recalibrate the machine if its correlation rates start to fall.** For example, more work is needed if the "match rate" falls from 80% of contacts to below 75%. AI and machine learning tools can be trained to help but may not recognize new issues and problems and will probably catch a smaller percentage of contacts over time.

- **Data-mine verbatim comments to find new trends and themes.** That reinforces the power of asking for verbatims.

Another pattern that can add insight is a customer's **PTC (propensity to contact)**, which can also refer to a growing body of research about a customer's **propensity to complain**. A customer's tenure with the organization, the number of products or services they have, and where they live each provides a different opportunity to learn.

- **The customer's tenure reveals important patterns.** Typically, first-time customers contact the company three to five times more than customers who have become used to the operations, products, or services. Answers to a high, early PTC are usually found "upstream" in sales and marketing processes. For example, the sales team may not have set expectations clearly or educated new customers properly about what will happen in the first few weeks after they start to use a

service or product. Geographic patterns can be layered over these contacts to show issues in logistics by site or to flag certain stores that
sell too aggressively or without enough personalization.

- **The number of products or services a customer uses changes their
  PTC.** If products are similar to each other, using more of them will
  produce a lower contact rate. However, if the products are different
  or keep changing, the contact rates will increase. Reporting by customer, and by each customer's different products and services, will
  start to reveal the patterns and suggest which products and services
  the company needs to address.

- **Where customers live and where they grew up also affects their
  contact rates.** Academic research into PTC reveals that customers
  in (or from) Japan tend to make far fewer contacts for the same reason
  than those in (or from) China or other Asian countries. In contrast,
  customers from Italy or Boston tend to contact a lot more for the
  same reason than those in (or from) northern European countries or
  the U.S. Northwest. Understanding these patterns is important if
  companies are to make sense of different geographic contact rates.

There are patterns everywhere. You just have to know where to look and
how to learn from them.

Looking outside the Lines

Perhaps the hardest patterns to look for are gaps or missing pieces, but these
patterns can be quite insightful. Frictionless Organizations research what
customers do *not* say that they would like them to say and what customers
do *not* do that they want them to do. For example, organizations might
research similar customer groups and determine that some of them are
not purchasing the same amount or types of products or services as are
others. This can lead to new insights about the "non-contacting" groups. For
example, it can show that some groups have had shared experiences that
make them less loyal and more likely to leave. These behavioral gaps can
be early warning indicators of customer churn.

Another missing pattern are customers who are not complaining but who
are looking to go elsewhere—called the silent sufferers. There are two ways
to identify these types of customers. The first is to talk to a cross-section of

customers regularly to check that issues aren't being buried or hidden. This might include monitoring external forums like social media. The second way is to reach out to customers affected by an issue that others have made contact about but they haven't. It's hard to look for "what's not there," but it can provide critical insights ahead of losing the customers.

◼ HINTS AND TIPS

There are several techniques that can make Learn more effective.

Get Data for Multiple Purposes, or Two for the Price of One

Some data-collection techniques can be used to obtain multiple insights rather than being treated in isolation. For example, some well-structured ·customer surveys probe for two or three key insights by doing the following: (1) including a satisfaction, CES, or NPS question, (2) asking how many attempts were required to resolve the issue (a repeat-contacts question), and (3) prompting open-ended feedback. The trick is to consider how investments in measurement can be minimized by combining multiple measurement types without burdening the customer with too many questions.

This idea in practice. A utility changed its quality assessments in a way that would provide multiple insights. The revised assessments were used to evaluate repeat work, confirm or track contact reasons and outcomes ("Was the problem resolved?"), and serve their original purpose of assessing process adherence and compliance. This gave the utility a monthly litmus test of key overall metrics, like repeat contact rates based on analysis by a trusted group of quality assessors.

Go Beyond Averages

Averages or aggregates are used extensively in all organizations, especially in customer support operations, and yet they hide myriad detail to the point that they can be misleading. A high NPS, for example, may still include a significant percentage of deep detractors who are damaging the brand. A contact center that answers 80% of calls in an average of

30 seconds may have hundreds of calls that wait for 10 minutes or more during certain periods of the day. As noted earlier, an overall customer churn figure of, say, 2% per month, looks very different when you break it down by reason, where the range could be from 0.3% ("We don't have to worry.") to over 12% per month ("All hands on deck!"). Therefore, it is useful to examine the entire range of data that make up the averages to see where the opportunities are and where not to have to spend precious time.

This idea in practice. A wealth-management business moved away from managing their customer contact centers' daily activities with a single "grade of service" figure. Instead, they published a "heat map" that showed the service level delivered by the contact center in each 15-minute interval throughout the day. Poor intervals were shown in red, good outcomes in green, and slightly below target in orange. This view showed that there were problems to be fixed during certain parts of the day and made it easier to spot recurring issues, such as a poor start and end to each day. This view led the operation to revise its staff rostering to address the visible problems.

Take Incremental Approaches

Case studies in other chapters have described data analytics that were successful for organizations such as Airbnb and Cable One. For organizations that haven't used these mechanisms, these tools can represent complex new capabilities and expensive investments; these organization can start by using manual mechanisms. A well-structured sampling exercise where contacts help frontline staff select from a list of 25 to 50 reasons will start to build an initial view of the opportunities. These data can then be used to "teach the machine" to obtain faster and deeper outcomes, thereby building credibility.

This idea in practice. An insurance business embarked on a five-week diagnostic exercise to assess the customer experience and identify demand-reduction opportunities across customer calls, email messages, and chats. They sampled 1,000 contacts, selected from a typical month, in proportion to the channels that customers used. This sample was more than enough to identify Eliminate, Digitize, and Preempt opportunities. It also created the first view of repeat contacts and was used to build the case for further investment in analytics and reporting.

Up the Involvement

Some CEOs who have wanted to get everyone focused on customer issues have sought ways to involve as many people as possible. Ironically, size and success can cause greater separation from the customer, and the bigger an organization becomes, the more removed many of its departments get from their customers. When that happens, organizations need mechanisms that involve everyone in order to reground them in customer issues. In Innovators and start-ups, often everyone has to "muck in" and help customers; for example, answering customer inquiries, shipping products, finding bugs in code, and reaching out to disgruntled customers. As we noted at the outset, becoming frictionless is a "whole of company" challenge.

This idea in practice. One telecommunication head insisted that his executive team spend one day a month in a customer-facing area such as in a retail store, in a contact center, or on the social media response team. The team didn't embrace the idea at first. However, after each immersion day, team members came back energized and overflowing with stories and ideas. "Did you know we do *X*?" and "I can fix *Y*!" became familiar comments at each executive meeting.

Create an Integrated Data Set and Repository

The data and the skills necessary for Learn actions usually reside in different departments. Marketing and products may own data sets like CLV, customer research, and customer win/loss data; IT may have the skills and knowledge in big-data analytics; and operations may have the data sets on customer contacts. Co-locating these functions and joining the data allows these departments to feed off of each other and to get insights across multiple data sets. The Learn processes are more effective when VOC, customer testimonials and stories, and customer experience data reside in a central data repository (now called data lakes) that departments across the organization can access and leverage.

This idea in practice. Trek Bikes uses an inventory of customer stories at its annual Trek World conference and in its training programs. The stories have become a core and anticipated aspect of Trek World, prompting dealers to want to share more stories about how their employees and mechanics have delighted Trek customers and created a frictionless experience.

Look for Mismatches

Mismatches and contradictions in data will reveal gaps and areas needing more research. For example, NPS, CES, or satisfaction scores may indicate that an organization has happy customers, but its revenues are falling. Perhaps the surveys are biased, unhappy customers are electing not to engage in various feedback processes (the silent suffers), or customers simply no longer need the products and services. These and other possible root causes merit the same attack squads introduced in chapter 3, "Eliminate."

This idea in practice. One organization noticed rising contact rates while complaint rates were stable or falling. What this showed was that the frontline staff were reluctant to identify and raise complaints. In effect, these customer complaints were hidden from senior management and only emerged later with external complaint bodies and a rising customer attrition rate. Looking at the different growth rates of contacts and complaints gave early warning of a larger hidden problem.

SUMMARY

The objective of Learn is to enable continuous monitoring and improvement to reduce friction for both the customer and the organization. There is great potential in using interactions across channels as a source of continuous learning, especially when those interactions include obvious pain points such as complaints and repeat contacts. Customer interactions contain copious real-time insights if they can be mined correctly. The process can yield an intimidating amount of data and require deep analysis, so it is better to start with samples or trial forms of analytics. It is important to include all channels so that a complete picture of customer interactions can be built and linked to revenue and all customer-related costs. While other mechanisms, like surveys, can be useful, they impose more effort on the customer and may not provide a complete or continuous picture.

An important aspect of Learn is to keep the right owners and departments engaged in these issues with clear and consistent sponsorship and aligned measurement. While stories and anecdotes can provide telling insights, it is more effective when executives get to experience customer issues regularly. Reporting that makes CPX, trends, and costs transparent and visual is also very helpful. Analytics and visualization are now so sophisticated that all organizations need to have effective Learn mechanisms in place. Finally, determining what customers are not saying or doing, which may require reaching out to silent sufferers, is both insightful and beneficial.

ASSESS YOUR NEED TO LEARN

If you answer no to any of these questions, then the ideas in this chapter apply to your organization.

Q1. Does your organization collect VOC from multiple mechanisms, not just surveys?

Q2. Is there a closed loop from unhappy customer voices within the organization and then back to the customers expressing these voices?

Q3. Is your organization reviewing weekly VOC insights and contact trends and taking actions?

Q4. Are there multiple department owners outside customer service who are responsible for different contact reasons and VOC pain points?

Q5. Do you analyze different types of data and look for unexpected missing data and movements?

Q6. Are you reaching out to the silent sufferers to understand what's on their minds?

Q7. Is your executive team engaged by data and frequent contact with customers to understand customer issues?

Q8. Are trends in contact rates, satisfaction levels, and customer complaints clear every week and month?

Q9. Are the meetings around VOC and contact rates sufficiently frequent to stay on top of the issues and track progress?

REDESIGN

9

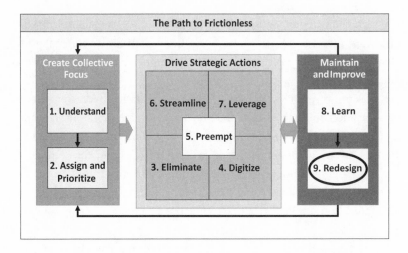

WHAT IS "REDESIGN" AND WHY IS IT IMPORTANT?

Organizations need to Redesign in order to improve their performance continuously and to deal with the implications of the actions described in the eight prior chapters (chapters 1–8). These improvement processes will prevent friction from recurring and help the organization react to external forces and competitor actions (see figure 9.1). The need to Redesign because of internal factors partially depends on the extent of the impact of the five strategic actions (chapters 3–7). The external drivers include the emergence of new customer needs, competitors, and organizations that influence customers' expectations (e.g., "last contact benchmarking"), all

FIGURE 9.1. Driving Forces for Redesign

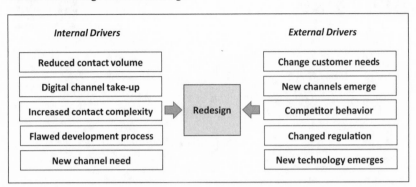

of which the company must respond to in order to stay relevant. In many industries, the cycle of disruption from these external drivers is more frequent, as barriers to entry are lower and the lines between industries are more blurred.

Redesign recognizes that the world isn't static. Successes through Digitize and Eliminate change the mix of interactions and force a rethinking of service and sales operating models. The more the mix of interaction changes, the more the service model will need to change. For example, the service model to handle high-volume, low-complexity transactions is not the same as that needed for high-complexity, low-volume transactions. As an organization automates routine transactions and reduces errors and problems, the skills and processes needed for the remaining contacts will be very different as those contacts will become more complex. Redesign is also a way to solve even deeper root causes, such as product design and testing that may not have been tackled earlier, including reasons parked in Streamline or bridged with Preempt. Strategic shifts in the marketplace may leave an organization with legacy structures, products, and processes that must change in order to stay relevant.

Redesign is a critical survival strategy in a world that is more dynamic now than at any point in history. No organization can afford to sit still, thanks to emerging technologies and disruptive businesses that are coming on fast and furiously. There are also more emerging technologies that impact business performance now than at any time in history (e.g., smartphones, speech and data analytics, AI and machine learning, and robotic process automation). These changes are all significant in their own right, but because they all are occurring at the same time, their impacts are colliding and magnifying.

It isn't just the Renovators that must respond; today's Innovators can become outdated and irrelevant far more quickly: Blackberry, Gateway, Yahoo, and Nokia are examples of how short-lived success can be. The pace of change today means that any company can be overtaken by the next wave of innovation. It has been a common trend that the first player in each new wave of technology has often not been the most successful, as subsequent Innovators have come to market with "a better mousetrap." Google was not the first search engine, Apple didn't invent the tiny audio player, and Netflix pivoted from DVD-by-mail to video-streaming when it realized that that was the innovation wave to ride. Clayton Christensen's *The Innovator's Dilemma* highlights waves of innovation and the need for companies to move from wave to wave.[1]

The speed of their initial go-to market programs can also drive the need for Innovators to change. Many Innovators get products to market quickly and then need to spend time fixing the "smoke and mirrors" models (also known as MVP releases) that they put in place to win market share. To get to market quickly, they may have had very inefficient and immature ways of handling the customers and business they created. If they don't fix these issues, the inefficiencies of highly manual processes will create costly and ineffective models as the organization scales.

The approach to redesign has three stages:

1. **Identify the need to redesign.** This stage presents techniques that can be used to assess which changes are significant enough to consider a redesign and what symptoms to look for.
2. **Realign the core.** The second stage applies methods to redesign different operating-model dimensions in response to internal and external drivers. The how-to section in this chapter presents examples of some, but not all, of these dimensions. It also describes examples of organizations that have changed their approach to product design.
3. **Make Redesign a recurring strategy.** The final stage describes the internal capabilities and talent needed for organizations to be able to challenge themselves. Redesign then integrates the techniques of Understand and Assign to produce a continuous improvement cycle.

If changes are treated as a one-off improvement, it's almost certain that in a short time, new issues and problems will have been created. Redesign forces a company to question daily why it does what it does—or, in Jeff Bezos's words, to work as if "it's always day one!"[2]

For large and successful organizations, Redesign is hard to achieve, because success breeds inertia: few of the most valuable companies today were in the top 20 as of 20 years ago, and 20 years earlier, the dominant companies were different again. We may think that the emergence of leaders such as Google, Facebook, Amazon, and Netflix is a new phenomenon, but the change in mix of the most dominant businesses has been constant over the last century. Companies that emerge with one wave of technology struggle to jump to the next wave. For example, most post offices didn't imagine overnight package delivery, allowing FedEx and DHL to create a new, lucrative market; the railroads didn't add long-haul trucking or air shipments, allowing many new players to enter; and the major car makers didn't expand quickly into electric vehicles, allowing Tesla to forge the way.[3]

Authors and researchers have articulated a range of factors that explain why redesign is hard. Jim Collins identified "organizational arrogance" as one factor preventing companies from spotting trends that might bring about their demise.[4] Australian researcher Dr. Robert Kay identified that it may be programmed into the organizations' DNA to ignore information that doesn't meet the framework that brought about their success.[5] These are both logical explanations that illustrate why there has been so much churn among the most successful major businesses and why Redesign is so important to keep an organization frictionless.

GOOD STORIES

There are many good stories illustrating how organizations have applied Redesign actions and, as a result, are continuously evolving to reduce effort and friction.

T-Mobile USA's Team of Experts

T-Mobile USA demonstrated Redesign capability at two levels. First, the company completed a radical redesign of its Postpaid mobile products to make itself a market Innovator that forced competitors to respond. It shocked its larger competitors when CEO John Legere tossed out the company's one-to-two-year service contracts, which were heavily tied into subsidized mobile devices. T-Mobile emerged as the "uncarrier," whereby customers paid for the device but had no contract and could switch at any time. This made it easier for customers to switch to T-Mobile and was an implied vote of self-confidence in their service and delivery. It said to customers that T-Mobile didn't need to lock customers in for fear of losing them, because everything worked so well. After T-Mobile faced howls of derision, along with predictions that the company would lose millions of subscribers and see its stock price tank, the exact opposite occurred. T-Mobile quickly added more new subscribers than its two biggest rivals and later acquired its smaller competitor Sprint. Now it is nearing the size of the top two U.S. mobile carriers, and the company's stock price has risen steadily.

That initial redesign was then tied into another critical redesign that Legere had in mind: he challenged the company's customer care team to figure out how to revolutionize how it supported customers, so that they would be able to offer superior service. After considering several models, T-Mobile USA hatched its **Team of Experts**, or **TEX** for short. Rather than staffing isolated skill areas (e.g., tech support or billing) with high rates of transfers between the skills, T-Mobile USA created teams of 45 agents with all of the relevant device, app, and network skills. They then organized the teams geographically, so that they had connections to the nearby company retail shops and understood local weather patterns and other regional differences. Each TEX team knew its assigned customers' history, and an agent might even speak multiple times with the same customer.

The results have been nothing short of amazing: 71% fewer transferred calls (dropping from 14% to only 4%, attacking one of the most dissatisfying events for customers), a 31% reduction in escalations, a 25% lower customer churn in its postpaid mobile services, a 56% higher NPS (going from 43 to 67), and a 48% drop in frontline turnover.[6]

Australia Post Packages Change in Reaction to Market Restructuring

Australia Post, like other national mail carriers, has seen a massive decline in its core mail-delivery business. Legislation in Australia means that

Australia Post has to maintain a large retail network and therefore has a high fixed cost. To avoid losing money, they had to renovate, and in doing so they have become a postal service Innovator.

First, they recognized that their retail network could play a key role in bill payment and identification services for utilities and government. With cameras now installed in many outlets, Australia Post plays a key role in many identity-checking or provision services (e.g., for passports). They also signed an agreement with banks to enable transactions in the regional post office network, and now this network is often the only source of financial services in small rural communities.

The organization also realized that its network and delivery capabilities had growth potential in line with e-commerce and online shopping. Seeing that parcels were expanding almost as fast as the mail business was declining, they decided to address the delivery needs of e-commerce companies. This led to allying with many online retail businesses for parcel delivery and enjoying continued rapid growth. Customers could pick up e-commerce packages at a nearby Australia Post outlet using installed drop boxes rather than require work or home delivery.

This combination of new services has rebalanced Australia Post's financial performance. The parcel and services business now generates twice the revenues of the old mail business. Their drop boxes provide a unique positioning for e-commerce delivery and give a revised purpose to its large network. The redesign of the whole business has turned around a potential loss-making government enterprise into an e-commerce enabler that helps their business partners reduce customer effort. The business remains profitable with double-digit growth (as of 2020 results) in the parcels business. The other services have also grown and given a revised purpose to a network of outlets that would have been reduced as mail has declined.

Qantas and Jetstar: If You Can't Beat Them . . .

Discount airlines like Ryanair and easyJet emerged as Innovators in the 1990s to challenge full-service airlines, following Southwest Airlines' success in the United States. These airlines offered simpler business models (e.g., a single-aircraft model type), could exploit cheaper airports, and had none of the overhead of a large incumbent workforce. In Australia, Qantas faced similar challenges as the incumbent player in Australia, since they had multiple aircraft types, pilots, and flight crews on inflexible contracts that locked in high costs and all the costs of servicing business and frequent flyers. New entrants were eating into Qantas's market share through the low-cost, one-plane-type model.

Qantas fought back by establishing a new brand and business that followed the recipe of the low-cost airlines. It set up the Jetstar brand with a single plane type and was able to hire staff using new, lower-cost contracts. It moved maintenance to cheaper locations and set up as much of a self-service model as possible, exploiting online booking and self-service check-in as default options and offering a no-frills product where customers paid for extras only if they wanted them. The separate branding made it clear that this was a different product and service. They even used different, lower-cost airports for some flights. They exploited Qantas's expertise in running an airline but kept most parts of the new brand separate.

Jetstar became such a profitable part of the Qantas group that it created Jetstar Asia, Jetstar Vietnam, and Jetstar Japan. The success of Jetstar allowed Qantas to redesign parts of its international and domestic network, as some routes were not profitable for a full-service airline but lent themselves well to a discount airline. This redesign enabled Qantas to use Jetstar group routes where customers were looking for discounted family travel. In effect, Qantas faced down Innovators by taking them on at their own game. In recent years, Jetstar has contributed to about 33% of the Qantas group's overall profitability. If good strategy is doing what your competitors least want you to, then the setup and execution of Jetstar has been a great strategic move.

Tesla Rethinks Everything

Until Tesla rolled out its snazzy two-seat Roadster convertible in late 2008, electric cars were stodgy, with minimal pickup and range. What has set Tesla apart from its now numerous rivals is that the company's founders and executives did not come from the automobile industry; instead, they imagined, designed, and delivered what they wanted to drive. This form of complete redesign has kept other manufacturers scratching their heads with wonder. Tesla's dramatic redesign is captured by this stark difference: "Yet a striking feature of the re-engineering of the auto [by Tesla] is the reduction in moving parts, from some 2,000 in a petrol engine to about 20 in an EV [electric vehicle] drivetrain."[7]

Other examples include the following:

- Tesla has showrooms, but all ordering is online, and it's quite simple to compare models and features.
- Refundable deposits make it easy (frictionless) to start ordering.
- Frequent communications before delivery help to preempt "When's my car going to be here?" contacts.
- "Customer Delivery" to the customer's home or office or the nearest company-owned service center with a full in-person tutorial that prevents the inevitable "How do I do X?" contacts.
- Owners of newer Tesla models (S, X, 3) can set the climate system to "Dog Mode," to maintain the heater or air-conditioner at a specific temperature while the car is parked. Meanwhile, a message on the large screen reassures passersby who might be worried about dogs in the car alone.
- Scheduled "firm upgrades" at 1:15 in the morning (or at another time selected by the owner) obviate the need to come into the dealership for routine items.

It is no surprise, then, that in one comparative survey, Tesla's NPS of 37 far exceeds that of the two largest U.S. automakers—General Motors (at 3) and Ford (at 9).[8] European and some Asian carmakers have a higher NPS but not yet for their electric vehicles.

AGL Rethinks the Service Model for Customers

The oldest Australian utility, AGL, originally called Australian Gas Light, could see that customer demand was changing with the creation of customer portals and mobile applications, making simple transactions increasingly rare in its assisted centers. AGL's service organization had been split into specialized skills like billing, credit, and moves to reduce the learning curve of new staff, but this required **SBR (skills-based routing)**, where customers would select the skill they needed from an IVR menu option. SBR models sound good, but customer problems often overlap these skills; customers struggle to identify the right option, leading them to the wrong skill, which requires agents to transfer them.

With the growth in complexity, as routine transactions were performed digitally, AGL chose to redesign their service model around that complexity rather than around its products or service. **Tiered service models** have existed in IT help desk and software functions for some time: Tier 1 support handles simple problems of all types and helps triage complex issues, while more experienced agents who have deeper skills reside in Tier 2. AGL used this Redesign opportunity to rethink all aspects of the process. They recognized that to offer an excellent service experience, customers' queries had to be analyzed and transferred fast if they had a complex problem. The Tier 1 agents were also tasked to educate customers on self-service options and achieved 60% to 70% resolution rates regardless of the problem. As a result, customers spent less time navigating the business with far less effort, ultimately experiencing less friction.

AGL then extended its Redesign thinking. By isolating harder problems to more experienced staff, they were able to provide those staff with greater authority to complete transactions with higher levels of delegation. This brought processes forward from the back office to the contact center and enabled greater immediate resolution. It also provided strategic flexibility for AGL. The Tier 1 role was well defined and enabled the business to off-shore some of these roles. Then they exploited technology to route likely repeat callers straight to the experienced operators in Tier 2, who were empowered to solve any outstanding problems. This set up customer service operations for success while also lowering costs, because problems were matched to the abilities of staff. AGL ended up with the lowest rate of complaints in the industry.

▰▰ BAD STORIES

The business world is full of examples of companies who should have seen new waves of technology coming and then redesigned their processes, but have not. These bad stories illustrate a few of those examples.

Rained On by the Cloud

Riding new technology waves can deliver great success, but staying on the waves can be a problem. A leading supplier of business-accounting software created a product for small and medium businesses that allowed users to run the software on multiple distributed and standalone devices. The product used complex technology layers to keep the software and databases in sync. It worked well at first but created complexity when new versions or releases occurred, because the businesses had to keep these distributed copies on the same version. Frustrated customers received complex release notes and often fired off support requests. Some customers even commented on social media sites that they always waited for the second or third release in the hope that "maybe that will be bug-free."

Innovative competitors entered the market with 100% cloud-based products. They had no distribution and release issues because they merely updated a centralized cloud-based version of the software. They had far lower rates of contact (CPX) and lower support costs. The original market leader was then forced to redesign its product to a cloud-based solution and create a migration path for customers from their distributed solutions to a cloud-based product. In effect, the company played catch-up with the new wave of technology. The Redesign came late and was expensive, showing the importance of staying on top of the best operating models and technology.

Mess for Less or Mess for Stress

Several major utilities embarked on technology-driven transformations, which promised greater automation and self-service, while simultaneously pursuing major offshoring strategies. The idea was that new core billing platforms, along with new digital customer access that was supported by cheaper offshore processing teams, would drive out costs and enable competitive advantage. One major utility knew that its billing processes and products were complex and hard to automate. They coined the term "mess for less" to describe the idea that the new technology and offshore teams would offer cost savings despite product and process complexity. In this case, the Redesign didn't go far enough.

The IT transformation took longer than expected and failed on many key metrics: bills were late or wrong for over six months after migration; there were backlogs in many processes; contact volumes jumped by nearly 40%; handle times increased; and the new offshore teams struggled with all the complexity. Onshore, this company had to add staff to handle a 50% greater workload (contacts were longer and had added volume). Complaints rose to the highest in the industry, and the business had to send squads of experts to their offshore operations to assist the transformation partner. The "mess for less" turned into a "mess for stress," and it took a further year for the business to recover. This demonstrates the value of redesigning and simplifying before making a major system change or offshoring.

Webex Misses, Zoom Scores

A veteran at Webex from even before Cisco acquired the company, Eric Yuan became disillusioned with the way that Webex was performing: "The problem, according to Yuan: The service simply wasn't very good. Each time users logged on to a Webex conference, the company's systems would have to identify which version of the product (iPhone, Android, PC, or Mac) to run, which slowed things down. Too many people on the line would strain the connection, leading to choppy audio and video. The service lacked modern features like screen-sharing for mobile." Yuan, who ran Webex's Engineering, was worried that "Someday, someone is going to build something on the cloud, and it's going to kill me." Later, "after a year of pestering his bosses to let him rebuild Webex, Yuan gave up and decided to leave Cisco in 2011."[9] While Cisco and Webex missed its chance to redesign its system, Yuan founded Zoom and, as they say, the rest is history.

▌ HOW TO REDESIGN

There are many different ways to approach Redesign across an organization's operating model. There are also many different aspects of any operation that can be redesigned; for example, processes, technologies, and the workforce. The approach in figure 9.2 suggests ways to make Redesign a systematic process rather than a one-off scenario. In the "Redesign the core" stage, locations and technologies are described in more detail, but this approach can cover any operating-model aspect. Location and technologies are used as examples of dimensions to consider.

FIGURE 9.2. The Redesign Approach

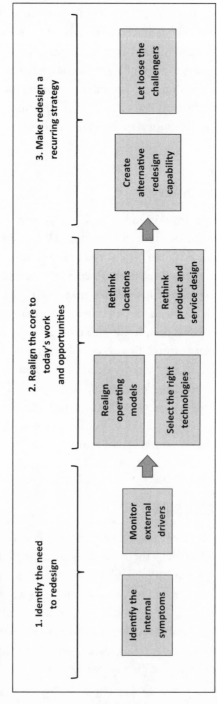

Identify the Need to Redesign

Identify Internal Drivers

There are several operational indicators that a service model isn't working well and merits Redesign:

- Longer contact handle times
- More repeat contacts or snowballs (see chapters 1 and 8)
- A higher growth in contacts per customer or per order (i.e., an increase in CPX) (see chapter 1)
- A rising number of complaints, especially ones that are retweeted or carry "Me, too!" comments
- New Digitize solutions that customers like but that aren't being adopted as expected
- A high staff turnover in frontline and back-office teams

Any one of these indicators signals that Redesign might be needed, and two or more mean a more detailed makeover is required.

A more subtle but powerful indicator, if an organization is using analytics to understand and track customer contact, is when these tools record lower match rates to customer contacts (e.g., falling from greater than 80% recognition of reasons to less than 70%). This suggests that new contact types are emerging that the business isn't tracking or addressing. Another indicator is when the number and percentage of null or failed searches on the organization's website is increasing; that's one reason Amazon, Red Hat, and other Innovators (and some Renovators) pore over this metric—it means customers can't find what they are looking for. Service redesign may be required if the business makes major changes to products, services, or channels that the front line needs to support. In other words, redesigning one area should necessitate redesigning all of its supporting services.

Identify External Drivers

There are obvious early warning signs when products and/or services are being left behind, including a decrease in key product and service revenues versus market trend; an increase in customer churn; a gradual decline in products purchased per customer; and a higher turnover of key product or marketing staff. Another early warning indicator is the emergence of new entrant Innovators with more specialized or technology-enabled businesses. It's often hard for dominant players to know whether to take these Innovators seriously. A degree of hubris in large companies can prevent them from seeing these start-ups as proper competition. However, the current wave of disruptors is of such interest to many banks that some have set up venture-capital arms to invest in the companies that may bring about their demise. They have made early stakes in many start-up fintech businesses, hoping to become major shareholders in any emerging successes or to buy out technology and bring it in-house.

A significant change in the external environment, such as new emerging technologies or significant new regulation, may force a rethink of everything from products to channels offered. For example, the expansion of broadband and then wireless technology has enabled new models of streaming services that have undermined many conventional cable TV companies. In the public sector, the emergence of electric vehicles has forced government licensing agencies to find ways to offset the expected decline of gasoline taxes to pay for roads and maintenance.

Realign the Core

Realign Operating Models

As noted earlier in this chapter, organizations that succeed with Digitize or Eliminate strategies will be left with a very different mix of customer contacts. The role of service functions will therefore change dramatically, requiring a total overhaul of the service model. Greater use of automated self-service means that routine transactions in assisted channels decline, and this leaves frontline service staff with a higher mix of more complex problems. The increasing use of Digitize solutions will also lead to the addition of new support channels. Customers using self-service on web or mobile platforms may expect to use web chat, SMS, TikTok, or some other form of messaging.

The following responses to such change can align the operating model to these trends:

- **Reorganize the service operations around greater complexity.** This could mean a tiered or layered model in which customer problems are triaged to the right area (see the AGL story in the "Good Stories" section of this chapter). It could also mean grouping expertise in new ways to make it more accessible for customers (see the T-Mobile USA Team of Experts story, also under "Good Stories"). Other organizations try to break down the operation into more specialized skills. This often leads to higher rates of transfer and lower rates of resolution, but it may be a necessary short-term answer.

- **Improve knowledge tools and access so that more complex problems and their solutions are documented and made available to the frontline team.** This may require a process to allow frontline staff to capture and codify new problems and their solutions, including permission to change entries in the knowledge tool or wiki sources. It could also mean increased access to experts outside the normal frontline service operations, often called Tier 3 support. Augmented agent tools have also emerged that help agents link to available knowledge better.

- **Increase training for staff so that they can support digital or automated solutions better and educate customers on how to use them.** In effect, part of the service role becomes that of a self-service guide, including possibly using co-browsing. This may mean redefining service processes to make appropriate use of the digital solutions and making frontline service staff experts in how the digital solutions work.

- **Enable frontline staff to manage and investigate problems.** With more complexity, the frontline staff may need to take problems offline and investigate them before getting back to customers. This sounds easy, but it needs a whole process of management and measurement to allow staff to do this effectively. Some companies temporarily assign frontline staff to IT or product teams to share their experiences and review new IT releases so they can also help critique releases for the customer.

- **Expand channel and resolution training to equip staff for the new channels that customers are using, along with their new problem types and solutions.** This may require a more incremental training curriculum to prevent it from being overwhelming, and support desks may be needed for periods to help new-hires when they join the business.

Select the Right Technologies to Disrupt or Improve Your Service and Offer

The last 50 years in business is littered with technologies and developments that were supposed to transform business but either didn't work or had a short shelf life, so it isn't easy to be on the leading edge (which is why it's often called the "bleeding edge"). The list of underperformers is long, from Betamax video to mini-computers. Even recent trends, like speech recognition and biometric identification, have grown much more slowly than analysts' predictions. Technology vendors have constantly pushed their solutions with amazing forecasted benefits and tried to jump on board the "hype cycles," so it isn't easy to pick winners.

There are four questions to ask that may help identify the right time to back an emerging technology:

When does this trend show signs of reaching a critical mass of customers who want to use it the first time but also, importantly, use it again?

For example, U.S.-based property and casualty insurance firm USAA, in lieu of dispatching an agent or inspector, asks its members to use their phone cameras to upload and send pictures, whether it be for a claim after an accident or for a value assessment on a new property. They waited until after the technology was in the hands of most customers, however, before offering this service. This approach comes with no risk and minimal investment while cutting costs and improving the customer experience.

*Does the business case stack up, factoring in **TCO (total cost of ownership)** regardless of customer adoption rates?*

Developing robotic solutions (like RPA, or bots) that automate manual processes might require a one-off investment to replace ongoing operational costs, but the net results can be very positive. A leading business-services provider connecting skilled contractors with their assignments was able to replace 75% of its schedulers with a bot, which freed up this staff to handle exceptions, improved both contractor and customer experiences, and reduced friction for all parties.

Will this technology enable flexibility rather than placing a onetime, one-option bet (aka, "Don't bet the farm!")?

Data analytics technologies add flexibility and deepen insights but are an example of technologies where companies can experiment before investing large amounts of capital. Organizations no longer have to place bets on a particular vendor, since there are many options to choose from. Most vendors offer analytics entirely in the cloud, giving the option of a "pay for use" model instead of requiring a major, upfront investment. Organizations can use them to test the capability and then run a series of experiments so they can figure out what works best and scale it or adapt. Another way to add flexibility is to add a platform or vendor that has capabilities that may be needed later. For example, many major customer-contact platforms can handle voice, email, chat, messaging, and various forms of automation. It may be sensible to use a provider with options like this that can be used later, even if not all options are in use on day one.

Are there ways to test and conduct trials?

Several of the leading speech analytics vendors offer free pilots so that organizations can try before they buy. For example, to help with Learn, send samples of contact data to an analytics provider and get them to pilot their methods to analyze this data. From this pilot, it's an easy step to expand to real-time data feeds to enable continuous monitoring. "Bake-offs" aren't popular with the vendor community, but they are probably the best way to identify the "best-fit" providers. By issuing the same business requirements to different players, the organization can assess not only their direct responses but their willingness to improvise or offer additional solutions.

Rethink Locations

Where to locate functions has always been a challenge, and it has become more complex since communication and transport capabilities have transformed nationally, regionally, and globally. This multifaceted design problem illustrates how complex it can be to redesign any operating model dimension. Many factors are colliding that make the question "Where in the world do we go next?" complex:

- Technologies are making it easy to perform service and administration functions from home or in remote locations (e.g., cloud-based technologies that provide access from anywhere for contact centers and work management).
- Greater workplace flexibility is being enabled by at-home work (e.g., an increase in part-time work, varied shifts, more work for employees with disabilities or those unable to commute).
- More staff are preferring to avoid long commutes and commuting costs through at-home working.
- Education and skills are increasing in emerging economies, such as those in Central America, India, the Philippines, Vietnam, Eastern Europe, and some African nations.
- Rates of labor arbitrage are changing across the world.
- Societies are becoming more multicultural, such that language skills are common and even required in an onshore environment.

Many companies relocated functions offshore to get away from constraints such as high rent, labor inflexibility, or stifling union agreements. Many are very happy with the decision while others have found the service quality doesn't match their expectations. Some organizations didn't offshore well because they moved complex work to a workforce that couldn't cope or didn't document it in enough detail for this transition. These organizations had to spend time fixing problems of their own making or migrating the work back onshore.

Globalization is now so well established that it is hard to ignore. The press in many countries paints offshoring as corporate greed and domestic economic vandalism. Done correctly, however, moving the right work in the right way to the right location can be almost invisible to the customer base and benefit the customer, shareholders, and staff alike. Move the wrong work, migrate it badly, or put it in the wrong place, however, and every customer will notice through greater effort and poor resolution. For example, one company relocated complex work to a workforce made up of recent graduates, and the handle times of the offshore team were 60% longer than those onshore, eating up all the labor arbitrage savings. Worse still, resolution levels were lower in this team (more snowballs), and customers hated the drawn-out experience. This is a good example of having the wrong work in the wrong place!

Additionally, two trends are driving work back onshore (in a practice also known as homeshoring or re-shoring). Increased complexity is making it more necessary to have the skills and knowledge of workforces with greater cultural context and experience. Each wave of automation is more likely to mechanize the simpler tasks and roles that were previously offshored for reasons of labor arbitrage. In short, automation may "eat" offshoring, leaving an increased complexity of work to be handled onshore.

An example of a location redesign was a major hotel chain that had offshored global reservations and guest support. However, an expiring lease in a major downtown location and a lack of space made them consider at-home work a major component of their location strategy (even before the COVID-19 crisis). They set up a **hub-and-spoke model** that used reduced office space in combination with at-home working. This was a win-win for staff and the business: staff relished the location flexibility and could choose to commute on days that suited them, while the company benefited from reduced rent, increased staff loyalty, lower staff churn, and greater shift flexibility.

Rethink Product and Process Design
Understand and Eliminate often show that an underlying cause of friction is the way organizations design products and processes. For example, data may emerge that show too many flawed products make it into production (e.g., software with bugs) or too much customer confusion caused by IT's digital solutions. Organizations are now using revised design and development techniques to try to address the root causes that allow these flaws to make it to market. Examples include agile methodologies and the use of usability labs.

Agile uses iterative techniques to build products or services (particularly IT products for websites or mobile apps) in gradual, incremental releases. The idea is to test, learn, and expand the product set in short sharp "sprints." This enables benefits such as the following:

- Flexible design that can be fine-tuned when customer feedback is received
- A design that can expand as the organization learns more about what works and what doesn't
- Getting products and services to market faster without extended design and development cycles
- The ability to place multiple bets when the needs of a market or customer group may be unclear
- Ways to market-test real solutions rather than concepts and mock-ups

As mentioned in Digitize, usability labs represent another way to test products. Several financial services companies have invested in "labs" that they use to test all products and services. This can be anything from a new app to getting customer feedback on a new product. These more scientific and customer-focused ways to test products and services are an attempt to create almost friction-free experiences, as the friction is removed at an earlier stage.

Make Redesign a Recurring Strategy

It is hard for organizations to constantly challenge how they work and are organized. It isn't easy to keep a business from getting complacent. Amazon's Jeff Bezos would often exhort every manager and staff member to "wake up every morning terrified [that another company would beat Amazon]."[10] Another factor that makes this hard is that organizations often need to sacrifice short-term profitability for longer-term gains. With stock market analysts often focused on quarterly returns, executives and boards will need to stand up to market pressures and place long-term bets when doing extensive redesigns that may appear counter to current business trends.

Create Alternative Redesign Capability

Large organizations have a tendency to not only oppose change but also to actively slow it down. One bank set up a "bank of the future" unit only to find that the "old bank" refused to share its budget and would not help trial new solutions. The bank eventually shut the unit down, claiming it could use the capital better elsewhere. However, this strategy of setting up a division to incubate innovations is a common strategy (see the "Hints and Tips" section at the end of this chapter). Another strategy is to invest in external organizations and to place bets on solutions being developed by external Innovators. All four major banks in Australia have investment arms that are helping incubate potential fintech Innovators. Other organizations have tried to partner in other ways. Some have tried co-sourcing capability through partnerships. Some use a strategy called insourcing, where they form joint ventures with technology organizations or processing specialists. Others use outsourcers because it allows an organization to compare internal and external capability. For example, some government departments have started using outsourcing partners so that they can benchmark internal and external performance. This strategy also allows them to draw on the expertise and points of difference of their outsourced partners, onshore as well as off.

Let Loose the Challengers

Many organizations contain "challengers," people who are constantly annoying their bosses and others with ideas about what could be different. For many managers, these people are annoyances since many of their ideas appear impractical or apply well outside their own department. Often, their ideas are plain wrong. However, these challengers may have the very Redesign ideas that no one else in the company can see. They are the constant "hackers" with no hackathon as an outlet. Organizations that recognize that they need to redesign frequently harness these people and back some of their ideas. It can be annoying and confrontational, but it might just save the organization from a lingering decline. Other companies try to tap into new ideas through things like hackathons or other brainstorm techniques.

Facilitating these challengers in the right way can produce great results. One bank, for example, was looking for a group of frontline reps to help rethink every process. The group they picked looked like a motley crew—troublemakers, frequent complainers, and those with variable performance scores; they were probably the least popular agents in the contact center. They turned out to be the perfect group to redesign and challenge the status quo. They loved questioning everything and brainstormed many improvements. They bonded as a group and became passionate advocates of their redesign. Their changes delivered a 25% improvement in the performance of the contact center and won "project of the year" within the bank. Many admitted afterward that they had been about to leave the bank, but this exercise gave their creativity an outlet. Some went on to take new roles in areas like training and continuous improvement.

HINTS AND TIPS

There are four Redesign hints and tips, as outlined next.

Bring the Outside In

Bringing the outside in means embedding customer thinking into the organization to counter the risk of being overconfident or self-obsessed. The antidote to this internal focus is to have techniques that bring customer ideas from the outside in. This can take various forms. Amazon had WOCAS ("What our customers are saying")—a structured process to get suggestions from the front line. Some companies have a customer advisory board, while others pay for open research. It can be as simple as inviting customers to talk to senior management or tapping complaints in a different way.

This idea in practice. A major bank told its executive team to listen to or read five complaints each month. This kept them well grounded in what was going wrong and what customers wanted changed. It also provided impetus and sponsorship for root cause analysis and improvement. This exercise in humility kept the executive team attuned to things that could go wrong in their business. Another company created quarterly Talk to a Customer days. On these days, every employee in the bank had to talk to a customer. Everybody was provided with customer names and numbers; no one was exempt, and they were given help and guidance. This meant that a large percentage of people in IT, finance, human resources, and many other areas that never dealt with customers had to do so. This exercise was positive in demonstrating the customer-first ethic of the executive team. It also surfaced many ideas and kept the whole workforce grounded in customer issues.

Force the Inside Out

Forcing the inside out means getting the organization exposed to new ideas via a process where executives and managers learn from other organizations to challenge their thinking. This could be mystery shopping at a new competitor or signing up to understand how they onboard new customers. Alternatively, it could be using an intermediary who can arrange in-depth site visits in a different industry to refresh the perspective of what "good" looks like; this can lead to obtaining valuable **OBP (outside best practices)**.

The risk is that overconfident companies will still find ways to dismiss or belittle innovations or better practices, or that the right managers will refuse to participate. Forcing people to identify what's better or to address the "What three things can we learn?" question is a way to encourage reflection. Those with a bad case of blinders may need some eye opening!

This idea in practice. A major bank wanted new and different ideas, so they engaged a recently retired entertainment industry executive to advise them on customer issues. As a former leader of some of the most successful theme parks, this executive had a very different perspective on what good experiences looked like and how to deliver them. The entertainment leader was renowned for continually delighting customers. While banking doesn't aspire to be so enjoyable, using the techniques applied to staff and CX design in theme parks brought this bank a completely different perspective. The bank learned a lot and put in place a raft of changes.

In another instance, a leading U.S. health insurance company fanned out its senior customer service team in a large shopping mall to try to return items to various retail stores without receipts. Some clerks recognized the products and accepted the items, while others refused and confronted the customers. The team then got back together to share their experiences and apply the positive lessons learned to make it easier for their patients, with less friction.

Hold Continuous Hackathons

Hackathons were originally created inside IT shops as a way for developers to break code or create new code under the pressure of a short time frame, freed up from their day jobs. Hackathons have now morphed into cross-business problem-solving and creativity days. The irony is that this started as a somewhat anarchic idea, in which developers were allowed free rein to break things and challenge the status quo, but in some organizations they have almost been institutionalized as a way to channel creativity. They have become almost mainstream, but they can still create different thinking.

This idea in practice. Atlassian represents this idea well. A global software company based in Australia, Atlassian makes tools for developers. It's always been an edgy business trying to anticipate the next wave of technology and developer needs. Its unusual business model includes not having a sales team and selling software online through reputation and word of mouth. From its inception, it has held quarterly hackathons called Ship-It Days. They throw together groups across departments with almost no rules. They claim many great ideas and products have come out of these hackathons, including Jira Service Desk, one of their leading products. The Atlassian team also cites the benefit of regularly bringing the business together in different ways and groups.

Ring-Fence the Future

Some organizations have hived off a separate business unit to be more innovative and to create change for the future. The goal is to protect new ideas from the conservative forces in the rest of the business. Others have set up a new business that reports separately to the CEO or managing director. Internal departments are also used at times, but they are often vulnerable to cuts and power plays. The arms-length businesses are more likely to survive. A final option is to acquire this challenge capability in another business and give it more control. This is also harder than it sounds, as existing forces within a business will often resist a new force just because it is different.

This idea in practice. Sometimes, however, ring-fencing works quite well. One bank set up a new subsidiary designed to house and test new ways of working in a more dynamic environment. It was a separately branded direct bank using all the latest channels and technology with none of the legacy of the old bank but piggybacking some systems. The "new" bank was set up to be digital, with only digital channels enabled. The new subsidiary has been the first to trial AI-enabled chat with a machine-learning engine. It was one of the first to offer a digital application for a home loan, and over time it has provided an interesting vehicle for the bank to trial new ways to do things. It has also attracted a customer base that like the edgy high-tech feel.

██ SUMMARY

Redesign concludes the nine actions to becoming a Frictionless Organization. Redesign can be a necessity for an organization where much has changed, but it is also critical to ensure a successful organization doesn't rest on its laurels. It's harder than it sounds because of the forces that make some organizations suppress issues and opportunities. Special expertise is also needed, because redesigning may lead down new paths that the business doesn't know well. This may mean hiring those with new skills or, at a minimum, those who think differently. It is not surprising that new executives or private equity owners often bring in their top team to drive change and improvement. When change is urgent, new management doesn't have time to analyze the skills of the existing team and nurture it; they often have to bring in trusted lieutenants to make change happen fast. That can be uncomfortable, but urgency requires this kind of action.

Redesign is hard, complex work and has risks. It may not be popular with shareholders who seek shorter-term profits. Staff may also resist the need to redesign, as they are comfortable with the status quo. Significant redesign can feel like a step into the unknown and, therefore, requires courage from the leadership team. Standing still can feel much more comfortable, but in a world of dramatic change, it is perhaps a false sense of security. Some shareholders and many staff are often risk averse, and this will increase resistance to redesign. Leaders have to show them that standing still may be the riskier path. Put another way, don't wait too long to redesign, or an Innovator will eat your lunch!

ASSESS YOUR ABILITY TO REDESIGN

Check how well you are able to redesign. If you answer no to any of these questions, some aspects of redesign are needed.

Q1. Does your organization reward risk-taking and innovation?

Q2. Are most of your new initiatives linked to customer requests or problems (versus internally driven fine-tuning)?

Q3. Do you look for new ideas outside the business all the time?

Q4. Are executives and managers concerned about disruption to the business and industry?

Q5. Do you find ways to trial technology without significant risk or expense?

Q6. Has your business changed significantly in the last 10 years?

Q7. Have you changed aspects of your service model as the mix of work has become more automated or digitized?

Q8. Do those who challenge existing thinking in your business get heard and their ideas funded?

START

10

Let's start at the very beginning.
A very good place to start. . . .

—Oscar Hammerstein, *The Sound of Music*

HOW DO YOU GET STARTED?

The case for becoming frictionless is compelling, but it might be hard to
know where to start. You might be intimidated by the lack of information
surrounding the friction in your company. On the other hand, you might
be overwhelmed by data or by the number of problems that need to be
solved. Or, you might think those problems are too urgent to solve by
going through the nine stages to becoming frictionless.

So how do you get started? First off, consider that you might not have to perform *all* of the actions defined in the prior chapters. For instance, maybe you already have great digital services in place, or maybe you have already eliminated many of the root causes of friction. Even so, it's still valuable to start with the Understand action because too often there is a surprising amount of friction that isn't well known and shared across the organization. That may seem an audacious claim, but keep in mind that many organizations have built cultures that hide problems and issues. One board member interviewed for this book said she learned to ignore the surveys and feedback fed to the boards she served on because she knew they were biased and designed to make the executive team look good. Another board member recognized that solid feedback surveys were not being used to attack problems, thereby biasing the results. The Understand action will address these kinds of issues by helping to build a common level of insight around what needs to change, creating momentum that can drive the remaining steps toward becoming frictionless. Similarly, a wholehearted focus on any one of the five strategic actions (Eliminate, Digitize, Leverage, Preempt, and Streamline) will add to the momentum.

If you do need to take more rapid actions, here are 10 steps you might take that can be achieved in four to eight weeks:

1. **Sample a small cross-section of contacts in one or multiple channels over two to three weeks with a small team.** Even from a few hundred contacts, you will learn a great deal about the reasons and begin to see opportunities.
2. **Examine last year's contact volumes using the CPX formula, normalizing the data against drivers such as number of orders shipped or total active accounts.** Trend these CPX data by week as well as year over year to discover whether the overall figures are rising (indicating more friction) or going down (indicating less friction).
3. **Assemble a cross-functional group of executives and maybe also board members to observe calls, chats, or other frontline interactions for two hours, to begin to figure out what customers and the staff are facing.**
4. **Select the most risk-averse process that your compliance team has forced on the front line that makes no sense to customers (e.g.,**

reading terms and conditions that they don't understand). Then cut it out or find another way to provide the information to customers.

5. **Complete a detailed root cause analysis on one major annoying reason to get to the heart of these situation.** Do this with the right people in the room, including those who built the processes and products. This major reason might be "Why is my bill wrong?" "Where is my refund?" or "Why did you send me this?" Use the Ishikawa fishbone diagram to collect all of the possible root causes and ask the five whys.

6. **Ask all senior executives and managers to use the company's self-service tools.** Ask them each to set up a new account, place an order, change details, and experience what customers have to do.

7. **Spend a day in a workshop to break down your most used form or process to make it simpler and quicker.** Maybe you'll even discover that it's not really needed at all.

8. **Unpack your most widely reported "average" customer experience metric (e.g., NPS, c-sat, or CES).** Study the customer impacts for the top 10% and the bottom 10%.

9. **Break down your frontline service levels and your "average" frontline performance metrics (e.g., AHT, ASA, FCR, or containment) for your main contact channels (e.g., contact center, retail shop, app, or web self-service) into the same top or bottom 10%.** For service levels, look at every 15-minute interval for every day of the week. Use "traffic light reporting" (red, amber, and green) to show when customers were served well or poorly and see what the patterns reveal.

10. **Have C-level executives mystery shop to get firsthand experience with the sales and service processes.**

THE QUINTUPLE WIN

The 10 actions should help you get started, but becoming totally frictionless will take more work—and, as we've seen, it isn't easy. It requires detailed and perceptive analysis, effective sponsorship, cross-departmental conflict resolution, smart design, and persistent implementation. It is worth the effort, however, because the benefits extend to all stakeholders. Consider the following five stakeholder wins:

- **Customers.** They get the products and services they want with less time and effort and without facing obstacles.
- **Organizations and shareholders.** They see lower costs to build and serve while also improving reputation and revenue growth.
- **Executive team members.** They unify their purpose and collective goals to reduce friction across the business. This complements and helps to reshape other changes, such as new waves of technology, new products and services, and mergers and acquisitions.
- **Frontline and other staff.** They have less friction to overcome and repair, so they can deal with happier customers and unite around the common purpose of serving customers better.
- **External regulators.** They see reduced complaints, better performance of industry members, and improved customer outcomes.

All of these wins might sound too good to be true, but the success of organizations that routinely attack friction is the ultimate proof: Amazon, Apple, Blizzard Entertainment, E.ON, Jetstar, N26, Red Hat, Tesla, Trek Bikes, Uber, United Airlines, Vodafone, and Xero, to name a few. We hope you are convinced that becoming frictionless should become a core part of your organization's strategy and everyday operations. But more than that, we hope that if you are convinced, you get started!

It takes a huge amount of work to make something seem like there was no work in it at all.

—Stephen Sondheim

NOTES

Preface

1. Chief Customer Officer Forum, Australia, where speakers' comments are kept confidential.

Introduction and Overview

1. ACSI is the longest-running and one of the most frequently cited cross-industry measures of customer satisfaction for U.S. companies: https://www.theacsi.org /national-economic-indicator/us-overall-customer-satisfaction
2. https://www.statista.com/topics/2169/call-center-services-industry-in-the-us/
3. https://www.gravysolutions.io/post/customer-churn-rate-and-retention-top-25 -stats-you-need-to-know
4. The full quote by accounting historian H. Thomas Johnson is even more meaningful: "Perhaps what you measure is what you get. More likely, what you measure is all you'll get. What you don't (or can't) measure is lost." Recounted by James Considine in "What you measure is what you get?" at https://www.isixsigma.com /community/blogs/what-you-measure-what-you-get/
5. See the e-estonia story at https://e-estonia.com/
6. https://watermarkconsult.net/blog/2019/01/14/customer-experience-roi-study
7. https://www.gravysolutions.io/post/customer-churn-rate-and-retention-top-25 -stats-you-need-to-know
8. https://www.jsk-solutions.com/downloads/If%20you%20want%20to%20 be%20loved.pdf
9. Carsales.com owns online sites in 10 countries.
10. https://triumphpau.com/
11. https://www.theguardian.com/business/2019/mar/05/long-read-aldi-discount -supermarket-changed-britain-shopping

Chapter 1

1. https://isosystem.org/wp-content/uploads/ISO-10002.pdf
2. https://hbr.org/2007/10/the-institutional-yes
3. Using standard assumptions, 100 agents $\times$ 6.5 hours per day $\times$ 5 days per week $=$ 3,250 handle-time hours $\times$ 60 minutes per hour $=$ 195,000 connect-time minutes $\div$ 6.25 minutes to handle each contact $=$ 31,200 conversations per week.

4. https://medium.com/@daviddacostamota/do-suporte-%C3%A0-experi%C3%AAncia-no-olx-portugal-986781703d1a
5. Author interview.
6. Limebridge Australia analysis.
7. Limebridge Australia analysis.

Chapter 2

1. Author interview.
2. Author interview.
3. https://www.reuters.com/article/australia-banks-inquiry/australias-commonwealth-bank-ceo-says-narev-told-him-to-temper-sense-of-justice-idUSL4N1XV014
4. Limebridge Australia analysis.

Chapter 3

1. https://www.gravysolutions.io/post/customer-churn-rate-and-retention-top-25-stats-you-need-to-know
2. Author interview.
3. https://www.jimcollins.com/concepts/bhag.html

Chapter 4

1. https://get.niceincontact.com/Q121-AI-Help-Cust-Help-Themselves-Infographic.html
2. https://www.forrester.com/blogs/your-customers-want-to-self-serve-its-good-for-them-and-good-for-you/
3. https://www.pymnts.com/news/retail/2021/80-of-consumers-interested-in-self-service-checkout-two-thirds-prefer-it/
4. Author interview.
5. https://www.xero.com/us/
6. Medallia webinar, February 2021.
7. Author interview.
8. https://www.blizzard.com/en-us/company/about/
9. Author interview.
10. https://www.redhat.com/en
11. https://asponline.com/redhat-2019-asp-top-ten-winner/
12. ASP community awards webinar 2020.
13. "Different people are suited to different things or situations," in www.google.com
14. https://www.nngroup.com/books/
15. https://www.iso.org/standard/52172.html

Chapter 5

1. https://www.aihw.gov.au/reports/cancer-screening/national-bowel-cancer
   -screening-monitoring-2020/contents/summary
2. https://www.health.gov.au/initiatives-and-programs/breastscreen-australia
   -program
3. https://electrek.co/2017/09/09/tesla-extends-range-vehicles-for-free-in-florida
   -escape-hurricane-irma/
4. https://www.cnbc.com/2021/01/29/tesla-service-now-includes-collision-repairs
   .html
5. Limebridge Australia analysis.
6. https://hbr.org/2004/07/staple-yourself-to-an-order
7. Driva Solutions analysis.
8. https://www.vulture.com/2013/04/timing-is-everything-the-comedy-of-bob
   -hope.html

Chapter 6

1. https://www.smithsonianmag.com/arts-culture/a-nike-shoe-now-a-part-of-the
   -smithsonian-4378596/
2. https://www.penguinrandomhouse.com/books/574956/a-complaint-is-a-gift-by
   -janelle-barlow-and-claus-mller/
3. https://www.1stfinancialtraining.com/Newsletters/trainerstoolkit1Q2009.pdf
4. https://www.customerthermometer.com/customer-surveys/survey-fatigue
   -statistics/

Chapter 7

1. Coined by former SAS Chairman Jan Carlzon; summarized in https://pdf-2516
   .firebaseapp.com/moments-of-truth-by-jan-carlzon.pdf
2. Analyzing customer value and determining appropriate segments is a separate
   marketing strategy that is covered in books such as those by Philip Kotler: https://
   www.pkotler.org/books

Chapter 8

1. Author interview.
2. Author interview.
3. Author interview.
4. Author interview.
5. Author interview.
6. https://learn.redhat.com/

Chapter 9

1. https://www.amazon.com/innovators-Dilemma-Technologies-Management
   -Innovation-ebook/dp/B012BLTM6I/ref=sr_1_1?crid=3VQHOOCW2HZP7
   &dchild=1&keywords=innovators+dilemma&qid=1632616206&sprefix
   =innovato%2Caps%2C314&sr=8-1
2. From Bill Price's years as Amazon's first worldwide VP of customer service on
   the "J-Team."
3. http://strategictoolkits.com/strategic-concepts/s-curve/
4. Jim Collins, *How the Mighty Fall*, 2009, https://www.amazon.com/How-Mighty
   -Fall-Jim-Collins/dp/1847940420/ref=tmm_hrd_swatch_0?_encoding=UTF8
   &qid=1632616379&sr=8-1
5. https://inceptlabs.com.au/
6. "Reinventing Customer Service," Matthew Dixon, *HBR*, Nov–Dec 2018: https://
   hbr.org/2018/11/reinventing-customer-service
7. https://customer.guru/net-promoter-score/tesla-motors
8. See also "The Software Engineer Will Fix Your Car Now," https://www.ft.com
   /content/bc813976-4fea-4ac3-afb8-4cd4eee0d462
9. https://www.forbes.com/sites/alexkonrad/2019/04/19/zoom-zoom-zoom-the
   -exclusive-inside-story-of-the-new-billionaire-behind-techs-hottest-ipo/?sh
   =24b2dc544af1
10. "I constantly remind our employees to be afraid, to wake up every morning terri-
    fied," the Amazon founder wrote in a 1999 shareholder letter. "Our customers have
    made our business what it is," he continued, "and we consider them to be loyal to
    us—right up until the second that someone else offers them a better service."
    https://www.cnbc.com/2018/08/28/why-jeff-bezos-wants-amazon-employees
    -to-wake-up-terrified.html

GLOSSARY

Above the fold: The visible part of a website's home page that does not require the customer to scroll down to see the rest of the content. The preferred location for customers to access their accounts and help pages.

ACSI (American Customer Satisfaction Index): A national survey of more than 100,000 customers every month in the United States. Used as a benchmark of attitudes toward companies across more than 50 industries and is the most commonly quoted U.S. business customer satisfaction survey.

Agile: An iterative approach to project management and software development that delivers work in small but consumable increments (called sprints). It can include the idea of a minimal viable product (MVP).

AHT (average handle time): How long it take **frontline agents** to complete an interaction, expressed in seconds or in minutes. Usually excludes after-call work (ACW) before agents address the next contact.

AI (artificial intelligence): A field of computer science in which computers are able to perform complex tasks formerly performed by human intelligence. Examples of AI include visual perception, speech recognition, decision-making, and translation. Often linked with machine learning.

ANI (automatic number identification): The U.S. term for technology that identifies the number from which the caller is calling and that either displays it or uses it to look up customer data, so that the agent does not have to ask for basic information. This enables **screen pops** that display the customer's information without data entry. (Internationally known as **CLI**.)

Assisted channels: Where a real person—not software or a bot—interacts directly with prospects or customers (as opposed to **unassisted channels**). Includes inbound calls, email, chat, social media, branches, or shops. Staffed by **frontline agents**.

Asynchronous messaging: Messaging platforms that enable contact without both parties needing to be active concurrently. For example, User A sends a message and then can continue with other unrelated tasks, while the responder can reply later. Typical mode for web chat, text, and social media messages.

Attack squads: Designated teams assigned to conduct root cause analysis on customer reasons and/or to design solutions to address (attack) the root causes. Usually composed of experts from the owner's Functional Organization and technology or IT.

Augmented agent solutions: Software that provides real-time recommendations to frontline agents during an interaction (e.g., a suggestion as to where the conversation might go next or the next best offer for the customer). Usually dependent on real-time speech analytics to interpret the conversation.

Autopop(ulate): See **screen pop**.

Best service: The core concept of Price and Jaffe's first book *The Best Service Is No Service*, which argues that customers rarely *want* to contact organizations for help or support but do so only because of frustration, confusion, or broken processes and products.

BHAG (big hairy audacious goal): Jim Collins's challenge for organizations to set ambitious objectives, instead of piecemeal or incremental gains, in order to stretch thinking and achieve more than expected.

Big data: Extremely large data sets usually used to analyze human behavior. A big data set for customers might include all of the interactions, purchases, and behaviors of customers in order to predict future behaviors such as likelihood to purchase.

Bot: Short for robot, a software program that performs automated, repetitive, predefined tasks and can do so faster than human users. See also **chatbot** and **RPA**.

BPO (business process outsourcer): Third-party companies that take over part or all of assisted or unassisted interactions with customers. Some handle customer contact, like phone calls, chats, or emails, while others manage processes like claims or data entry. Also called **outsourcers**.

C2C (customer-to-customer): Interactions in which the customer assists or advises other customers. Includes shared help sites, blogs. and forums.

CES (customer effort score/customer effort): The amount of time and energy that customers have to invest to use the products and services of a company. The CES is often gauged on a five- or seven-point scale, but definitions vary by organization.

Channel(s): The contact medium that customers use to deal with an organization. Includes **assisted channels**, such as inbound phone calls, emails, chats, branches, or shops, and social media, as well as **unassisted channels** where customers self-serve, such as mobile phone apps, web portals, chatbots, and IVR systems.

Chatbot: An **AI**-driven automated interaction tool usually provided by organizations on their website to answer routine queries using webchat. See also **bot**.

Churn: The rate of customer turnover in an organization, expressed as a percentage of all customers (monthly or annually). Sometimes called attrition.

C-level: Any senior executive whose title begins with the word *chief*, starting with the CEO and often including a COO (chief operating officer), CFO (chief financial officer), CIO (chief information officer), and CCO (chief customer officer).

CLI (caller line identification): Technology that identifies the number from which the caller is calling and either displays it or uses it to look up customer data, so that the agent does not have to ask for basic information. Known as **ANI** in the United States. Also used for **screen pops**.

Click and collect: A process in which one orders online and picks up the purchased item in a designated retail shop.

CLV (customer lifetime value): A process to calculate the total revenue and profit return that a company can obtain from a given customer over the entire span of their relationship.

Co-browsing: The ability for the frontline agent and customer to view the customer's screen or another shared screen at the same time, so that the agent can diagnose problems and guide the customer.

Containment rate: The percentage of customers attempting an unassisted channel who do not require subsequent assisted support (i.e., contained in self-service).

CPX (contacts per *X*): The number of customer-initiated, assisted contacts divided by a key denominator of business size or growth, such as orders or accounts. For example, a CPO (contact per order) of 14 equals 14 agent-handled or assisted contacts for every 100 orders. The *C* in CPX can also stand for *costs*.

Customer journey mapping: Annotated documentation of the steps a customer takes to complete a complex or important process, such as joining or upgrading. Used to educate stakeholders on the complexities and pain points of the process. Can include key steps highlighted as **moments of truth**.

CX (customer experience): The customer's reactions and responses to all interactions with an organization's products and processes. Improvements in CX are often viewed as the number one objective for companies, ahead of price or product.

Data lake: A repository of a wide range of data or inputs awaiting analysis.

Deep detractors: The sum of **NPS** scores $0 + 1 + 2$, the lowest of the 11 offered NPS scores and subset of detractors (0 through 6). They represent the most seriously upset customers who warrant special attention.

Design thinking: An interactive, solutions-based process centered on user needs.

Digital native: Organizations that are only online or that started after the internet became commercially viable in the late 1990s.

Digitization: The use of digital technologies such as websites, bots, or mobile applications to automate and refine processes and interactions.

DIWM (do it with me): When frontline agents walk customers through some form of self-service, such as website-based forms. Related to **co-browsing**.

Downgrading or down-selling: A form of **rightsizing** where the customer is moved to a lower-cost product or plan that better matches their need.

Downstream costs: All of the work and expenses required to complete the process or compensate the customer after an assisted contact (e.g., refunds, trouble tickets sent to another department, or technician visits [truck rolls]).

Dumb contacts: Bill Price's term to depict unnecessary or unwanted customer contacts caused by underlying mistakes, confusion, or product defects.

FCR (first-contact resolution): The percentage of customer contacts that are resolved without any follow-up by the customer or by the agent to the customer. This can include a transfer between staff on the interaction.

Fishbone diagram: Causal diagrams created by Kaoru Ishikawa that show the potential causes of a specific event and enable a structured decomposition of possible causes. Used to conduct root cause analysis.

Five whys: A root cause analysis process developed in the 1930s in Japan by Toyota's founder. Requires asking five why questions in succession to get to the root causes.

Frontline agents: Staff who interact directly with prospects or customers on calls, emails, chats, social media, branches, or shops.

(GM) General Managers: A profit-and-loss-responsible executive within a large corporation; or in some countries, the senior-most executive responsible for all operations.

Golden 30 seconds: Bill Price's term for the customer's opening comments on a call or the first part of a chat thread or the subject line of an email message from the customer. Quickly conveys the essence of the problem the customer is facing.

GOS (grade of service): See also **service levels**. Used to measure what percentage of contacts are answered in a defined period (e.g., 80% answered in 30 seconds).

Hub-and-spoke model: The placement of frontline agents in smaller locations surrounding or networked into a central site to enable shorter commutes and lower rents.

IVR (interactive voice-response system): A phone-based system that enables the customer to enter digits or speak to navigate menu options or obtain automated information, such as an account balance or order status.

Joined up: Making sure that all customer and interaction data are available at the same time in all channels, instead of being siloed or in separate operations, which usually confuses or frustrates the customer.

KPIs (key performance indicators): The measures used to motivate desired outcomes. Often part of a manager's or agent's performance scorecards as well as contract requirements with BPOs.

Last-contact benchmarking: Bill Price's term for the customer's comparison of this organization's experiences with the best equivalent experiences that they have had recently.

Lateral thinking: As coined by Edward de Bono, follows nonlogical steps to get to solutions by "coloring outside the lines" and/or bringing into play disparate ideas.

Look for common: Seeking and leveraging the same root causes for different contact reasons. Creates a multiplier effect so that, as the organization implements solutions for these common root causes, multiple contact reasons are addressed.

Me2B: A business model explained by Price and Jaffe in *Your Customer Rules! (2015)* in which customers take control of the relationship with businesses, dictating the products and services they want, the price they'll pay, and the way they want to interact.

ML (machine learning): A branch of artificial intelligence in which systems can learn from data, identify patterns, and make decisions with minimal human intervention.

Moments of truth: Key points in a process that make or break the outcome for the customer.

Multichannel: Multichannel (versus **omni-channel**) means the ability to offer sales and services via multiple interaction mechanisms, such as call centers and digital forums, but with limited integration between channels. Also see **omnichannel**.

MVP (minimum viable product): A product or software development methodology that deliberately releases the product or service in a limited form with the objective of getting to market quickly and soliciting customer feedback in order to refine the product.

NPS (net promoter score): A survey technique defined by Fred Reichheld in the book *The Ultimate Question* to measure a customer's likely loyalty to a business. It asks the customer how likely they are to recommend the company on an 11-point scale. The NPS counts those who scored 9 or 10 as promoters minus those who score 0 through 6 as detractors, yielding a net number from −100 to +100.

Null search: A situation in which a customer attempts to obtain information in a search field for which there is no answer; therefore, the customer's need is not met.

OBP (outside best practices): Bill Price's technique to profile operations against the best practitioners in any industry.

Omnichannel: Where contact channels are fully integrated so the customer can start an interaction in one channel, complete it in another channel, and move between channels seamlessly.

Outsourcers: Third-party companies contracted to deliver services of any type. Also called **BPOs**.

Owner: A senior executive or head of a department whose function either caused the customers to make contact or is best positioned to find a solution for that contact reason. Also called a **reason owner**.

PaaS (Platform as a Service): A third-party provider delivers hardware and software tools to users over the internet.

Personas: A defined customer segment that shares similar needs or demographics that make them easy to identify (e.g., Empty Nesters, Fantasy Readers, Gray Nomads, Avid Runners).

Predictive analytics: Analytics that collect, sort, and test data inputs to make predictions about future events, such as what customers will do next (e.g., which customers will not renew their contracts).

Propensity to complain: The tendency for customers in different geographies, or with different demographics, to express frustration with various frequencies for the same reason. Research shows that the PTC can be five times different among varying regions or countries.

PTC (propensity to contact): The tendency for customers in different geographies, or with different demographics, to contact the organization for support for the same reason.

QA (quality assurance): A process whereby organizations score frontline agents based on criteria used to assess the contact, such as compliance, manner, and process. Typically involves sampling a limited number of historic interactions as part of a coaching and development program.

RCA (root cause analysis): An analysis of the underlying driver or drivers behind customer contact. Uses techniques such as Ishikawa fishbone diagrams and the Five Whys.

Real-time speech analytics: A type of AI that interprets conversations as they occur. Can be used to monitor a live-agent conversation or accept speech-based requests and data (e.g., Amazon's Alexa, Apple's Siri).

Reasons: Why the prospect or customer contacted the organization, either to ask questions, seek support, or express frustration. Sometimes also called customer **contact reasons** or customer contact reason codes, these are usually articulated early on in the contact, within the **golden 30 seconds**.

Rightsizing: Matching the most appropriate product or service to customer needs.

RPA (robotic process automation): An application of technology that automates a business process (e.g., an automatic response to an email, a process to transcribe data from forms to systems).

SaaS (Software as a Service): A cloud-based provisioning of software that enables both code and data to be accessed over the internet by end users and customers.

SBR (skills-based routing): A workforce management technique that divides frontline agents into groups around capabilities or skills and connects customers to those groups based on their specific needs.

Screen pop: A system by which the customer's record or details are displayed to the agent (using **ANI** or **CLI**) as a customer call arrives, so that the agent need not ask customers for their details. Sometimes called **Auto pop(ulate)**.

Service levels: Measures the speed of response or work completion (e.g., the percentage of calls answered in X seconds, email responses within Y hours, or forms processed within Z days of arrival). Also called **grade of service (GOS)**.

Silent sufferers: Those customers who do not contact the company to ask questions, seek support, or express frustrations where others do.

Skyline: A report developed at Amazon to show the rate of contact by reason codes and associated activity-based costing. Now refined to include downstream costs, owners, and target customer experience metrics.

Smart routing: See **SBR**.

Snowballs (also called repeat contacts): Bill Price's term to represent repeat contacts (as the snowball grew with each further contact). The snowball rate is the complement of resolved contacts or FCR.

Speech analytics: The ability to apply **structured analytics** or **unstructured analytics** to recorded calls in order to understand things like call reasons, customer sentiment, and satisfaction. See also **text analytics**.

Structured analytics: Analytics that start with a defined list of reasons, key words, or other search criteria to mine against a data set of recorded calls, collected text, or other interaction histories. See also **unstructured analytics**.

STS (sales through service): A strategy that encourages frontline agents to introduce an offer during a service interaction. Also called crossselling and upselling. Sometimes referred to as "service to sales."

Survey fatigue: A decline in the rate of customer survey responses over time, as a result of sending too many surveys or requesting too much information.

TCO (total cost of ownership): The overall cost of a technology from the organization's point of view, including initial purchase cost, implementation cost, usage costs, and operational costs.

Take-up rate: Self-service completion as a percent of self-service and assisted support for the same reason.

Test and learn: An iterative process to pilot or test multiple options or solutions, gather results, and apply lessons learned.

TEX (T-Mobile USA's team of experts): Clusters of agents with different skills serving the same customers in the same geography.

Text analytics: The ability to apply **structured analytics** or **unstructured analytics** to any or all collected text, including emails, chats, social media texts, responses to open-ended questions, agent notes, and speech converted to text. Used to assess customer sentiment, satisfaction, and contact reasons. See also **speech analytics**.

Tiered service models: Models in which contact complexity is split out to different groups of frontline agents based on their tenure or training, with the goal of matching contact complexity to the tenure of the agent. For example, Tier 1 new agents handle routine or simple contacts, whereas Tier 2 experienced agents are assigned to contacts with greater complexity.

tNPS (transactional NPS): Uses the same 11-point scale as NPS but focuses on the interaction that immediately preceded the survey request.

Top-issues management: A process to manage key issues or reasons and analyze their trends and impacts.

Two-way text messaging: The ability for the organization or the customer to respond using text messaging or SMS functionality and have a dialogue. One-way text messaging is a broadcast of information where the customer can't respond.

Unassisted channels: Contact mechanisms where a bot or program (e.g., IVR, app, portal, kiosk, etc.) interacts directly with prospects or customers. See **assisted channels**.

Unstructured analytics: Analytics that produce reasons, key words, or other themes from the entire range of the data set. (See **structured analytics**.)

V-I matrix (value-irritant matrix): A 2×2 assessment technique, developed over time by Price and Jaffe's colleague Peter Massey, that classifies contact reasons based on whether they are valuable or irritating to the customer and organization: the Eliminate quadrant has contacts irritating to both customer and organization; Leverage has contacts valuable to both; Digitize contacts are valuable to the customer only; and Streamline is valuable to the organization only.

Visualization: An advanced reporting capability that embeds multiple display options, drill-down analyses, what-if scenarios, and other decision-making insights.

VOC (voice of customer): The art and science of listening to what the customer is telling the company, either directly through the contacts they make or indirectly through surveys and research.

Warm transfer: When the frontline agent remains with the customer while transferring that customer to another agent. Cold transfers are those where an agent drops the customer into another queue and hangs up.

Whole-of-business problem: Recognizes that customer issues and contact reasons require every functional executive and the CEO or MD to focus attention and devote resources. Counters the traditional argument that customer service can fix all the problems.

Wiki: Online posting tool originally designed for numerous experts to crowdsource content, including Wikipedia.

WOCAS (what our customers are saying): Early Amazon process to collect **VOC** from frontline employees with whom the customers interact on a regular basis.

ACKNOWLEDGMENTS

First off, we would like to thank the rest of our LimeBridge global partnership with whom we have spent many memorable days in meetings and conferences and working together on client projects: Joseph Kort of Activeo France and Singapore; MD Ramaswami at Celtycs India; Osamu Taniguchi at e-partners in Japan; Peter Massey of Budd UK; Peter Morrison at LimeBridge Australia; and Stephan Pucker at WOCAS Germany. We owe a particular vote of thanks to Peter Massey, who was the original creator of the V-I framework referenced in chapter 2, which also inspired much of the framework for this book.

Over the past 20 years, as consultants and advisors to organizations ranging from pre-revenue pups to global giants, we have been fortunate to work with some terrific clients and fantastic colleagues. These clients have inspired us and always challenged us to design frictionless experiences for their customers. In particular, Bill would like to thank Ana Paraschivoiu, Antonio Veiga, Emre Ergun, Evrim Ozkurt, and Kim Hiltz at Vodafone; Chip McDonald at Cable One; David da Costa Mota, OLX Portugal; Leah Monica of Costco; Laurie Koch, Trek Bikes; Scott Wesson, UDR; and Todd Pawlowski, Blizzard Entertainment. David would like to thank Anthony Sinclair of AGL, our longest-standing client; Sharyn Baker at BT Financial; Kerry Crowley, Link Services; Andrew Porter of Domain; and Matt Paterson, nib Group. Some of those folks have been clients multiple times.

We would also like to thank these customer support executives who shared their stories and passion for delivering frictionless experiences, including Antony Welton, T-Mobile New Zealand; Bryan Stoller, United Airlines; Carmen Beissner, N26; David Nygaard, BestBuy; Desiree Madison-Biggs, Airbnb; Harvey Trager, Fortive; Kristin Rodig, E.ON; Megan Jones and Ted Mitchell, Red Hat; Melanie Schefer Bräker, Swisscom; Michael Baker, UnitedHealthcare; and Troy Stevenson, Uber.

There is no way we could have delivered our consulting recommendations to our clients if it weren't for our impressive consulting colleagues, all of whom share deep domain expertise in what Bill likes to call "We've been there." Across Bill's company, Driva Solutions, this list includes current and former colleagues Anant Kumar, David Sims, Doug Cassell, Ed Wong, Fernando Salas, Gary Qualls, Henry Rodriguez, Jim Folk, John Rushing, Linda Chidester, Maria Contreras, Pat Larson, Scott Tweedy, Sharon McCarthy, Wes Pitman, and Zulma Pereira. As mentioned, we have worked closely with our LimeBridge partners on joint projects, so Bill adds Margarita Hermann from Activeo and Markus Pollmann and Ralf Graf from WOCAS. Across David's company, LimeBridge Australia, this list includes Michael Hazel, Luke Hannemann, Helen Moses, John Spooner, Toni Stent, and Steve Garrett. David's business partner, Peter Morrison, continued to support the idea of a third book and put up with David's ramblings and his cartoon and white-paper ideas.

The book would not be the same without Jon Kudelka's unique cartoons. Jon lives on the island of Tasmania and is a multiple award-winning political cartoonist for various Australian newspapers. He and David get together every year to poke fun at customer-facing parts of organizations and come up with the cartoons you see here. David hatches the ideas, and then Jon adds his unique visual humor and style. Their partnership now goes back 17 years, and they have constructed well over 200 cartoons together. Thanks, Jon.

We have been very fortunate to be reunited with Neil Maillet, the editor of our first book, as our editor for this book. Along with his colleagues Catherine Lengronne, Jeevan Sivasubramaniam, Maria Jesus Aguilo, Michael Crowley, and Valerie Caldwell, Neil has staunchly supported our ideas and helped to refine the message. Without Neil's steady hand, we would certainly not have created this work in this form. We would also like to thank Sarah Romney, Sarah Jane Hope, and Simon J. Blattner, who reviewed and provided extensive editorial advice on an early version of the manuscript; it was great to get critiques at that stage. Without Lynn Everett's, Katelyn Keating's, and Susan Geraghty's sharp eyes and clarifying edits, ours would be a far less readable book.

Our journey was inspired by numerous stories from Bill's friend and business-school classmate Ed Forman, and from a long walk with Bill's friend Ben Slivka, both ardent critics of bad service and friction as well as strong supporters in the belief that the best service is no service. Ben told Bill that he had experienced so many bad stories, many of which he sends to Bill, that our books needed to be updated. Ben also reviewed an early version of our draft and provided invaluable comments. Bill's good friend and neighbor Jerry Ruthruff rounded out the final version with critical comments and suggestions for the reader not used to so many acronyms.

Bill would also like to express his deep appreciation for his wife, Lori's, constant support during the pandemic, when he retreated to his home office to have long Zoom calls with David; write, rewrite, and edit the chapters; and perfect the image that is now the book in front of you.

David is still surprised that his wife, Sue, agreed that he should write a third book, but her support has been inspirational. She and their son, Patrick, had to put up with his ramblings about good and bad stories on their long walks during the 250 days of lockdowns in Melbourne, and still came out supportive. Thanks, Team Jaffe!

David would also like to thank Bill for enabling this unique partnership. We've written three books now, and this time we were never able to get together in person. It's a unique partnership and one that we both value and get a great deal from. It's fun, stimulating, and above all collaborative. Like all good couples, we can annoy each other, but we seem to heal any creative differences with little effort. There is so much mutual respect in the relationship that we always come out stronger. Thanks, Bill!

When David agreed to help Bill chronicle the Amazon story back in 2004, we embarked on this 18-year research and writing experience together, and what a ride it's been! David quickly grasps details and holds clearly the big picture at the same time, adding terrific tables, tips, and stories from Australian and New Zealand organizations. Our weekly Zoom calls, challenges to each other, multiple edits, and laughs along the way have made this our easiest book to write. Good on you, mate!

INDEX

SMS, 52*f*
snowballs
    management of, 42–43*f*
    prevention of, 140
    process (Amazon), 42, 160
Soccer Without Borders (nonprofit), 13
Sondheim, Stephen, 250
Southwest Airlines, 226
Sparklight Internet, 55
speech analytics, 186*f*
Speth, Ralf, 221
S&P 500 Index, 4
Sprint, 225
Start, 247–250
    how to Start, 247–49
    stakeholder wins, 249–50
    steps, 248–49
Stevenson, Troy, 82
Stoller, Bryan, 101
Streamline, 149–69
    analytics, 167
    antithesis of, 156
    assessment of need to Streamline
        (questions), 168–69
    automation, 164
    avid runners (Nike), 152–53
    bad stories, 155–57
    complaint handling, 160–61
    complaints team (unqualified), 155–56
    complaints threat, 155
    defective products (Amazon), 153–54
    description of, 149–52
    Eliminate versus, 150–51
    exceptions (isolation of), 165–66
    frontline teams, 166
    good stories, 152–55
    hints and tips, 165–67
    how to Streamline, 157–165, 158*f*, 163*f*
    location in path to frictionless, 149*f*
    market challenges during pandemic
        (Vodafone Romania), 153
    network fault (energy business), 154–55
    open-ended questions, 161–62
    root cause analyses, 159
    smart design, 166–67
    special cases, 150
    streams, 152
    vehicle recall, 156–57

STS. *See* sales through service
Sydney Morning Herald, 56

Target, 8
Team of Experts (TEX), 225, 235
Tesla, 9
    battery power for customers fleeing
        Hurricane Irma, 129
    climate systems set to "Dog Mode," 228
    distinction of, 227–28
    reduction of "range anxiety," 128–29
    showrooms, 228
    success of, 250
test and learn approach, 89
TEX. *See* Team of Experts
text analytics, 38*f*
text messaging, 138*f*
tiered service model (AGL), 155, 228–29
Tiffany's, 9
TikTok, 234
T- Mobile USA
    as Renovator, 13
    Retail stores, 54
    team of experts, 224–25, 235
    web self-service, 55
tNPS. *See* transactional Net Promoter
    Scores
top-issues management, 197
toxic revenues, 124–25
Toys R Us, 8
transactional Net Promoter Scores (tNPS),
    27*f*
Trek Bikes, 176, 216, 250
TriumphPay, 8
two-way text messaging, 144

Uber, 11
    as digital native Innovator, 98
    elimination of defects, 82–83
    as example of Frictionless Organization,
        12
    as Innovator, 8, 13, 98, 119
    as non-contact business, 78
    original model of, 82
    revenue growth of, 82
    success of, 12, 250
    UberEats, 82
unassisted channels, 52

ABOUT THE AUTHORS

 **Bill Price** is the coauthor of *The Best Service Is No Service* and *Your Customer Rules!* He is the founder and president of Driva Solutions LLC based in Bellevue, Washington, USA, whose tagline is "Creating and sustaining highly effective customer contact strategies and operations, locally and globally." In 2002, he cofounded the LimeBridge Global Alliance and later formed the Global Operations Council, whose members shared best practices and worst experiences. For five years he was also a partner with Antuit, a big-data analytics company, developing its customer experience analytics practice.

Price started his career with McKinsey & Company in its San Francisco and Stockholm offices, serving global clients and working on what turned into *In Search of Excellence.* He became CFO and COO at an early-stage IVR service bureau called Automated Call Processing Corporation in San Francisco, whose network routing division was acquired by MCI in 1991. He then built MCI Call Center Services' automation, consulting, and agent outsourcing businesses through the 1990s. He was named one of the first Call Center Pioneers by *CRM* magazine in 1997. In early 1999, Price joined Amazon.com as the company's first worldwide VP of customer service, working closely with Jeff Bezos and his other direct reports to create what has become one of the most successful customer experience companies in the world.

Price is a frequent keynote speaker, graduate-school instructor in marketing and global business management, board member, and advisor to CustomerThink, with more than 50 posts. He graduated from Dartmouth College and the Stanford Graduate School of Business, and lives with his wife, Lori, in Bellevue, Washington. He maintains a weekly running regimen, a summertime kayaking passion, and a range of collections. His daughters, Erika and Rachel, have returned to Seattle after completing graduate programs in primate communications and aeronautical engineering, respectively, and are the apples of his eye.

David Jaffe is the coauthor of *The Best Service Is No Service* and *Your Customer Rules!* from Melbourne, Australia. He is the consulting director and founder of LimeBridge Australia, the specialist customer experience business and operations consultancy. He launched the Chief Customer Officer Forum in Australia in 2004, and it remains an active network of customer experience leaders that meets twice a year.

Jaffe started his consulting career in London with Accenture (then Andersen Consulting) and transferred to Australia in 1990 to marry his wife, Sue. He became an associate partner and led the CRM practice in Financial Services before joining A.T. Kearney as a principal. In 2001 he left to create a new consultancy to specialize in customer-facing operations, which became LimeBridge Australia, and became a member of the global LimeBridge alliance. He has consulted over 100 companies in Australia as well as companies in India, New Zealand, Hong Kong, the Philippines, Singapore, the United Kingdom, and the United States.

Within LimeBridge Australia, Jaffe leads thought-leadership development and has written nearly 100 white papers. He is responsible for all client projects, research, and marketing. David has spoken at numerous conferences in Australia, Asia, and North America. He is also on the board of Orienteering Victoria and is active in the sport. He is proud of his daughter, Rebecca, who is now a lawyer for the Australian government in Canberra; and of his son, Patrick, who is an economist working on environmental issues for the Victorian government. David is also a keen choral singer, Orienteer, and after-dinner entertainer with a rural property 80 kilometers from Melbourne.

Berrett–Koehler
Publishers

Berrett-Koehler is an independent publisher dedicated to an ambitious mission: *Connecting people and ideas to create a world that works for all.*

Our publications span many formats, including print, digital, audio, and video. We also offer online resources, training, and gatherings. And we will continue expanding our products and services to advance our mission.

We believe that the solutions to the world's problems will come from all of us, working at all levels: in our society, in our organizations, and in our own lives. Our publications and resources offer pathways to creating a more just, equitable, and sustainable society. They help people make their organizations more humane, democratic, diverse, and effective (and we don't think there's any contradiction there). And they guide people in creating positive change in their own lives and aligning their personal practices with their aspirations for a better world.

And we strive to practice what we preach through what we call "The BK Way." At the core of this approach is *stewardship,* a deep sense of responsibility to administer the company for the benefit of all of our stakeholder groups, including authors, customers, employees, investors, service providers, sales partners, and the communities and environment around us. Everything we do is built around stewardship and our other core values of *quality, partnership, inclusion,* and *sustainability.*

This is why Berrett-Koehler is the first book publishing company to be both a B Corporation (a rigorous certification) and a benefit corporation (a for-profit legal status), which together require us to adhere to the highest standards for corporate, social, and environmental performance. And it is why we have instituted many pioneering practices (which you can learn about at www.bkconnection.com), including the Berrett-Koehler Constitution, the Bill of Rights and Responsibilities for BK Authors, and our unique Author Days.

We are grateful to our readers, authors, and other friends who are supporting our mission. We ask you to share with us examples of how BK publications and resources are making a difference in your lives, organizations, and communities at www.bkconnection.com/impact.

Dear reader,

Thank you for picking up this book, and welcome to the worldwide BK community! You're joining a special group of people who have come together to create positive change in their lives, organizations, and communities.

What's BK all about?

Our mission is to connect people and ideas to create a world that works for all.

Why? Our communities, organizations, and lives get bogged down by old paradigms of self-interest, exclusion, hierarchy, and privilege. But we believe that can change. That's why we seek the leading experts on these challenges—and share their actionable ideas with you.

A welcome gift

To help you get started, we'd like to offer you a **free copy** of one of our bestselling ebooks:

www.bkconnection.com/welcome

When you claim your **free ebook**, you'll also be subscribed to our blog.

Our freshest insights

Access the best new tools and ideas for leaders at all levels on our blog at ideas.bkconnection.com.

Sincerely,

Your friends at Berrett-Koehler

Certified

Corporation